THE LITERATURE OF EMIGRATION AND EXILE

Edited by James Whitlark
and Wendell Aycock

Texas Tech University Press

STUDIES IN COMPARATIVE LITERATURE
NUMBER 23

Copyright 1992 Texas Tech University Press

All rights reserved. No portion of this book may be reproduced in any form or by any means, including electronic storage and retrieval systems, except by explicit, prior written permission of the publisher.

This book was set in 10 on 12 Garamond and printed on acid-free paper that meets the guidelines for permanence and durability of the Committee on Production Guidelines for Book Longevity of the Council on Library Resources.

Printed in the United States of America

Library of Congress Cataloging-in-Publication Data
The Literature of emigration and exile / edited by James S. Whitlark and Wendell Aycock.
    p. cm. — (Studies in comparative literature ; no. 23)
    Includes bibliographical references.
    ISBN 0-89672-263-5 (cloth). — ISBN 0-89672-264-3 (paper)
    1. Exiles in literature. 2. Emigration and immigration in literature. 3. Literature—History and criticism. I. Whitlark, James, 1948- . II. Aycock, Wendell M. III. Series: Studies in comparative literature (Lubbock, Tex.) ; no. 23.
PN56.5.E96L58 1992
809'.93355—dc20   91-9313
                                                    CIP

92 93 94 95 96 97 98 99 00 / 9 8 7 6 5 4 3 2 1

Texas Tech University Press
Lubbock, Texas 79409–1037 USA

Preface

The purpose of Studies in Comparative Literature is to explore literatures of various cultures and linguistic groups in comparison with one another and to compare literature with other disciplines or fields of study. First published in 1968, volumes of the series originally derived from annual symposia founded by Wolodymyr T. Zyla, under the auspices of the Interdepartmental Committee on Comparative Literature at Texas Tech. In subsequent years, the series flourished, and volumes have been devoted to the study of authors (e.g., Kafka, Camus, Shakespeare), genres (e.g., the short story, science fiction), movements, themes, and historical periods (e.g., surrealism, mythology, the Spanish Civil War), and comparative art forms and disciplines (e.g., film and literature, literature and anthropology, literature and medicine).

This volume explores the literature of emigration and exile which is a topic that is both ancient and modern. The topic is one that appears in all literatures and invites the student of comparative literature to see parallels in a human experience that transcends temporal and geographic boundaries. Whether their exile was voluntary or not, writers have often found their voices most meaningful in a foreign land, and the literary world benefits from these voices. The writers of the following chapters examine these poetic, fictional, and biographical voices from such settings as ancient Turkey, renaissance Italy, modern Spain, Central and South America, Eastern Europe, China, Canada, and elsewhere. This volume cannot be all–inclusive, but it does indicate the universal nature of the topic.

STUDIES IN COMPARATIVE LITERATURE
TEXAS TECH UNIVERSITY PRESS

*James Joyce: His Place in World Literature

*From Surrealism to the Absurd

Franz Kafka: His Place in World Literature

Modern American Fiction: Insights and Foreign Lights

*William Faulkner: Prevailing Verities and World Literature

Joseph Conrad: Theory and World Fiction

Albert Camus' Literary Milieu: Arid Lands

Ethnic Literature since 1776: The Many Voices of America, Part One and Part Two

Ibero-American Letters in a Comparative Perspective

Classical Mythology in Twentieth-Century Thought and Literature

Shakespeare's Art from a Comparative Perspective

The Teller and the Tale: Aspects of the Short Story

Calderón de la Barca at the Tercentenary: Comparative Views

Johann Wolfgang von Goethe: One Hundred and Fifty Years of Continuing Vitality

Women World Walkers: New Dimensions of Science Fiction and Fantasy

Myths and Realities of Contemporary French Theater

War and Peace: Perspectives in the Nuclear Age

Film and Literature: A Comparative Approach to Adaptation

Literature and Anthropology

The Spanish Civil War in Literature

The Body and the Text: Comparative Essays in Literature and Medicine

The Literature of Emigration and Exile

*Out of print

Contents

Introduction	1
Petrarch's Temporal Exile and the Wounds of History 　Dolora Wojciehowski	11
Triple-Tiered Migration in *The Book of Dede Korkut* 　Warren Walker	23
Paradigms of Exile in Donoso's Spanish Fiction 　Janet Pérez	33
The Bitter Air of Exile: Russian Émigrés 　and the Berlin Experience 　Shoshanah Dietz	43
Creating the "Canamerican" Self: The Autobiographies 　of American Women Immigrants to Canada 　Helen M. Buss	51
Exile and Intertextuality in Maxine Hong Kingston's 　*China Men* 　Shu-mei Shih	65
Gender in Exile: Mothers and Daughters 　in Roberto G. Fernández's *Raining Backwards* 　Mary S. Vásquez	79
The Reader of Exile: Skvorecky's *Engineer of Human Souls* 　Robert S. Newman	87

"Home is a Place Where You Have Never Been":
The Exile Motif in the Hainish Novels
of Ursula K. Le Guin   105
   Frank Dietz

Cultural/Familial Estrangement: Self-Exile
and Self-Destruction in Jay McInerney's Novels   115
   Jefferson Faye

Bradbury and Atwood: Exile as Rational Decision   131
   Diane S. Wood

Daniel Moyano's *Libro de Navíos y Borrascas:*
The Expression of Territorial Exile   143
   Linda L. Hollabaugh

When the Gods Abandon Us: Dissolution
in *The Hill of Devi, Pharos and Pharillon,* and *Alexandria*   157
   Kathleen Collins Beyer

Parricide and Exile: Tracing Derrida in Augusto Roa Bastos'
Yo El Supremo   169
   John Incledon

Notes on the Authors   181

 Introduction

To go into exile was written neither in my mind nor in my heart. I tore myself by force from the soil upon which I stood. (Tabori 1972, 43)

Thus wrote an Egyptian named Sinuhe 4000 years ago. Exile, emigration, expatriation, ostracism, and nomadic migration are presumably even much older than that, yet foreigners (*los despistados*, "the disoriented" as the Spanish mischievously nickname them) commonly receive more condescension than understanding from new neighbors. Vestiges of prejudice or provincialism thwart even the academic investigation of alienation. Consider, for example, Terry Eagleton's *Exiles and Émigrés: Studies in Modern Literature* (1970). He starts his book by deeming the situation "odd" that immigrants from various parts of the English-speaking world (and beyond) have contributed significantly to its literature (9). He ends asserting that the works of even his favorites (Conrad, James, Eliot, Pound, Yeats, and Joyce) must have been "substitutes for genuine 'objectivity' and imaginative penetrations" *because they were expatriates* (219). His book, nonetheless, is one of so few, general, theoretical explorations of exilic literature that, almost inevitably, scholars regularly cite it. Another frequently mentioned theoretical work, Michael Seidel's *Exile and the Narrative Imagination* (1986), does not suffer from chauvinism, but does (like Eagleton's) limit itself to a few examples, all of them English–language. Thus, in an area (exilic literature) where bilingualism is the norm, Seidel, despite some creditable insights, also seems slightly parochial. Aside from these two volumes, the examination of exile and émigré literature is dominated by relatively specialized studies, as even a brief list of recent books may indicate: *La Emigración y el Exilio en la Literatura Hispanica del Siglo Veinte* (1988); *Alien Tongues: Bilingual Russian Writers of the "First" Emigration* (1989);

Shifting Ground: Spanish Civil War Exile Literature (1989); *Hero and Exile: The Art of Old English Poetry* (1989).

There is thus room for a comparative literature volume such as the following. Each of its essays takes a point of departure from some work of specialized scholarship, yet opens the study to wider implications. These are all the easier to see because of the juxtaposition of essays about literary works from different languages but with related or strikingly contrasting themes.

Ancient descriptions of exile were typically lugubrious, e.g., Ovid's *Tristia* and *Epistulae ex Ponto* or the biblical psalms lamenting Babylonian captivity (e.g., 137). In medieval Christianity, as in the Catholic antiphon *Salve Regina*, all mundane existence was considered *exilium* from Paradise (Tabori 1972, 31). The exemplary Renaissance figure Petrarch, however, deemed a man "desidiosus ac mollis [lazy and soft]" not to leave home some time in life.[1] Based on Petrarch's seeing his very existence as exile (including birth, subsequent wandering, as well as his distance from the classical period), A. Bartlett Giamatti has argued, "Unlike Ulysses, who wandered but came home . . . Petrarch . . . was never at home save in books" (13). In "Petrarch's Temporal Exile and the Wounds of History," the first essay in our collection, Dolora Wojciehowski subtly transcends Giamatti, showing that one book by Cicero, far from being a haven from exile, almost killed Petrarch. Her point is that Petrarch repeatedly put it on a shelf in such a way that it would strike his foot in the same place, eventually causing a dangerous wound, which he associated with its author (a figurative father to him). She cites Freud's "oedipal complex" and Bloom's "anxiety of influence"—unavoidable allusions for a psychoanalytically oriented reader encountering a "swollen foot" (i.e., *oedipus*) caused by a paternal author. Then, as an equally figurative resolution of this anxiety, she adds that Petrarch calls partaking of Virgil, Horace, Livy, and Cicero "ingestion" of the latter. This image might, I suppose, also have had eucharistic resonances for Petrarch, since he found Cicero and Jesus comparable: "Christus equidem Deus noster, Cicero autem nostri princeps eloquii [Christ is truly our God, but Cicero is our prince of eloquence.]" At any rate, she well demonstrates how not even books *per se* could entirely relieve Petrarch's exile, which he apparently saw as a necessarily arduous pilgrimage toward the heavenly Jerusalem.

Petrarch's eternal wound or brand ("stigma perpetuum") is worth considering in the light of other essays in our volume. In Wojciehowski's analysis, Petrarch feels *both* in competition with and exiled from the patriarchs of classical literature—a masculine rivalry, even to the one opponent's wounding the other. All the essays, in varying degrees, bear upon a current topic of controversy: whether or not suffering from exile is more a male than female tendency. For Petrarch, at least, exile must be painfully hard (even to a seemingly self-inflicted wound), thereby avoiding that unmanly softness of which he so scornfully spoke.

Was this masochistic *machismo* something new in the history of human attitudes? In the introduction to his translation *The Book of Dede Korkut* (1972, x), Warren Walker explains that the Oghuz, who wandered Central Asia from the ninth to the thirteenth centuries, quite as dedicated to hardiness as Petrarch, also called those who abandoned the nomad life "yatuk [lazy]." Based on research subsequent to that volume, Walker has contributed our second essay, "Triple-Tiered Migration in *The Book of Dede Korkut*" (the three tiers being spatial, religious, and cultural). The Oghuz group-movements (which form the background of that epic) serve as an intriguing contrast to and comparison with Petrarch's paradigmatically individualistic exile. While Wojciehowski's Petrarch is plagued by a father figure from antiquity, the Oghuz epic is attributed to the benevolent poet/shaman Korkut called "Dede" ("grandfather") or "Ata" ("father"). Despite his miraculous power to paralyze the ungodly, he is not one to injure his figurative or literal descendants. Instead (according to the work's sixteenth-century prologue writer), he reassuringly prophesies that the ruler to whom the prologue is addressed ("my khan, may Allah preserve you") is part of a dynasty destined to last until Judgment Day. In other words, no noticeable "anxiety of influence" afflicts the sixteenth-century Turkish editor (1972, 3). Nor should any. *The Book of Dede Korkut* is as much an act of collective forgetting as of collective memory. Its previous anonymous redactors *already* softened or disguised early legends, at least partly so as not to bring anxiety to later listeners or readers. The chief source of potential disturbance was that the Oghuz's original animism would make them infidels in the eyes of their Islamic descendants. To diffuse this potential, the redactors carelessly or deliberately falsified history, for instance, by anachronistically mixing the names of Moslem saints amid animistic apostrophes. Although both the Oghuz and their enemies the Kipchak actually shared a common culture, "Korkut" denounces the latter as infidels and cannibals. So little consistency exists within the epic that, as Walker emphasizes, one character is killed three times! As we shall see in other essays, the price a traveler pays for avoiding culture clash is an insouciant inconsistency. There may be other prices as well. The Oghuz women, for example, originally were respected for wisdom and even military prowess. After leaving their original homeland, they accepted the veil, headcovering, harem, and polygamy required in their new area.

Janet Pérez's "Paradigms of Exile in Donoso's Spanish Fiction," the next selection, masterfully combines important themes found in the first two essays. Like Wojciehowski's, it focuses on an individual author; like Walker's, it also involves a group—in Donoso's case, Latin-American exiles and expatriates, whom Pérez believes have "a shared, a collective experience." Thus, she seeks not what is idiosyncratic in Donoso's work but the "Paradigms" of his far-flung, emigré community. And as the Oghuz resorted to inconsistency to record their collective experience, so Latin-American fiction is famous for its fantasy and paradox, its paradigms sounding like a list of almost anything that now is or ever was once considered a mental illness, particularly any conceivable identity crisis. In describing this medical nightmare, Donoso uses "schizophrenic" in its old sense of split personality, not in its current clinical one. Like Wojciehowski's Petrarch, Pérez's Donoso even sees exile in terms of "implied castration."

Donoso, though, appears almost cheerful when compared to the subjects of Shoshanah Dietz's "The Bitter Air of Exile: Marina Tsvetaeva, Vladimir Khodasevich, and the Berlin Experience." One of the more optimistic of these Russians, Ivanov, sings: "How good it is that there is no tsar . . . no Russia . . . no God. How good it is that there is nobody . . . nothing." Have they brought Russian nihilism with them? Have they succumbed to that German attitude that transformed the word *Elend*, originally meaning "foreign land," into a term for misery? Dietz plausibly suggests that the Russian émigré nihilism is at least partly the result of their temporary condition in Berlin with no desire for or hope of sinking roots.

Coming from Dietz's rendition of the agonized verses of Marina Tsvetaeva (and Anna Akhmatova), one may be surprised by the next essay "Creating the 'CanAmerican' Self: The Autobiographies of American Women Immigrants." Helen M. Buss begins it with a controversial pronouncement: "[The] dark view of relocating in a new land is not one I have found typical of women. . . ." How can Buss's voluminous research on Canadian-American women yield results so different from Shoshanah Dietz's investigation of Russian émigrés in Berlin? First, of course, there is the contrast between temporary Berliners and people who long to stay in the open spaces of Canada. More interestingly, though, Buss's essay is a feminist re-vision of Hallvard Dahlie's *Varieties of Exile: The Canadian Experience*. Dahlie theorizes that many of his expatriate countrymen's autobiographies are more cheerful than those of ancient exiles because the modern Canadian experience of relocation is not as "negative or punitive" (1986, 3). Astutely seeing how often Dahlie has cited women's autobiographies for these more positive attitudes, Buss provides case studies of women who have profited in one way or another from relocation. From her examples, one may realize how the very sexist stereotypes that normally hinder women may sometimes, ironically, help émigrées. Buss's Elizabeth Johnston, for instance, was kept by eighteenth-century views of women from affecting the major issues of her time. Thus, she largely avoids "the subject of political or military events," thereby focusing on domestic matters essential to successful settling. Another sexist stereotype traditionally held against women is alleged inconsistency, while Buss archly contends that women adjust better than men *because* the women "are able to hold contradictions in their personalities." Indeed, Buss's encomium of women in transit could be extended to émigrés in America such as the wife of the minor German writer Erich Juhn. He was so impressed by the speed of his wife's adaptation to New York that he wrote a poem concluding "Das starke Geschlecht is die heutige Frau [The strong sex is the woman of today]" (1983, 83).

The next essay, Shu-mei Shih's "Exile and Intertextuality in Maxine Hong Kingston's *China Men*," provides a further reason why some women have adapted relatively smoothly to exile: they were already used to second-class status. The Chinese male émigrés had something new to learn, for, as Shih remarks, "[Almost universal] sexism saw femininity as a negative quality, and [American] racism imposed that negative quality on [Chinese-American males]." Shih analyzes how Kingston highlights this racism and sexism by counterpointing her main narrative with "intertexts." These are rewritings of traditional Chinese stories, such as "The Ghostmate" about a scholar kept as concubine by a beautiful ghost (the word "ghost" or "demon" being the literal translation of the Chinese word *kuei,* meaning "foreigner"). In Kingston's retelling, the tale becomes (among other things) an allegory of the unfulfilled sexual desires of Chinese men legally long prevented both from bringing Chinese women to the states or from marrying non-Chinese women. When the Chinese wives did arrive, some were the kind of dynamic forces that Buss describes, but that story is more fully told in Kingston's previous book, *The Women Warrior,* than in *China Men*.

Mary Vásquez's "Gender in Exile: Mothers and Daughters in Roberto G. Fernández's *Raining Backwards*" provides another kind of complement to *China Men*. Fernández's book is a male author's version of dynamic (and other) émigrées. A "self-abnegating Latin grandmother, family counselor, repository of family values," Mima (one of the main characters) manages a successful business as well (allegedly) as a number of lovers. One of her sons becomes Pope. The other son, though, is a drug runner and terrorist, while she herself seems to be having growing difficulty reconciling the two "codes" of American and Latin culture.

This vision of émigré (or émigrée) and exile literature as embodying "complex codes" is pursued by the next essay, Robert S. Newman's "The Reader of Exile: Skvorecky's *Engineer of Human Souls.*" It applies to these codes a brand of reader-response criticism. Particularly, it treats the problems of liberals' bewilderment at certain expatriates' books that condemn left-wing ideas (because the expatriates know firsthand the bleakness of enduring the fruition of such ideology in Eastern Europe). Newman applies his method to Skvorecky's "cynicism," "humor," and even "schizophrenic" condition (in Donoso's old sense of the word). Skvorecky's protagonist proclaims, "I am speaking in paradoxes, and they are only partially true I know, but they rouse the intellect out of its winter's sleep of adaptation." By implication, the paradoxes of expatriate literature differ from unconscious inconsistencies of the community in that the former articulate and call attention to the muddle of the latter. Newman ends by quoting expatriate Skvorecky quoting expatriate Evelyn Waugh, "The artist must always be . . . a reactionary" (i.e., in reaction against the thoughtless adaptations of the group).

The main point of Newman's Skvorecky is that when people try to construct a utopia (as the communists did in Eastern Europe) they trample on human liberty. Frank Dietz explores this notion further in his "'Home is a Place Where You Have Never Been': The Exile Motif in the Hainish Novels of Ursula K. Le Guin." For Dietz's Le Guin, utopia (i.e., a perfect society) can never be a literal place but only an "ever present utopian horizon," an incentive for social experiment, not stagnation. Thus, ironically, Le Guin's liberal (indeed anarchist) orientation resembles Skvorecky's "reactionary" one. Dietz shows how Le Guin's novels about the interplanetary settlements of the "Hainish" become more theoretical, going from a "pragmatic" understanding of exile to a "moral" one. Le Guin, however, makes one concession in her ethical imperative to live in spiritual exile, ever exploring the "utopian horizon": she gives her heroes an "ansible," a futuristic communication device that puts them instantly in touch with the home base.

Jefferson Faye's "Cultural/Familial Estrangement: Self-Exile and Self-Destruction in Jay McInerney's Novels," however, uncovers tendencies suggesting that any mass communication system may give society a coherence that could seem utopian but actually becomes a source of alienation, particularly for intellectuals. In analyzing *Bright Lights, Big City* (1984), *Ransom* (1985), and *Story of My Life* (1988), Faye dwells on McInerney's treatment of television and tabloids: slick, exploitative, pseudo-homes away from home, in a world of travel, relocation, and loneliness. Far from McCluhan's benevolent "global village," McInerney's media appear in such forms as a Japanese television show dedicated to the weekly reenactments of gang rapes, double suicides, love-triangle murders, etc. Where such shallow sensationalism takes the place of family and more deeply rooted-culture, the sensitive will already be in exile before they leave home.

Diane Wood's "Atwood and Bradbury: Exile as Rational Decision" continues this theme of emotional expatriation. The future Americas depicted by Ray Bradbury's *Fahrenheit 451* (1967) and Margaret Atwood's *The Handmaid's Tale* (1985) have made indoctrination by mass communication virtually or entirely compulsory and have outlawed reading—for everyone in Bradbury's novel, for one entire class of women in Atwood's nightmarish American theocracy called "Gilead." As Wood explains, in both books, these conditions have come about largely through public apathy. A scholar in Atwood's book, though, notes "racist fears provided some of the emotional fuel that allowed the Gilead takeover to succeed as well as it did" (305)—racism being a form of xenophobia, the fear of emigrants who seem physically different from the main population. Indeed, in *A Handmaid's Tale* any difference of culture, of faith, and most particularly of gender opens one to persecution.

Linda Hollabaugh's "Daniel Moyano's *Libro de navios y borrascas*: The expression of Territorial Exile" concerns a portrayal (part fiction, part autobiography) of those fleeing a real persecution in Latin America. The novel's protagonist is, as Hollabaugh notes, "ashamed of evading reality" yet, as she also shows, the experiences that drove him from homeland are so harrowing that he finds himself unable or unwilling to render them fully into words. At one time a violin teacher in the Conservatorio Provincial (La Rioja, Argentina), the expatriate Moyano makes his protagonist an emigrating violinist whose experience is almost as much rendered in musical as verbal terms (comparable to the complex interrelationship of music and expatriation in Thomas Mann's *Dr. Faustus*).

A common concern with autobiography ties Hollabaugh's essay to Kathleen Beyer's "The Interplay Between E. M. Forster's Indian and Egyptian Writings"—an investigation of travel literature, a vast but largely neglected genre. As a key to Forster's orientalism, Beyer scrupulously documents his attitude toward the East as found both in published works and in unpublished manuscripts housed in Texas and Cambridge. The resulting picture helps establish to what extent Forster's sense of "things falling apart" came from the personal "muddle" that inspired his wanderings and to what extent it accurately reflected his surrounding world.

The culminating essay, John Incledon's "Parricide and Exile: Tracing Derrida in *Yo, el Supremo* by Augusto Roa Bastos" ties together many of the preceding themes. According to Susan Handleman, the French-Algerian world-traveler Jacques Derrida is "another in the line of Jewish prodigal sons" for whom Writing ("Écriture—Scripture?") is a kind of exile or exodus (1982, 166). Incledon begins with his own uncommonly lucid explanation of the relationship of exile and Derridian Deconstruction. Even this beginning is valuable to our collection, related as it is to the complex dichotomy of written words and spoken (televised) presentations, which preoccupies Faye and Wood. Still more interestingly, Incledon shows how the author of *Yo, el Supremo* deliberately used Derrida's notions to (un)structure that celebrated experimental novel. Like Faye, Incledon analyzes exile where it is not literally present, in Incledon's case, a fictional version of Paraguay, hermetically sealed by a totalitarian dictator. Because of Derrida's love/hate relationship with Lacan, figurative exile becomes ambiguously oedipal (as in Wojciehowski's Petrarch). Like Dietz's and Wood's chapters, it concerns the tragically unsuccessful attempt to establish a utopia, but like Hollabaugh's and Beyer's, it touches on the complex relationship of fiction and fact.

Above all, Incledon points to one of the most important aspects of literary exile and emigration, the tie between alienation and "differ*a*nce" in language. Donoso has said:

> The homeland of a writer is not really a place, but a language. The return voyage to Ithaca is an effort to regain one's vernacular, which the intervening silence of years and space has rendered powerless, and plug into it again, even when one lives abroad (1980, 11).

But as Pérez reveals, Donoso found even language slipping away from him in his own version of differ*a*nce and alterity, his "linguistic schizophrenia"—an experience particularly of our century. Seeking that Ithaca (to which Donoso alludes), the original Odysseus could communicate even with the dead who came "ex Erebeus [from Erebus]" (1970, 718) at his summoning. In the end, they return to their proper place and he (eventually) to his. Today, though, how many know (or even believe in the existence of) their proper place? And faith in communication, taken for granted in *The Odyssey* (or *The Book of Dede Korkut*), seems to have drifted away. The tides of relocation (particularly modern travel) have washed together the flotsam and jetsam of traditional cultures and religions[2] profoundly affecting literature.

James Whitlark

Notes

1. Petrarch 1859-63, 90; 1975, 71. See also, 1984, 15.
2. For some of the chief effects of alienation on religions in literature, see my *Behind the Great Wall*.

Works Cited

Atwood, Margaret. *A Handmaid's Tale*. Boston: Houghton Mifflin, 1986.
Beaujour, Elizabeth Klosti. *Alien Tongues: Bilingual Russian Writers of the "First" Emigration*. Ithaca: Cornell University Press, 1989.
Donoso, Jose. "Ithaca: The Impossible Return," *The City College Papers*, Number 18, February 1980.
Eagleton, Terry. *Exiles and Émigrés: Studies in Modern Literature*. New York: Schocken Books, 1970
Giamatti, A. Bartlett. *Exile and Change in Renaissance Literature*. New Haven: Yale University Press, 1984.
Greenfield, Stanley B. *Hero and Exile: The Art of Old English Poetry*. Ed. George H. Brown. London: The Hambledon Press, 1989.
Handleman, Susan A. *The Slayers of Moses: The Emergence of Rabbinic Interpretation in Modern Literary Theory*. Albany: University of New York Press, 1982.
Homer [attributed]. *Ilias; Odyssee*. Eds. J. C. Bruijn and C. Spoelder. Haarlem: H. D. Tjeenk Willink & Zoon, 1970.
Lichtblau, Myron, ed. *La Emigración y el Exilio en la Literatura Hispanica del Siglo Veinte*. Miami, Florida: Ediciones Universal, 1988.
Michael Seidel, *Exile and the Narrative Imagination*. New Haven: Yale University Press, 1986.
Petrarch, Francesco. *Epistolae de rebus familiaribus et variae*. Ed. Joseph Fracasetti. 3 vols. Florence: Typis Felicis Le Monier, 1859–63.
——. *Rerum familiarium libri I-VIII*. Translated by Aldo S. Bernardo. Albany: State University of New York Press, 1975.
Pfanner, Helmut F. *Exile in New York: German and Austrian Writers after 1933*. Detroit: Wayne State University Press, 1983.
Sümer, Faruk, Ahmet E. Uysal, and Warren S. Walker, trans. *The Book of Dede Korkut: A Turkish Epic*. Austin: University of Texas Press, 1972.
Tabori, Paul. *The Anatomy of Exile: A Semantic and Historical Study*. London: Harrap, 1972.
Ugarte, Michael. *Shifting Ground: Spanish Civil War Exile Literature*. London: Duke University Press, 1989.
Whitlark, James. *Behind the Great Wall: A Post-Jungian Approach to Kafkaesque Literature*. London: Fairleigh-Dickson University Press/Associated University Presses, 1991.

Petrarch's Temporal Exile and the Wounds of History
Dolora Wojciehowski

There is virtually no form of exile—spatial, temporal, spiritual, social, and/or psychological—that the fourteenth-century poet Francis Petrarch did not claim to have experienced. Undoubtedly one of the most virtuosic exiles of the last thousand years, Petrarch explored chasms of alienation previously unfathomed. As the late Bart Giamatti argued, "Petrarch's whole existence, his sense of himself, would be determined by his obsession with origin and exile; by his conviction that he was displaced and marginal" (13). Fortunately Petrarch documented his experiences and feelings prolifically, leaving for posterity volumes of letters, meditations, and poems about, above all, his sense of dislocation. I will briefly present several Petrarchan notions of exile before analyzing the ways in which these notions shaped his artistic production.

Possessed of a strong sense of alienation, and, perhaps, an equally strong desire to think of himself as alienated, Petrarch sought to establish certain credentials as an expatriate. He described his originary exile as one inherited from his parents. His father Ser Petracco, a notary and public official, and his mother Eletta were forced to leave Florence in 1302 as a result of the political conflict between rival Guelf factions, the Blacks and the Whites; this ongoing struggle between the factions had resulted in Dante's exile two years earlier (1963, 14–15). Along with many other Florentines, they relocated for a time in Arezzo, where Petrarch was born in 1304. In a 1350 letter to his friend Lodewyck Heyliger, nicknamed "Socrates," Petrarch describes his birth as the first of several harrowing experiences of exile. In this letter, part of a collection known as the *Familiares*, or *Letters on Familiar Matters*, Petrarch compares his wanderings to those of a still more famous expatriate, Ulysses:

> Ulixeos errores erroribus meis confer: profecto, si nominis et rerum claritas una foret, nec diutius erravit ille nec latius. Ille patrios fines iam senior excessit.... Ego, in exilio genitus, in exilio natus sum, tanto matris labore tantoque discrimine, ut non obstetricum modo sed medicorum iudicio diu exanimis haberetur; ita periclitari cepi antequam nascerer et ad ipsum vite limen auspicio mortis accessi. (1933–42, I.1.145–147, 149–153)

> [Compare my wanderings with those of Ulysses; if we were equal in name and fame, it would be known that he traveled no longer or farther than I. He was a mature man when he left his hometown.... But I was conceived in exile and born in exile. I cost my mother such labor and struggle that for a long time the midwives and physicians thought her dead. Thus I began to know danger even before I was born, and I crossed the threshold of life under the loom of death.] (1966, 18–19)

In this passage Petrarch attempts to upstage the peripatetic Ulysses by asserting that his own exile not only began at an earlier stage of life than did the Greek hero's, but also that his exile began before he was born. Petrarch links his actual birth in exile to the notion of birth *as* exile, his mother's labor pains and near death standing metonymically for the poet's future crises—that is, a lifetime of alienation, loss, and frustration.

In the *Familiares* and elsewhere Petrarch routinely depicts himself as a man never completely at home, always removed from some idealized haven. Generally, though, Petrarch figures that haven in non-spatial (i.e., figurative) terms. Thus, it is not necessarily an actual home or homeland that he craves, but often a spiritual one. For example, he writes in 1352 to his ascetic brother Gherardo, a Carthusian monk:

> Adeo michi magnifice visus es et melioris status desiderium ac stimulos incutere et presentis lapsus frena substringere, ut luce clarius videam ubi sim quo ve ire sit necesse quantoque miser absim intervallo ab illa patria nostra Ierusalem ad quam nisi nos nostri immemores fuscus et luteus carcer facit, semper in hoc exilio suspiramus. (1933–42, X.5.10–16)

> [I thought that you most excellently stimulated me to a desire of a better condition of life, and that you imposed proper restraints on my backslidings, in order that I might better recognize where I now stand and whither I must go and how far I am distant from Jerusalem, our home, for which in our exile we must always yearn, unless we are distracted by the filth and darkness of our prison] (1966, 101)

Removed from the heavenly Jerusalem by the very fact of his being alive, Petrarch here defines exile as the condition of having a body. Merely to exist, then, is to be imprisoned in the foul cell of corporeality, exiled from the world of pure spirit.

Such medieval "contemptus mundi" themes recur throughout the *Familiares*. Petrarch writes to his friend Giovanni Boccaccio in 1350:

> ... et quamvis cum corpore nostro quedam nobis innata familiaritas sit, per quam multa in suo corpore fert quisque suaviter que in altero fastidiret, ego tamen raro unquam in alieno cadavere ut nunc in carne propria cognovi quam nichil, imo vero quam miserum et vile animal est homo, nisi ignobilitatem corporis animi nobilitate redemerit. (1933–42, XI.1.67–73)

> [Although our innate familiarity with our bodies is such that we can bear in them what is repulsive in others, I never learned from any corpse the lesson of my own flesh, that man is a vile, wretched animal unless he redeems the ignobility of the body with the nobility of the soul.] (1966, 104)[2]

While Petrarch does not invent or even revive the convention of scorning the bodily prison, he adapts that convention in unique ways to his overall themes of exile. Thus, the notion of the mutability of the flesh becomes for Petrarch not some proof of the predicament of man- or womankind in general, but rather, further proof of his own personal dislocation from some transcendental center.

Arguably, though, the most significant form of dislocation for Petrarch was temporal. For Petrarch has been credited with, among other things, inventing the notion of the Dark Ages, a bleak and desolate stretch of centuries far removed from the pure "radiance" of the past— removed, namely, from classical antiquity.[3] Doomed to contemplate the glories of Greece and Rome from a vast temporal distance, Petrarch lamented his exile from an age he considered far superior to his own, and agonized, too, over yet another sort of exile—his exile from the future. Indeed, Petrarch generated not only a version of the Dark Ages, but also a version of the period concept we now call the Renaissance. In his epic poem *Africa* he wrote to his readers:

> At tibi fortassis, si—quod mens sperat et optat—
> Es post me victura diu, meliora supersunt
> Secula: non omnes veniet Letheus in annos
> Iste sopor! Poterunt discussis forte tenebris
> Ad purum priscumque iubar remeare nepotes.
> (*Africa*, IX, 453–457)

> [But if you, as is my wish / and ardent hope, shall live on after me, / a more propitious age will come again: / this Lethean stupor surely can't endure / forever. Our posterity, perchance, / when the dark clouds are lifted, may enjoy / once more the radiance the ancients knew.] (1977, 239)

In these lines Petrarch asserted his belief that a remarkable recovery of the past was already underway in his own time, and that a new era was fast approaching. Unfortunately Petrarch found himself at the threshold of this "better age," but knew he would not live long enough to cross it. Describing Petrarch's sense of historical isolation, Thomas Greene writes, "the discovery of antiquity and simultaneously the remoteness of antiquity made of Petrarch a double exile, neither Roman nor modern, so that he became in his own eyes a living anachronism" (8). Overwhelmed by this pain of temporal exile, Petrarch compensated for his sense of historical alienation in many ways—for example, by writing wistful letters to dead Roman authors (e.g., his beloved Cicero) and to posterity, thereby attempting to bridge those temporal removes which marked his distance from a brighter past and future.

We have seen in these last few excerpts from his letters that Petrarch represented himself as historically isolated. Let us now consider one figure he used to convey the pain of that displacement—namely, the figure of the wound dealt him by history, and specifically by the prince of Latin eloquence, Cicero. In certain curious letters Petrarch wrote of his wounding—the literal wound, in fact, that had been inflicted by Cicero, Petrarch's favorite Roman author. That is to say, Petrarch had been wounded by a book. We might take the odd series of episodes presented in these letters as not just an academic's nightmare about the dangers of libraries, but also as an allegory of poetic imitation. In so doing we may further understand the connections between Petrarchan exile and the problems of literary influence.

On October 15, 1359, Petrarch wrote to his friend Neri Morando that he was having problems with his foot, which had been wounded by a falling book. Having placed a large volume of Cicero's letters next to the door of his study, standing on the floor of the library, Petrarch surprised himself one day by catching the book with the edge of his gown. He was dealt a small wound on the left leg. In his account of the accident, Petrarch personifies the book, attributing hostility to it: He says to his friend, "Ceterum vir ille de quo loqui ceperam, michi ab ineunte etate tam carus semper et tam cultus, Cicero, qualiter modo mecum luserit, hinc audies! (1933–42, xxi.10.103–105) [Listen to the trick Cicero played on me—Cicero, whom I have loved and cherished since boyhood!]." (1966, 170) He claims to have said to the book itself, "Quid re est, mi Cicero, cur me feris? [What's this, my Cicero? Why are you wounding me?]" In the letter Petrarch adds ironically:

> Ille nichil, sed eodem postridie redeuntem rursum ferit rursumque cum iocis erigitur in suam sedem. Quid te moror? Lesus iterum atque iterum expergiscor, et quasi indignantem humi esse, altius attollo; sed cum iam crebra concussione repetiti loci fracta cutis nec spernendum ulcus extaret, sprevi tamen . . . . (1933–42, XXI.10.116–121)

> [He didn't say a thing; but the next day when I entered the room he smote me again, and jokingly I put him back in his place again. Well, to cut it short, I was repeatedly injured and taken by surprise; and as he seemed to be angry at standing on the floor, I put him higher up. But since the skin was broken by the repeated blows on the same place the sore was not to be disregarded. However, I did disregard it . . . .] (1966, 170)

And because he refused to treat the wound for a long time, Petrarch says that he has come close to causing permanent damage to his leg. He describes to Morando the putrescence of the wound with a certain relish, as well as his blasé attitude toward the festering sore, about which his doctors had expressed great concern.

The following August, nearly a year later, Petrarch describes to Boccaccio the continuing leg crisis. He writes, "vulnus illud Ciceronianum de quo ludere solebam, ludum mihi vertit in luctum. [The wound dealt me by Cicero, about which I used to joke, turned from jest to earnest.]"[4] He reports that the medicines and procedures recommended by his doctors had made things considerably worse, so Petrarch threw them out in order to allow the power of the "coelestis medici [Celestial Physician]" and a young servant to bring him back to health. And he remarks with irony, "Indelebilem memoriae meae notam et stigma perpetuum Cicero mihi meus affixit. [My Cicero has impressed an indelible mark on my memory and a permanent brand on my body]."[5]

What are we to make of this curious set of events? It is striking that Petrarch mentions that he is repeatedly wounded. Yet even though he keeps returning the book to its post by the door, he is "taken by surprise" at each wounding. Why, we might wonder, didn't he move the book in the first place, and why, moreover, did he, albeit jokingly, accuse the book of hostility—hostility provoked by the lowly station that Petrarch has accorded Cicero? One might, of course, read the wounding as a mere accident, the absurdity of which Petrarch points out through his personifications. But humor, arguably, is a polyvalent map of the unconscious, as Freud contended; hence we might read Petrarch's irony as a mode of representing the fact that he stages his wounding several times over.

The compulsion to repeat is, of course, central to Freud's theory of neurosis. Having endured some trauma, a psychic wound, the neurotic "is obliged to *repeat* the repressed material as a contemporary experience instead of . . . *remembering* it as something belonging to the past."[6] The examples of the repetition compulsion that Freud gives are of trauma victims who relive in their dreams some earlier horror, and of an infant who perpetually restages his mother's departure in the form of a game. It is tempting to speculate on Petrarch's repetition of his own injury in the fall of 1359 as a case of Freudian *Wiederholungszwang*, or repetition compulsion. In particular, we might ask, what was it about Petrarch's relation to Cicero—what repressed narcissistic wound—that might have returned in another, literalized form?

First of all, Petrarch's lifelong adoration and emulation of Cicero is well known: "Amavi ego Ciceronem, fateor, et Virgilium amavi . . . ita quasi ille michi parens fuerit, iste germanus." (1933–42, XXII.10.31–32, 34–35) ["I loved Cicero, I admit, and I loved Virgil. . . . I loved Cicero as if he were my father, Virgil as my brother"] (1966, 191). Or, in that same letter to Morando in which he describes his wound, Petrarch writes, "Christus equidem Deus noster, Cicero autem nostri princeps eloquii" (1933–42, XXI.10.70–71) ["Christ is truly our God, but Cicero is our prince of eloquence"] (1975–85, 186). These comments are but two samples of Petrarch's effusive, though not always uncritical, appreciations of the great Latin dialogist, whose writings were for Petrarch the epitome of rhetorical style and philosophical excellence.

At this point it is useful to consider Petrarch's Ciceronian wound in terms of Harold Bloom's theory of the anxiety of influence—that is, the way in which a poet structures in familial terms, Oedipal terms, his relation to his literary precursors. In brief, such anxiety is produced by the weight of a particular history—specifically, by the weight of an inescapable rivalry with the literary forebears that one has chosen to emulate. The anxiety of influence produces one of two outcomes. This anxiety either paralyzes a poet's creative impulses or else it is mastered by his psychic defenses, in which case the poet becomes a "strong reader" of his literary inheritance.

It is possible, of course, to read this episode in Petrarch's ongoing struggle with Cicero to *be* Cicero (indeed, Petrarch is emphatic about his desire to imitate his great Roman precursor) as an example of one of Bloom's "revisionary ratios"—that is, as one of the stages of resolving the conflict between poet and precursor. Bloom writes of "kenosis," or "repetition and discontinuity," as one form of poetic defense against such anxiety. Kenosis, he asserts, involves an act of abasement on the part of the poet; in Petrarch's case, such abasement takes the form of a literal wounding of the poet by his precursor, a wounding that Petrarch seems compelled to repeat several times. "Kenosis," Bloom writes, "appears to be an act of self-abnegation, yet tends to make the fathers pay for their own sins, and perhaps for those of the sons also" (91). By this reasoning, we could say that Petrarch stages a wounding by the father, and, crucially, blames father Cicero in his fantasy of the book's hostility.

What is accomplished by this literal wounding and, perhaps, the symbolic mutilation of the dutiful son, who nearly loses his leg until another father (God, the "Celestial physician," in Petrarch's telling) steps in to heal it? In some sense the result of this defense is the vindication of the son through the guilt of the father/book. This displacement of aggression, the wounding of the son by the father, not only represents a stage of the poet's struggle with his precursor, but also appears to make possible several resolutions in Petrarch's psychic life. We detect in these results further evidence of the agonistic relation of Petrarch to his main literary model.

The first of these resolutions is suggested by a telling second letter to Neri Morando that Petrarch wrote before dawn on October 15th, 1359, just after he had told his friend of his wounding by the book. In this second letter Petrarch describes one of his own fans, a goldsmith from Bergamo, who has become obsessed with Petrarch and his works. The goldsmith, Petrarch relates with pleasure, has bought Petrarch's books, displayed Petrarch's portrait in his house, and, inspired by the poet, has given up his business for literary pursuits. The point of this narcissistic letter? Petrarch expresses his rivalry with Cicero; if the Roman author had devoted admirers, then so does Petrarch. "Ne autem solum Ciceronem diligi ab ignotis credas, unum illis adiciam" (1933–42 XXI.11.4–5) ["But to prove that Cicero is not the only person who has unknown admirers, I shall give you an example."] (1966, 171).

Petrarch confesses that he was persuaded by the goldsmith's "obsecrationibus et lacrimis [beseechings and tears]" to visit Bergamo, where his presence bestowed upon his host preternatural happiness:

> Ibi noctem illam egimus: nec unquam, puto, letiore hospite ulla nox acta est; tanta enim letitia gestiebat, ut timerent sui ne forte in morbum aut amentiam verteretur, sive, quod multis olim accidit, etiam in mortem. (1933–42 XXI.11.87–90)

> [There I passed the night. And never, I think, was a night spent under the auspices of a happier host. In fact he was so transported that his friends were alarmed for fear that he might fall ill or become unhinged, or that he might even die of joy, as has happened to many in times past.] (1966, 173)

The next day, Petrarch says, "honoribus et concursu hominum pulsus abii" (1933–42, XXI.11.91) ["I departed, loaded down with honors and surrounded by a great swarm of people."] (1966, 173). Petrarch's exuberant pleasure at the goldsmith's adulation and at the growing cult of Petrarch is clearly differential; that is, in his own mind it exists in relation to the cult of Cicero, as practiced both in antiquity and in Petrarch's own day—most notably by Petrarch himself. The story of Petrarch's wounding by Cicero is succeeded by the story of Petrarch's taking the place of Cicero. Not only does Petrarch play the role of the idolized mentor in the second letter, but he, like Cicero, threatens (though inadvertently) the health and well-being of his devotee. It seems no accident that the two letters were written together.

A second form of resolution of Petrarch's anxiety vis-à-vis Cicero concerns Petrarch's actual writing practice—specifically, his theory of poetic imitation. In 1359 (the year of the wounding) Petrarch writes an intriguing letter to Boccaccio on the matter of literary rivalry and imitation. Speaking of poetic imitation, he declares that he never borrows or lifts the words of his precursors, "nisi vel prolato auctore vel mutatione insigni, ut imitatione apium e multis et variis unum fiat" (1933–42, XXII.2.99–101). ["I quote the authors with credit, or I transform them honorably, as bees imitate by making a single honey from many various nectars"] (1966, 183). With this famous metaphor, Petrarch naturalizes the poet's relation to his precursors; what could be more innocuous or sweeter, he suggests, than bees making honey of their floral "subtexts."

Using a similar metaphor Petrarch describes how he has ingested his own precursors—Virgil, Horace, Livy, Cicero:

> mane comedi quod sero digererem, hausi puer quod senior ruminarem. Hec se michi tam familiariter ingessere et non modo memorie sed medullis affixa sunt unumque cum ingenio facta sunt meo, ut etsi per omnem vitam amplius non legantur, ipsa quidem hereant, actis in intima animi parte radicibus, sed interdum obliviscar auctorem, quippe qui longo usu et possessione continua quasi illa prescripserim diuque pro meis habuerim, et turba talium obsessus, nec cuius sint certe nec aliena meminerim. (1933–42, XXII.2.75–83)

> [I ate in the morning what I would digest in the evening; I swallowed as a boy what I would ruminate upon as a man. These writings I have so thoroughly absorbed and fixed, not only in my memory but in my very marrow, these have become so much a part of myself, that even though I should never read them again they would cling in my spirit, deep-rooted in its inmost recesses. But meanwhile I may well forget the author, since by long usage and possession I may adopt them and regard them as my own, and bewildered by their mass, I may forget whose they are and even that they are others' work.] (1966,182–183)

In this account of poetic imitation, anxiety is sublimated by digestive transformation—another defense against the wounds of history. "One might argue," writes Thomas Greene, "that already in these digestive and apian analogies there lies in germ the obsessive analogy of a rebirth. The metamorphosis of the ancient into renewed modern life within the poet's consciousness constitutes a kind of renascence" (99). It is not only antiquity that is reborn through the poet's digestion of the past, but also the poet's sense of his own identity in relation to that of his precursors, whose identities, not coincidentally, have been suppressed by the digestive process. This metaphor of digestive transformation, a figure of enormous popularity in the Renaissance, suggests in this letter a resolution to the crises of temporal exile, of historical and poetic belatedness—that is, the poet's temporal distance from antiquity, as well as his sense of distance from the greatness of his precursors. Petrarch obliterates the distinctions between his own age and classical antiquity, and between himself and his precursors, through a set of metaphors that neutralizes poetic rivals (in more ways than one) by *naturalizing* his imitation of them, and that obscures the problem of temporal difference by representing it as an ahistorical digestive process. The figures of digestion and mellification remove poetic rivalry, imitation, from the problematic context of anxiety and loss; thus these figures of ingestion are in a certain sense the figural opposites, and resolutions, of the wounds of history.

In a letter written in September of 1360,[7] just one month after he told Boccaccio about his recovery from the wound, Petrarch suggests a third form of resolution to the Ciceronian conflict. There he writes of his rejection of profane literature in favor of more spiritual offerings:

> Amavi ego Ciceronem, fateor, et Virgilium amavi, . . . hos ita quasi ille michi parens fuerit, iste germanus. . . . Sed iam michi maius agitur negotium, maiorque salutis quam eloquentie cura est; legi que delectabant, lego que prosint . . . . (1933–42, XXII.10.31–32, 34–35, 40–42)

> [I loved Cicero, I admit, and I loved Virgil . . . I loved Cicero as if he were my father, Virgil as my brother. . . . But now I must think of more serious matters. My care is more for my salvation than for noble language. I used to read what gave me pleasure, now I read what may be profitable.] (1966, 191)

What the wounding makes possible, arguably, is Petrarch's permanent exile—that is, his liberation—from father Cicero, for here again the poet figures his relation to his precursors in terms of the family romance. Here that love of Cicero and Virgil is placed in the past tense, and Petrarch suggests that a rupture in the family's unity has occurred—a rupture tenuously motivated by Petrarch's renewed interest in whatever is *not* Cicero and not Virgil. What I am suggesting is that Petrarch resolves, for a time, his lifelong battle with his chosen precursors by means of several defenses: the wounding, a repetition of the father's vengeance against the son; the replacement of the father by the son (via the cult of Petrarch); the metaphor/fantasy of consuming the father (whom the poet absorbs as an innocuous foodstuff); and lastly, the rejecting of the beloved father for the more "profitable"—i.e., less threatening—fathers of the Church.

As Giamatti argued, Petrarch's sense of himself was wholly bound up with his sense of displacement, "for only in perpetual exile could Petrarch gain the necessary perspective on himself truly to determine, or create, who he was" (13). Certainly exile was necessary for Petrarch; the question, though, is why? I have suggested that the wounding of Petrarch, to a large degree staged by the poet, has much to teach us about the psychic necessity of his exile. Indeed, Petrarch's avowed marginality, his temporal displacement, was a necessary fiction enabling his desire to become, in Bloom's terms, a "strong reader." As Thomas Greene says, "The precursor constitutes the present; he determines the atmosphere the poet breathes. Between the precursor and follower, no discontinuity can intervene, since for Bloom discontinuity would be freedom" (31). Perhaps we can say that for Petrarch exile was the primary fantasy of discontinuity that allowed the poet some relief from the tremendous anxiety he seemingly felt because of his "belatedness"—that is, his exile.

It may seem a contradiction that of the resolutions described above, the figuring of imitation as digestion seems to ignore or obliterate exile, while this third resolution insists on Petrarch's permanent exile from his classical, non-Christian precursors. But radical discontinuity on the one hand and undifferentiated continuity on the other are two responses to the same problem of influence and represent different strategies for dealing with an anxiety-provoking—that is, a wounding—precursor. Can we say that Petrarch's fantasy of poetic discontinuity, which he figured as exile, was successful for him? Petrarch's defenses were, apparently, only marginally successful. Despite such defensive strategies, Petrarch never abandoned his obsession with his own illnesses, pain, and frustration. Throughout his life he remained in his own mind wounded in one way or another. The desire to write and to emulate remained for him essentially traumatic: to write, for Petrarch, *was* to be wounded. In the letter to Neri Morando describing the falling book, Petrarch closes by writing, "Ita dilectus meus Cicero cuius olim cor, nunc tibiam vulneravit. Tu integer et illesus, vale" (1933–42, XXI.10.177–178). ["My beloved Cicero has now wounded my leg as he once did my heart. Farewell, O you who are healthy and unwounded."] (1975, 188). The irony of Petrarch's figures of exile, together with his metaphors of compensation, is that they mitigated, but did not finally quell the violence of poetic filiality.

Notes

1. Not only was Petrarch born in exile, but he also chose to remain in exile, as Giamatti discusses. In 1351, when Giovanni Boccaccio brought Petrarch a letter from the governors of Florence that offered him a university chair, as well as his lost patrimony, Petrarch refused to return to Florence. See *Exile and Change* 14.

2. A wound on Petrarch's leg, inflicted by a kick from a horse, occasioned this letter to Boccaccio. Petrarch's contempt for the flesh, he says, is evoked by the overpowering stench of his wound. Cp. the themes of 1933–42, XXI.10, also discussed in this essay.

3. For a discussion of the novelty of Petrarch's conception of history, see Theodor E. Mommsen's classic essay, "Petrarch's Conception of the Dark Ages," *Speculum* 17 (1942): 226–242, and Erwin Panofsky's *Renaissance and Renascences in Western Art* (1960; New York: Harper & Row, 1969), 10–13.

4. This miscellaneous letter, numbered XXV, has been drawn from *Epistolae de rebus familiaribus et variae*, ed. Joseph Fracassetti, 3 vols. (Florence: 1863) 3:368. Bishop 215.

5. This is the author's translation of a line not excerpted by Bishop.

6. *Beyond the Pleasure Principle*, in Vol. 18 of *The Standard Edition of the Complete Psychological Works of Sigmund Freud*, ed. James Strachey (London: Hogarth Press, 1955), 1–10, 18. The above quoted description of the repetition compulsion continues: "These reproductions, which emerge with such unwished-for exactitude, always have as their subject some portion of infantile sexual life—of the Oedipus complex, that is, and its derivatives . . . ."

7. The dating of this letter has not been established with certainty, though Wilkins dates it September 18, 1360. See *Petrarch's Correspondence* 85.

Works Cited

Bishop, Morris. *Petrarch and His World*. Bloomington: Indiana University Press, 1963.
Bloom, Harold. *The Anxiety of Influence: A Theory of Poetry*. New York: Oxford University Press, 1983.
Freud, Sigmund. *Beyond the Pleasure Principle*. In Vol. 18 of *The Standard Edition of the Complete Psychological Works of Sigmund Freud*, ed. James Strachey. London: Hogarth Press, 1955.
Giamatti, Bart. "Hippolytus Among the Exiles." *Exile and Change in Renaissance Literature*. New Haven: Yale University Press, 1984. 12–32.
Greene, Thomas. *The Light in Troy: Imitation and Discovery in Renaissance Poetry*. New Haven: Yale University Press, 1982.
Mommsen, Theodor E. "Petrarch's Conception of the Dark Ages," *Speculum* 17 (1942): 226–242
Panofsky, Erwin. *Renaissance and Renascences in Western Art*. 1960; New York: Harper & Row, 1969.
Petrarca, Francesco. *L'Africa*. Ed. Nicola Festa. Florence: G. C. Sansoni Editore, 1926.
———. *Epistolae de rebus familiaribus et variae*. Ed. Joseph Fracassetti. 3 vols. Florence: Typis Felicis Le Monier, 1859–63.
———. *Le Familiari*. Eds. Vittorio Rossi and Umberto Bosco. 4 vols. Florence: G. C. Sansoni Editore, 1933–1942.
———. *Letters from Petrarch*. Ed. and trans. Morris Bishop. Bloomington: Indiana University Press, 1966.
———. *Letters on Familiar Matters*. 3 vols. Ed. and trans. Aldo Bernardo. Baltimore: Johns Hopkins University Press, 1985.
———. *Petrarch's "Africa"*. Eds. and trans. Thomas Bergin and Alice Wilson. New Haven: Yale University Press, 1977.
Wilkins, Ernest Hatch. *Petrarch's Correspondence*, Medioevo e Umanesimo 3. Padua: Editrice Antenore, 1960.

Triple-Tiered Migration in *The Book of Dede Korkut*
Warren Walker

One of the many epics of the widely distributed Turkic peoples, *The Book of Dede Korkut* is the oldest literary masterpiece of the Turks of present-day Turkey. Beneath its episodes of love, war, internecine struggle, and interface with the world of the supernatural lies its unifying theme of migration: physical movement from Central Asia to the Caucasus and Middle East, religious progression from animism toward Islam, and the cultural journey from open-range tent life of the steppes to the more structured existence of permanent settlements and solid buildings. The trip takes centuries, and both story and text are as errant as the quasi-historical scenario.

The protagonists of *The Book of Dede Korkut* are the Oghuz, a confederation of twenty-four Turkish tribes divided into two branches of twelve tribes apiece, the Inner Oghuz and the Outer Oghuz. The name of the latter suggests that they were the guardians of the borders of the Oghuz territory, though in the epic there is little distinction between the two branches until a civil war erupts between them in the tragic last episode of the work. Once part of the Göktürk Empire of far eastern Asia, the Oghuz, numbering several hundred thousand people, had gone their own way sometime before the ninth century to establish a homeland in the broad area between the Amu Darya (Oxus River) and the Syr Darya (Jaxartes River), east of the Caspian and south of the Aral Seas. (Most of this land now lies within the Uzbek and Kazakh Soviet Socialist Republics.) There these pastoral people found ideal climatic and topographical conditions for the breeding of livestock: camels, cattle, goats, horses, and sheep. Ibn Fadlan, an emissary of the caliph at

Baghdad, passed through their area in 921 (the period of the epic's origin) and reported seeing numerous beys (feudal barons) with flocks of 100,000 sheep and herds of 10,000 horses (1972, 17).

The Oghuz epic eventually took its title from a historical person named Korkut, incorrectly thought to be the composer and first singer of the twelve narratives which comprise the work. *Dede* means *grandfather;* Korkut was also at times called *Ata,* meaning *father.* Actually, however, the present title is a latter-day creation, probably the interpolation of a scribe; for at least 300 years after its tenth-century origin the epic was referred to simply as *Oghuz namah*—Oghuz legend. Although there is a bard/shaman named Korkut who is an important character within the epic, it is most unlikely that he was its "author." Like many other folk epics, *The Book of Dede Korkut* is a set of long prose-and-verse ballads selected from a much larger body of floating narratives which countless minstrels had been singing over a considerable period of time. The selection was made and given a framework by some unidentified "Homer," an enterprising minstrel with a good sense of organization. Even then the oral text could not be considered fixed, for it is in the very nature of minstrelsy for individual performers to accept or reject given episodes, to develop their own variants, and thus, within certain limits, to alter the tradition. It seems clear that some such narrative license was exercised by the singers of Oghuz exploits. How, otherwise, can one account for inconsistencies and duplications within the present form of the epic? In the second tale Bamsi Beyrek with the Gray Horse is described as ". . . he who fled from Parasar's Bayburt Castle" (1972, 24), but in the sole surviving text he makes no escape until the third tale, and then it is from a different castle. Indeed, nowhere in the existent tales does he ever flee Bayburt Castle. To cite just one instance of duplication here, Shökli Melik, most hated enemy of the Oghuz, is killed three times, under different circumstances, in three different sections of the epic.

Exactly when the epic was first written down is unknown, but it was not until the first quarter of the fourteenth century that a written text was reported. Ebu Bekr Ibn Devadari, author of an important history of the Middle East, read and partially summarized a text of that time being used by Oghuz minstrels. Although only Devadari's notes on it—published by Köprülü (279)—now remain, this book can be considered the first transcribed "edition" of *The Book of Dede Korkut.* There is no way of estimating how many redactions of that "edition" may have been made before the second known written "edition" (the basis for all modern editions) appeared in the last quarter of the sixteenth century. This second "edition," written in the dialect of Eastern Anatolia and

Azerbaijan, was long neglected until its rediscovery in the Dresden Library early in the nineteenth century. Then it was to be almost another century before the first complete text of that "edition" was transliterated and published in book form by Kilisli Rifat at Istanbul in 1916. Had it never been reproduced in either manuscript or book form, however, the work would not have been entirely lost, for several episodes in the epic are still very much alive in the oral tradition in Turkey and in the Turkic republics of the Soviet Union.[1]

The Prologue of the epic seems clearly to be the handiwork of the sixteenth-century editor. It quite properly projects the action that follows backward to a much earlier time, so much so, in fact, that the writer assumes the role of antiquarian. This retrospective focus is maintained throughout the tales by explanations of customs and practices "in the time of the Oghuz." Inasmuch as the Oghuz became generally known as Türkmen or Turkomans after their conversion to Islam, the very use of the word *Oghuz* sounds an echo of yesteryear. The Prologue also serves to introduce the Middle Eastern scene (by the use of place names of the area) and to emphasize the Moslem *Weltanschauung* of that later time. Just as *Beowulf* was an essentially pagan work with an overlay of Christianity, *The Book of Dede Korkut* is a patently pagan epic with an ambience of Islam superimposed upon it. Islamization of Central Asia was just beginning in the tenth century, and the heroes of the narratives are more nominal than practicing Moslems. They may testify frequently to the Oneness of God, and they may battle to convert the infidel, but, in truth, their own faith is but skin-deep. They do not issue the five daily calls to prayer; they do not observe the required fasting and asceticism during the month of Ramadan; they do not make the usual Moslem preparations for death; and they do not make, plan to make, or even discuss the recommended pilgrimage to Mecca.

There follow then twelve tales, each an artistic entity unto itself but related to the rest of the epic by theme and shared dramatis personae.[2] The physical migration of the Oghuz westward resulted from pressure upon them from both the north and the east. Because of population growth among many other Turkic tribes, these remote kinsmen pushed into the Oghuz homeland in Central Asia. Most readily identifiable (both historically and linguistically) of these intruders were the extensive communities of Kipchak Turks. These were the enemies against whom the historical Oghuz were struggling in the tenth century, and these were the infidels whom the Oghuz of the epic engaged in battle. If the Oghuz were able to blunt the Kipchak thrust and relinquish territory to them only step by step, they were far less effective against the Mongols, whose Golden Horde swept through Asia into Europe in the thirteenth century, attacking simultaneously Byzantines and Russians (the latter of whom they conquered). The Oghuz religious and cultural migrations were concomitants of this compulsory trek to the Caucasus and Asia Minor.

With all the zeal of the newly converted, the Oghuz maligned the Kipchaks as barbarous infidels, "men with the savage religion," (1972, 75) who "have cooks who prepare human flesh" (1972, 74). But ironically, except for their veneer of Islam, the Oghuz were in their customs, practices, and lifestyle quite similar to these adversaries. The Kipchaks were animists, and the Oghuz sometimes reverted to that religious position when they were under extreme duress. Thus (in II) when his household and camp have been destroyed and his family and best troops carried away into captivity, Kazan appeals to elements of nature for explanation and consolation. Curiously, his apostrophe to the waters of a stream contains allusions to details of Islamic history.

> Oh, water that gushes from under the rocks;
> Oh, water that tosses the ships made of wood;
> Oh, water once sought by Hasan and Hüseyin;[3]
> Oh, water, a treasure for gardens and vineyards;
> Oh, water so cherished by Ayshe and Fatma;[4]
> Oh, water, the drink of all beautiful horses;
> Oh, water drunk deeply by thirsty red camels;
> Oh, water near which lie the flocks of white sheep—
> Do you know what disaster has come to my camp? Oh, speak!
> May my luckless head be a sacrifice to you![5] (1972, 28)

Crossing the stream, Kazan meets a wolf. Before he addresses this wild creature, he says to himself, "This wolf has a blessed face. He may know. Let me speak to him" (1972, 28). A wolf with a *blessed* face? For many centuries before the time of the epic the wolf had been the most important totemic animal not only to the Oghuz but also to many, perhaps most, Turkic peoples,[6] and in pre-Moslem Turkic mythology there are accounts of benevolences bestowed by Bozkurt (Gray Wolf), including a miraculous rescue from destruction of a whole generation of Turks. Annual ceremonies celebrating this miracle continue to this day in Central Asia and even (according to Mustafa Uslu, 23–29) in the eastern provinces of modern Turkey. Kazan's final expression of grief and dismay is made to a sheep dog. After each of these apostrophes by Kazan, the narrator demurs: "But how could the water [wolf, dog] inform him?" (1972, 28,29)—quite likely interpolations of the fully Islamized sixteenth-century editor/scribe. In the same tale Kazan's son, Uruz, praises a tree in verse lines beginning, "Be not offended, O Tree, that I call you 'tree'" (1972, 33). Both his apology for not having a more worthy name for the tree and the whole tone of his eulogy echo the reverence of the numerous tree cults among Turks during their animistic years.[7]

When Seghrek, the hero of X, discusses with his wife the possibility of his death in battle, he gives her instructions concerning his last rites: "Slaughter my horse and give my funeral feast" (1972, 149). This terse comment is not meant to suggest that his horse was to be the main fare at the feast. Rather, the horse was to be killed so that it, along with its owner's weapons, could be buried in the same grave with Seghrek—hardly a Moslem funeral practice! Studies ranging from Mahmut of Kashgar's eleventh-century primary work, *Divani Lugati Turk* (I, 338–339), to Abdülkadir Inan's recent "Orta Asyadaki Türk Kültür Izleri" (4,817–4,821) testify amply to this ancient Turkish custom.

No other character in the epic has greater ambivalence between the old and the new, between the animistic past and the Moslem present, than the titular author, Dede Korkut. The opening paragraph of the Prologue places him in the animistic period and attributes to him some of the qualities of the shaman.

> Shortly before the time of the Prophet [570–632] there appeared in the Bayat tribe a man by the name of Korkut Ata. He was the wise man of the Oghuz people. He used to prophesy and bring reports from the unknown world beyond, having been divinely inspired. Korkut Ata was an adviser of the Oghuz people in all vital matters, and nothing was done before he was consulted. Whatever advice he gave was accepted and acted upon (1972, 3).

His familiarity with the "unknown world beyond" enables him alone of all the Oghuz to negotiate with the otherworldly monster Tepegöz in VIII. He was also the bard of the Oghuz who immortalized each of their adventures portrayed in the epic by reciting and singing its story immediately after the conclusion of its action. In these performances he always accompanied himself on the *kopuz*, a three-stringed lutelike instrument thought to be the forerunner of the *saz*, an instrument used by Turkish folk minstrels today. At the end of a narrative, he sometimes emphasizes the identity of the protagonist, as he does in III: "Let this Oghuz legend be Beyrek's" (1972, 69) and in V: "Let this legend be Delü Dumrul's" (1972, 97).

But if Dede Korkut had lived "shortly before the time of the Prophet," he could neither have been a real-life character in a tenth-century literary work nor have played the public role (outside the epic) credited to him by several major historians. Beginning in the early fourteenth century with Reshid ud-din, these historians described him as having been a statesman, a competent diplomat, and an adviser to such ninth- and tenth-century kings as Inal Sir Yabgu, Kayi Inal Khan, and Tuman, all of whom reigned in the Central Asian city of Yeni Kent. The credibility of such historians is somewhat eroded by their insistence on his remarkable longevity: 250 years! Korkut was later incorporated into

Islamic hagiography as a Moslem saint, and in what had been the Oghuz homeland, he became the object of a cult. According to Chadwick and Zhirmunsky (310), his legendary tomb remained till this century a tourist attraction at what is now the station of Khorkut on the Tashkent-Kazilinsky Railroad.

Regardless of his equivocal historicity, there is also the post-animistic side of Korkut in *The Book of Dede Korkut*. After reciting a legend and dedicating it to its protagonist, Korkut prays for the welfare of "my khan," a device which enables succeeding minstrels to pray for their respective khans too.

> Let me pray for you, my khan. May your snow-covered mountains remain standing and your strong shade trees be not cut down. May your beautiful running streams never dry up, and may Almighty Allah never allow you to lie at the mercy of the wicked. May your white horse never slip while running. May your fine steel sword never be nicked while being struck. May your glittering spear never be broken in combat.
>
> May the resting place of your white-bearded father and white-haired mother be in paradise. May Allah keep you loyal to your faith. May those who say "Amen" see the face of Allah. (Sümer, 39)

The one unmistakable miracle that Dede Korkut performs—paralyzing the arm of the ferocious Delu Tundar as he is about to kill the bard—is achieved by praying and invoking the name of Allah. There seems to be little doubt that much of the Moslem content was added by the sixteenth-century editor. Inasmuch as he was a resident of the Erzurum area (judging from his dialect), we can infer that his religious outlook was as far removed from that of the tenth-century Oghuz as his geographical location was from Turkestan.

Transfer from the early Central Asian world of animism to the Moslem world of the Middle East and from a tribal political structure to that of the Ottoman Empire brought marked social and sociological changes. The Oghuz were first organized in a *comitatus* arrangement. All the beys owed allegiance to an absolute ruler—Bayindir, Khan of Khans, in the epic—who was the unquestioned ultimate authority in all important decisions and, at the same time, the wise and benign protector of his people. To him was brought all of the tribal income, and he, in turn, parceled it back, according to his best judgment, to his supporters. He made this redistribution of wealth at sumptuous banquets which he held periodically. Consistent with the nomadic ethos of the time, much of that income derived from the spoils of war, the payment of tribute, and the booty taken during forays against infidel groups. (The word *plunder* did not then have all the negative connotations it later acquired.) Kazan, next in Oghuz status, followed a somewhat similar practice. As Bayindir's son-in-law and military commander-in-chief—his title was Beylerbey, Bey of Beys—Kazan received a hefty portion of the rewards dispensed. In order to avoid any ill will over this, he annually gave most of it to his followers in what was known as a "plunder banquet." After feasting the beys at length, Kazan would remove his family to a safe place and then invite his guests to plunder his tent, taking whatever they wished of his household goods and weapons. In post-tribal times this looting free-for-all was replaced by the presentation of gifts to departing guests.[8]

The move to Moslem territory also produced a sharp decline in the status of women via the veil, the head covering, the harem, polygamy,[9] and exclusion from most public life. Before Islamization and its accompanying Arabian influence, Turkish women, according to Mahmut of Kashgar (I, 374), had no such restrictions imposed upon them. Nor were they stereotyped as having inferior intelligence. They were sometimes pictured as being wiser than their husbands; Dirse Khan (II) and Begil (IX) survive periods of crisis only because they follow the sage counsel of their wives. Furthermore, Oghuz women sometimes exhibited considerable physical prowess. Of the twenty-odd women in *The Book of Dede Korkut*, three—Banu Chichek (III), Burla Hatun (IV), and Seljen Hatun (VI)—engage successfully in armed combat against male antagonists. The third of these Amazonian girls is so strong that "[she] was able to stretch the strings of two bows at the same time, one with her right hand and one with her left" (1972, 99).

Most displaced people suffer some degree of culture shock, and undoubtedly the historical Oghuz experienced this variety of psychological dilemma. The wonder is, however, that *The Book of Dede Korkut* itself, through whatever intentions or inadvertencies, retains some of the same split response. The enemies against whom the Oghuz fight in the Middle East are Georgians, Greeks, and a tribe related to the Circassians, but all of the specific infidels identified have Kipchak names: Shökli Melik, Bugajik Melik, Kara Arslan Melik, Demir Yayla Kipchak Melik, Sunu Sandal Melik, Ak Melik Cheshme, Arshin Ughu Direk Tekur, and Kara Tekur. (*Melik* was a title used by the Kipchaks.) Many of the battles of the legendary Oghuz are waged to capture such castles as those at Trabzon, Bayburt, and Tortum (in Turkey), and Tatyan Castle (in Georgia), or to secure such a strategic mountain defile as Demir Kapu Dervent (Iron Gate Pass), on the route northeast from Azerbaijan to the Caucasus. But except for these military sites, many of the place names are Central Asian. Oghuz shepherds still take their flocks to water at Emet Stream (a tributary of the Syr Darya); Oghuz hunters pursue their quarry in the Karachuk Mountains (close to the Syr Darya); and Oghuz horsemen ride not the spirited Arabian steeds favored in the Middle East but the slower, sturdier Kasilik mounts bred in the bottomlands of the Amu Darya and Syr Darya. The feet of the heroes had wandered far, but their hearts had never left home!

Notes

1. For annotated bibliographies of the Beyrek (III), Delü Dumrul (V), and Tepegöz (VIII) tales still narrated in the *cante fable* fashion in Turkey, see Gökyay (xliv–lxxi), Ergin (102–104), and Öztelli (1,771–1,773). For several texts of these surviving tales see holdings of the Archive of Turkish Oral Narrative, Texas Tech University.

2.   I.   The Story of Bugach Khan, Son of Dirse Khan

Domestic troubles; lengthy childlessness of couple ends (through supernatural intervention) with birth of son; ironic Oedipal conflict almost ends in tragedy.

      II.   The Sack of the House of Salur Kazan: War.

      III.   The Story of Bamsi Beyrek, Son of Kam Büre

The great love story of the epic; marriage delayed by several obstacles, including fifteen-year captivity of male romantic lead, Bamsi Beyrek.

      IV.   The Story of the Capture of Uruz Bey, Son of Kazan Bey

      V.   The Story of Delü Dumrul, Son of Duha Koja

Conflict between brave but reckless Delü (Mad) Dumrul and Azrail, the Angel of Death; Alcestis motif included.

      VI.   The Story of Kan Turali, Son of Kanli Koja

Love story, elaborated through dangerously difficult suitor tests.

      VII.   The Story of Yigenek, Son of Kazilik Koja

Sixteen-year captivity of Kazilik Koja ended when Yigenek reaches maturity and captures castle in which his father is imprisoned.

      VIII.   The Story of Basat, Killer of the One-Eyed Giant

Execution of monstrous oppressor of Oghuz' people by young hero.

      IX.   The Story of Emren, Son of Begil

After Begil leaves Council of Bayindir on point of punctilio, he breaks leg—Divine punishment?—in hunting accident; helpless, he is saved from death at hands of enemies by divinely aided son; later returns to Council.

      X.   The Story of Seghrek, Son of Ushun Koja

Release of Eghrek from captivity by brother, Seghrek, when latter reaches maturity.

      XI.   The Story of Salur Kazan's Captivity and His Rescue by His Son, Uruz

Capture of Oghuz military commander and rescue, years later, by his son.

      XII.   The Story of the Revolt of the Outer Oghuz against the Inner Oghuz and of the Death of Beyrek

Civil war which threatens to be Oghuz. *Gotterdämmerung:* Kazan prevails and restores order.

These stories, as well as others which Dede Korkut was said to have sung at Oghuz banquets, are often referred to within the epic as legends. Most of them would indeed qualify for inclusion under that rubric as it is defined by Kenneth and Mary Clarke in their *Introduction to Folklore:* "Narratives about persons, places or events including real or pretended belief are legends" (24). If at least some possibility of historicity is the basic criterion, then V and VIII are not legends. Delü Dumrul's conflict with the Angel of Death in V has parallels in the folklore of many peoples. The tale of the one-eyed giant Tepegöz has more folkloric dimensions than its closest analogue, namely, the Polyphemus episode in *The Odyssey*. The Greek epic gives no account of the origin of its Cyclopean figure, but *The Book of Dede Korkut* shows Tepegöz to be the offspring of a mortal man and an otherworldly lover, a water nymph. The use of the Demon Lover motif here is analyzed most thoroughly by Walter

Ruben in his *Die 25 Erzählungen des Dämons* (244–253). Ordinary human beings cannot cause the death of this partly supernatural being, a task finally accomplished by a most extraordinary mortal. The slayer, Basat, had been suckled and reared by a lioness—another widely distributed fantasy of the folk imagination.

Slightly more than a third (35%) of *The Book of Dede Korkut* is in verse, these lines comprising much of the dialogue. The narrative is, for the greater part, in prose. It is likely that versions of the epic earlier than the surviving written text had a higher proportion of verse. Throughout the epic a number of metaphorical passages are repeated with such regularity that they have a formulaic quality. Human welfare and security (or the lack of same) are often expressed in terms of objects of the pastoral scene: mountain pastures, streams of clear running water, shade trees. In X, for example, Seghrek's mother indicates favorable change of fortune with these lines:

> If the mountain that lies out yonder
> Once fell, now it rises again;
> If the beautiful swift-running stream
> Once dried up, now it rushes again;
> If the branch of the large spreading tree
> Withered once, it grows green once again.
> (Sümer, 147)

There is no chronological order or sense of sequence in these tales, nor does the theme develop from the beginning of the epic to its end. Whatever amplified resonance it may have in the later narratives is largely a matter of cumulative effect. All three levels of migration are ever-present, but they do not actually progress from I through XII. Time is a clearly discernible element only within the context of individual narratives, especially in the five captivity legends (III, IV, VII, X, XI). The fifteen-year imprisonment of Bamsi Beyrek (III) and the sixteen-year detention of Yigenek's father (VII) foreground time with the emphasis of a waiting game. But the passage of time within the context of the total work is merely implied, primarily by the establishment of new campsites. Six of the tales (I, II, III, IV, VII, IX) begin with the same formulaic opening:

> Khan Bayindir, the son of Kam Gan, arose and had his bright tent set up on the black earth. As the many-colored canopy rose toward the sky, silk carpets were laid down in a thousand places. (1972, 40)

Wherever this occurs, it reflects a lapse of time, for the erection and striking of the huge domed tent (*otagh*) of Central Asia were not undertaken merely for exercise! No dates appear in the epic, nor are there any indications of the length of the intervals between stopping places of the Oghuz.

3. The sons of Ali, the fourth Caliph. Hasan succeeded Ali but was forced to abdicate. His younger brother, Hüseyin, was martyred in the desert near Kerbela while trying to recapture the caliphate for the family.

4. Although these are probably the two most common female names in Islamic lands, they refer to two specific women when they are used alone without further identification. Ayshe was Mohammed's favorite wife. Fatima (sometimes shortened to *Fatma*) was the Prophet's favorite daughter, the wife of Ali, and the mother of Hasan and Hüseyin.

5. An expression commonly used by someone asking another person for help. The sense is this: "If you will help me in this matter, I shall be so indebted that I'd give my life for you if need be."

6. See Banks and Rahmet (*passim*).

7. See Ülkütashir's book on Turkish tree lore.

8. The modern guest at a dinner already feels obligated to his/her hosts. To prevent causing the guest embarrassment by giving him still more, hosts giving such parting presents often say, "This is for the rental of your teeth." See Walker and Uysal (58).

9. It is somewhat ironic that the only instance of polygamy in the epic occurs in that work's greatest love story (III).

Works Cited

Bank, W., and G. R. Rahmet, Eds. *Oghuz Kaghan Destani*. Istanbul: Istanbul University Press, 1936.

Chadwick, Nora K., and Victor Zhirmunsky. *Oral Epics of Central Asia*. London: Cambridge University Press, 1969.

Clarke, Kenneth, and Mary Clarke. *Introduction to Folklore*. New York: Holt, Rinehart and Winston, 1963.

Ergin, Muharrem. "Dede Korkut Üzerinde, II," *Turk Dili ve Edebiyati Dergisi*, 6 (1954): 102–105.

Gökyay, Orhan Shaik. *Dede Korkut*. Istanbul: Gökyay, 1938.

Ibn Fadlan. *Rihle* [921], ed. Zeki V. Togan. Leipzig: Deutsche Morgenländische Gesellschafte, 1939.

Inan, Abdülkadir. "Orta Asyadaki Türk Kültür Izleri," *Turk Folklor Arashtirmalari*, 10 (1967): 4,817–4,821.

Köprülü, Fuad. *Ilk Mutasavvuflar* [1918]. Istanbul: Diyanet Ishleri Bashkanlighi Yazinlari, 1966.

Mahmut of Kashgar. *Divani Lugati Turk* [1074], ed. Besim Atalay, 3 vols. Ankara: Türk Dil Kurumu, 1939.

Öztelli, Jahit. "Dede Korkut: Bamsi Beyrek'in Sivas Söylentisi," *Türk Folklor Arashtirmalari*, 5 (1958): 1,771–1,773.

Reshid ud-din. *Jami-ut tevarih* [14th century], ed. Ahmet Atesh. Ankara: Türk Tarih Kurumu, 1957.

Rifat, Kilisli. *Kitab-i Dede Korkut ala Lisan-i Ta'ife Oghuzan*. Istanbul: Asar-i Islamiye ve Milliye Tedkik Encümeni Neshriyati, 1916.

Ruben, Walter. *Die 25 Erzählungen des Dämons*. Helsinki: Academia Scientiarum Fennica, 1944.

Sümer, Faruk, Ahmet E. Uysal, and Warren S. Walker. *The Book of Dede Korkut: A Turkish Epic*. Austin: University of Texas Press, 1972; reprinted in paperback, 1991.

Uslu, Mustafa. "The Neuruz Motives in Turkish Culture," in *Neuruz* (Ankara: Anadolu Press Union, 1988), 23–29.

Ülkütashir, M. S. *Turk ve Islam Geleneghinde Aghach*. Ankara: Türk Etnografya ve Folklor Derneghi Yayinlari, 1963.

Walker, Warren S., and Ahmet E. Uysal. *Tales Alive in Turkey* [1966]. Lubbock: Texas Tech University Press, 1990.

Paradigms of Exile in Donoso's Spanish Fiction
Janet Pérez

Donoso's numerous and prolonged absences from Chile cannot all be properly termed exile, because he was an expatriate before choosing self-exile. Something of a nomad, he first left Chile in 1943 at age nineteen, spending four years in Argentina and Patagonia where he worked as a goatherd before returning to Santiago to complete his secondary education. Less than two years later, he enrolled at Princeton and began his literary career with a short story written in English. After obtaining his degree, he prolonged his stay abroad with travels through Mexico and Central America, finally returning to Chile in 1952 where he remained for six years—the longest period of residence in his native land after adolescence. He returned to Buenos Aires in 1958, spending two years, and met his future wife (whom he married in 1961). Four more years in Santiago (1960–64) saw him established as a journalist, literary critic, editor and lecturer, gaining incipient recognition as a writer. His departure in 1964 for a writers' congress in Mexico initiated a prolonged self-exile interrupted only by brief visits in 1975 and 1980. After a stint as writer in residence at the University of Iowa, 1965–67, Donoso moved to Mallorca in 1967. Spain became his principal residence thereafter, and, beginning in 1970 with *El obsceno pájaro de la noche*, his works have been published in Spain. He lived in Barcelona, in the Mediterranean resort of Sitges, and the isolated Castilian village of Calaceite. During almost half a century, Donoso spent a scant dozen years in Chile.

His nomadic existence led a reviewer for *the New York Times* in 1977 to comment that he "sounds like a man without a country or a history of his own" (1977, 14). Donoso was preparing to return to Chile in 1973 when the military coup forced him to cancel the trip. Visiting his homeland in 1975, he found the new regime so oppressive that he "exiled himself to Spain, never to return" (Schwartz 104–05).

Spain under Franco was not known for its liberalism, and if Donoso chose to live there, his reasons were not primarily political. In an interview with Graciela Carminatti (published 1982), Donoso affirmed:

> ... llevaba la conciencia de que Chile era un país limitado que me imponía reglas literarias que no me gustaban, yo quería usar mis propias máscaras, no las impuestas por el país ... yo esencialmente salí de Chile por eso, porque quería perder relación con un barrio, con una casa, con un modo de vida, quería elegir lo propio ... (57)

> [I was aware that Chile was a limited country which imposed literary rules I didn't like; I wanted to use my own masks, not those imposed by the country ... I left Chile essentially for that reason because I didn't want to be identified with a neighborhood, a house, a way of life—I wanted to choose my own.]

Still earlier, he had discussed the strength of Chilean identity:

> Indiscutiblemente, 'chileno' explica muchas cosas. Significa tener un mundo muy ordenado, muy estructurado ... Es decir, la característica de Chile es que es un país cuyas fronteras son tan infinitamente naturales ... que no hay duda de que Chile tiene una *identidad* (1971, 525). [Undoubtedly, being "chilean" explains a lot. It means having a very orderly, very structured world. That is, Chile is a country whose borders are so infinitely natural that there can be no doubt as to its identity].

Such affirmations explain Donoso's expatriation, but insofar as they reveal the depth of his attachment to his native soil, they also indicate why exile could not be easy.

And distance alone does not guarantee the psychological independence of the émigré. Donoso's diaries and notebooks written from 1967 to 1975 are a veritable archive of nostalgia and homesickness for Chile, only intensified by the coup in 1973. Literary uncertainty gave way to fear of reprisals by the regime. His internal suffering during these years led, as Gutiérrez Mouat observes, to the writing of *Casa de campo* (6), an allegorical novel of social and political oppression set in a vague, unnamed, primitive, tropical land which observers had little difficulty in recognizing as Chile, despite the presence of multiple disguises. Logically, the exile experience may be reflected in nostalgia for the distant homeland (portrayed realistically or metaphorically) or by the presence of the land of exile in the exiled writer's works; both expressions appear in the writings of Donoso. Only the reflections of Spain, his most lasting home in exile, will be examined here. In addition to the portrayals of Spain, such motifs as criticism of the distant homeland and the presence of compatriots and other exiles are constant and obsessive.

Donoso himself has talked at length of the exile experience in his own work and that of his generation. A lecture on the subject of exile, given in New York in English, was significantly entitled "Ithaca: The Impossible Return," alluding to the *Odyssey* as the prototype of exilic experience:

> Exile—and I shall use this word, perhaps inappropriately, meaning both political and voluntary absence from one's own country—exile, then, is . . . a shared, a collective experience, from which I think the greater part of Latin American contemporary fiction derives its strength . . . .living isolated, as an expatriate in Spain in the sixties and seventies, remote from the shattering experiences of those who stayed behind in my country—or in my continent, for that matter—is the strongest collective experience I have ever undergone . . . .(6)

Donoso observed that his case is not exceptional, as the major Latin American novelists of his generation wrote the most important part of their works in exile, including Cortázar, García Márquez, Vargas Llosa, Roa Bastos, Fuentes, Cabrera Infante, and Manuel Puig.[1]

Exile is not only enforced absence from the homeland and separation from family or loved ones. Donoso described other practical consequences quite graphically:

> There are hordes of Argentinians in exile in Europe, lawyers washing dishes, professors of philosophy from Uruguay tending bars, long queues to get working-permits, marriages broken up, Chileans like me who have lost or are in danger of losing their identity, architects making *empanadas* to sell, little, unattractive bead necklaces no longer in fashion, *batik*, toys, pictures, anything. I know the political incertitude, the terror which suddenly strikes down when news of more killing suddenly arrives, and the ambivalent guilt of the few who have been able to make a go of it at their own thing, the lack of security, of faith in everything but especially in words, the frustration of being considered fifth-class citizens in France, of hating Swedish weather notwithstanding the security offered, the gradual loss of everything . . . yes, I've known this sorry crowd in Eastern and Western Europe alike. ("Ithaca" 15–16)

Essentially everything enumerated here appears in *El jardín de al lado* (1981), but also figures in Donoso's short fiction published in Spain, the *Tres novelitas burguesas* (1973), which paint the politico-social and cultural environment of Catalonia and provide the first unequivocal literary evidence of Donoso's reactions to the intellectual and psychic ambience of the Peninsula.[2]

Directly or metaphorically, these novelettes reflect exilic experience. "Chattanooga Choo-Choo," a critique of materialism, drugs, and easy eroticism among the haute-bourgeoisie of contemporary Barcelona, includes a drunken Latin American writer who appears uninvited at a party to fight with a publisher because his novel isn't selling—a motif repeated in *El jardín de al lado*. The two insult and choke each other, until the writer is thrown out bodily, rejection or ejection being paradigmatic of the exile's situation. The exiled writer loses a crucial element which affects him as artist to a degree not found in the case of other exiles: his public. Donoso suffered acutely from this loss, as is seen symbolically in the sterility of the painter in "Atomo verde #5," an allegorical representation of the exiled artist's frustration due to separation or distance from the homeland: his "seed" will bear no fruit. The writer's separation from his "native" public also has its effects on language and communication. Donoso indicates that he suffered language problems approaching "linguistic schizophrenia" (1982, 14):

> I began to become unable to use the unquestioned, 'natural' Chilean-Spanish vernacular which, no matter how literary it became, I had used without qualms up until then... But academic Spanish, or even the Spanish of the streets and everyday life ... was just as foreign, just as unmanageable for me (1982, 13).

Schizophrenia as a metaphor for the splitting in two of the authors torn between homeland and home-in-exile is anticipated in *El obsceno pájaro de la noche* when the narrative consciousness, symbolically dubbed "El Mudito," finds his works and identity preempted, his ability to communicate paralyzed to such an extent that he cannot even protest when he is rolled up in a ball of trash and thrown away.

The third novelette, "Gaspard de la Nuit," introduces other motifs common to several of Donoso's works written in exile, with homosexuality, schizophrenia, sterility, absence, estrangement, the double and role reversal being among the most noteworthy. These are paradigms of exile or metaphors of exilic experience. Motifs of dismemberment and disintegration are probable metaphors of painful separation from the homeland, while the frequent presence of gays alludes expressionistically to loss of a once-orderly world, the exile's almost schizoid difficulties in communication and pervading sense of estrangement. In the *Tres novelitas burguesas,* as well as *El jardín de al lado,* schizoid personalities abound, together with other identity problems, emblematic of the situation of the exile, eternally estranged in a land not his own.

Donoso uses numerous literary devices to communicate the sense of alienation and estrangement suffered by the exile, including a vanguardist tendency of the Spanish novel of the 1970s and 1980s, self-conscious or self-reflexive writing, a sub-genre characterized by constant unveiling of the fictitious condition of the fiction, revealing the mechanisms of literary production (Alter 3), and emphasizing the act of writing, the presence of books, manuscripts, libraries, and a variety of literary activities. All are prominent in *El jardín de al lado,* a metanovel which deliberately fuses and confuses the planes of life and literature, blurring the margins between the lives within the fiction and life beyond.[3] The author is simultaneously creator and creature, novelist and fictional character, and "his" novel is at once the one the reader holds, the work-in-progress whose genesis the text depicts, and a representation of the extra-literary existence of the author, his persona or mask. By adopting the form of self-conscious fiction or the metanovel, Donoso creates a paradigm of the unreal or unnatural existence of the exiles in a model which permits him to show how the mask (or identity-in-exile) has become the person, usurping pre-exilic identity. The problem of the relationship between author and text, text and reader, author and reader is a leitmotif in *Casa de campo*. That work includes an encounter between the novelist per se and one of his characters, who criticizes various details, a variant of the self-criticism found in *Don Quixote* and—among important Spanish precursors of this century—in Unamuno. Like these literary forebears, Donoso in *El jardín de al lado* presents his literary theories or comments on them, another characteristic of self-reflexive writing, apparently enjoying his exposure of the fictitious nature of the narrative. Donoso exploits to the maximum the ambiguity inherent in the relationship between author/narrator/character, and (as in Casa de campo) repeatedly defrauds reader expectations, mocks literary conventions, and destroys all illusion of reality.

But it is not only on the literary level, with echoes of Spain's classic writers and its "new novel" that Donoso reflects his homeland-in-exile. *El jardín de al lado* contains much explicit evidence of Spain's presence, its cultural climate, politics, intellectual atmosphere, geography and society. The novelistic topography is concrete, its toponomy specific, with abundant names of Mediterranean resorts, Madrid streets, and Spanish publishers. Spanish gastronomy is omnipresent, with multiple references to Spanish wine and such archetypes of Spanish cuisine as olive oil, white asparagus and fried *calamares*. The traditional aristocracy, titles of nobility and hereditary wealth at one extreme are balanced by numerous servants, maids, street vendors and other representatives of the lower end of the economic scale. Peninsular politics appear in repeated mentions of King Juan Carlos, the transition to democracy, and the neo-Fascist representatives of the "bunker," supporters of the late dictator. Spain's linguistic presence makes itself felt in the lexicon, and in case some readers might miss these intrusions, Donoso comments repeatedly upon their equivalents in Chile.

Donoso's residence in Spain also manifests itself thematically via the presentation of numerous Latin American exiles living in the Peninsula, their inter-cultural conflicts, and pervasive sense of rootlessness. The negative effects of Spain's massive tourist invasion form another repetitive theme of *El jardín de al lado*. The title itself is worthy of note, the "garden next door" or "neighbor's garden." By suggesting a garden belonging to someone else, not the property of the narrative consciousness, the title immediately insinuates the exile's alienation, and through the image of someone else's garden, the notion of being outside looking into an alien enclosure. Insofar as the garden is an allusion to Eden or earthly bliss, the alienation of property conveyed by the title suggests the loss of paradise or expulsion from the garden, another powerful metaphor of exile. The symbolic significance of gardens is similar to that of houses, according to Cirlot, who associates both with the feminine aspect of the universe (110, 146), and houses have been recognized as having exceptional symbolic significance in earlier works of Donoso. *El jardín de al lado* presents characters whose provisional dwellings (usually hotel rooms or apartments) are changed on short notice and who may occupy a house temporarily but with full consciousness that it is not a home.

Donoso divides *El jardín de al lado* in six numbered parts, the first and last of which take place in Catalonia, a geographic framing device which endows the novel with a vaguely circular structure by returning to the point of beginning. Reiteration in the final section of characters and scenes from the initial section constitutes a form of interior duplication, a characteristic of self-reflexive literature. Sections 2, 3, 4 and part of 5 take place in Madrid and in Morocco, insofar as the action of the novelistic present is concerned with retrospective scenes from the past of the narrative consciousness, Julio Méndez, an exiled Chilean novelist, the persona and occasional mouthpiece of Donoso. His recollections are usually triggered by Proustian flashbacks in response to a perception or an object related to an analogous experience in the past. The novelistic present is the summer of 1980, while the most remote past is the youth of the narrator in Chile some three decades before. Chile and Spain—past and present—alternate almost rhythmically in the metanovelistic text (the novel in gestation), mixing recollection and projection, a confusion of memory and desire in the disordered consciousness of an exile on the verge of an identity crisis.

Méndez, a professor of English literature, jailed for a week during the most recent revolutionary coup, fled to Spain in terror upon release, spending the next decade in somewhat sordid circumstances in the artistic colony of Sitges among an agglomeration of Latin American exiles, mostly political refugees. With the summer influx of European tourists, Julio and his wife Gloria accept the invitation of a Chilean painter to spend the summer in his luxurious Madrid flat in exchange for caring for his dog and Siamese cat. Tempted by the opportunity to live among sumptuous furnishings, each plans to use the tranquility to complete some writing: Julio works on a new version of his rejected novel of imprisonment, Gloria on a translation. The neighboring garden of the title, visible from several windows, is a private park surrounding the mansion of the Duque de Andia. The "neighbor's garden" is not simply the ducal park, but a metaphor of the exile's situation: he must live in the garden of another; his homeland has become the garden of someone else and no longer belongs to him. The ducal property is doubly alien, as the house and writing table from which the garden is contemplated are only loaned, and the garden represents an inaccessible world of aristocracy and wealth, a world from which the exiles are excluded for social reasons in addition to their political status.

The motif of the garden is dual or parallel: Julio as a child and adolescent would contemplate the deteriorating garden of his parents' home, filled with ancient trees and a variety of botanical specimens reflecting a more prosperous past during the life of his father, a liberal senator. This garden, symbolic of family memories, past innocence and youthful idealism, contrasts with Julio's present frustrated ambitions, incipient age, and envious spying upon the ducal garden and its jet-setters, as pool parties and other activities trigger associations with events of his past and the garden in Chile. Counterpoint or alternation between the two gardens emphasizes the schizophrenic existence of the exiled writer, intensified by inauthenticity: whatever political impediments may have existed regarding Julio's return have long since ceased to exist, but he resists returning without having published anything in Spain. While his brother Sebastian insists that Julio come because their mother is dying, Julio sits before his forgotten manuscript enthralled by the life of leisure unfolding before his eyes. The schizophrenic aspect of exile is underlined by the use both of mirrors (as the writer contemplates himself) and the window, which serves at times as a mirror. The use of narrative mirroring reinforces this allegorical image: there are the two gardens, one mirroring the other, and two novels, one a mirror of the other; various other parallels and repeated passages as well as a whole intertextual fabric of literary allusions, citations, parodies, and intercalated tales (told by other exiles) constitute further mirrors or fragments of mirrors.

Three long months of summer in Madrid abound in recollections, as Julio's mental woolgathering reveals his inertia, the stagnation of his marriage, and the absolute absence of inspiration in his literary task. His consciousness flows between past and present, as he carries on a mental dialogue with his brother in Chile, his dead father, and himself, thinking of his moribund mother and meditating on the scene before his eyes. The Mexican exile writer Jorge Ibarguengoitia, in a brief essay on his own exile experience, begins and ends with the words, "Yo paso los días en Paris y las noches en Mexico" [I spend the days in Paris and the nights in Mexico],[4] much the same situation as that of the protagonist of *El jardín de al lado*, whose body is in Spain while his soul is in Chile. Julio and Gloria depend on alcohol to get through the days, and on tranquilizers and sleeping pills to make it through the nights. Abuse of drugs and alcohol are leitmotifs as important as those of the literary world, memories and the generation gap. The stimulus necessary for Julio to finish his novel comes when Gloria suffers a deep depression and possible suicide attempt, coinciding with the death of his mother and his brother's wish to sell the paternal home, the only "root" connecting the exile to Chile. Sending his revised novel to a Barcelona publisher, Julio receives another rejection, but lacks the courage to confess his failure. He informs Gloria that the novel has been accepted and proposes a trip to Marrakesh, where their son is living. Purloining a painting belonging to their host, he sells it to a dealer in the Rastro. The crime, the trip which resembles running away, and his mother's recent death combine to produce a desperate identity crisis which Julio decides to solve by adopting the identity of a beggar, a semi-conscious addict—a solution which would amount to a symbolic suicide, echoing Gloria's failed attempt in Madrid. Determined to implement the identity change, he disappears for a night, but obviously lacks the strength to carry out his plan and returns to his wife the next day.

The final section surprises the reader by changing narrator and narrative viewpoint. The narrative, presented heretofore from Julio's perspective, proves to be a novel written by Gloria, accepted by the same publisher who rejected her husband's work. Gloria's words reveal aspects of his wife unknown to Méndez despite a quarter-century of matrimony, offering another mirror for self-reflexivity, a new and different version of the gestation of the self-conscious metanovel. Instead of being a novel within a novel, the text proves to be the novel of another novel about the literary birth of still another novel. Gloria, if a "character" in Julio's novel, is an autonomous creation, capable of creating her creator, and effectively usurping his creative function. Donoso shows the exiled writer completing the process of becoming a non-entity, incapable of ending the indignity, his identity finally supplanted entirely by that of his wife. With no home to return to, his *machismo* crushed and his hopes as a writer dashed, the exile is only the shell of the man who fled Chile.

Emphasizing the motifs of alienation and estrangement resulting from exile is the generation gap and resulting separation and lack of communication between parents and children. "Pato," the son of Julio and Gloria, has left home and calls himself Patrick, a change of name symbolizing his rejection of all that his parents represent as well as his national identity. Similarly, his friend "Bijou" has rejected his name and cultural and sexual identity; a Chilean, he pretends to be French and is an exaggerated homosexual and transvestite ("Pato," as his name suggests, has also joined the gay revolution). Homosexuality in the younger generation, a variant on the problem of identity and motif of schizophrenia in several works of Donoso, appears as yet another attempt to deal with the alienation of exile.

Problems of identity in exile are reflected in other ways. One of the protagonist's friends is a psychiatrist, constantly called upon to pull him out of depression. Julio and his wife are frequently troubled by forgetting the names of friends in Chile. Foreign words proliferate—words in English, French, Italian, and German—with all that language implies for cultural identity. One family of exiles are described as "socios propietarios de una *boutique* afro-hindu-folk-western-hippie-protesta: con sus cabelleras afro o engominadas según la moda del año, vestidos de blanco ala ibicenca" (40) [owners of an Afro-Hindu-Folk-Western-Hippie-Protest style boutique, with their afros or hair styled with mouse in the fashion of the moment, dressed in white, Ibiza-style]. What is most evident in the description is the absence of any authentic original trait.

Literal exile is itself a frequent subject, with the protagonists and a majority of characters of *El jardín de al lado* being exiles or expatriates. Motifs of wandering, restlessness and longing for return are so abundant in certain sections as to be omnipresent. The plight of the exiles—economic hardship, loss of status, alienation, and goallessness—are also repetitive motifs. In addition to literal portrayals of all of these, Donoso employs symbolic or metaphoric images to convey the crisis produced by exile: schizophrenia becomes a paradigm for splitting in two of the authorial persona, torn between the distant homeland and the home-in-exile. Homosexuality and sterility symbolize the exile's incapacity for normal, intimate, intellectual, and literary intercourse with his public due to obligatory estrangement. Enforced association with what is statistically a non-normal society (that of other exiles) is likewise symbolized by homosexual relationships. Motifs of dismemberment and disintegration are paradigms of painful separation from the homeland, family, and roots. A myriad of identity problems, personality disturbances, and psychosomatic ailments are emblematic of exilic alienation and estrangement.

The symbolic garden, with its transparent allusion to Eden and the exile's expulsion from Paradise, becomes the dominant, sustained metaphor of *El jardín de al lado*. The protagonist's non-participatory contemplation of the neighboring garden is paradigmatic of the situation of the exiles, outsiders in the land of exile, excluded by their situation from work in their own professional gardens.

It is no coincidence that a major emphasis of *El jardín de al lado* as a self-conscious and self-reflexive text is precisely the writer's craft. The focus upon Julio's progressive loss of control of his art, and by extension, his livelihood and his identity, allows Donoso to present another consequence of exile, impotence or implied castration. Julio's *machismo* is erased or neutralized by revelations of the final chapter: not only is his work rejected, but he himself becomes a character in his wife's novel, his very identity and objective existence in question. Thus, form is made to mirror content, as Donoso converts reflexivity and interior duplication into still more powerful paradigms of exile.

Notes

1. Schwartz includes much the same list, but names Donoso, adds Sarduy and Lezama Lima, and mentions Onetti's stay in Madrid.

2. *El obsceno pájaro de la noche* (1970), Donoso's first novel published in Spain, unquestionably portrays Chile and the socio-psychological environment of Santiago, despite its hallucinatory, surrealist passages, and a certain deliberate vagueness in the use of toponymy.

3. Robert Alter points out that the self-conscious novel "systematically flaunts its own condition of artifice," and states that "from beginning to end, through the style, the handling of narrative viewpoint, the names and words imposed on the characters, the patterning of the narration, the nature of the characters and what befalls them, there is effort to convey to us a sense of the fictional world as an authorial construct set up against a background of literary tradition and convention" (xi).

4. "En primera persona: exiliados," *Vuelta 81* (Mexico) 81:7 (August 1983), 34–35.

Works Cited

Alter, Robert. *Partial Magic: The Novel as Self-Conscious Genre.*. Berkeley: University of California Press, 1975.
Broyard, Anatole. "The Exile Who Lost His Tongue." *New York Times* 26 June 1977: 14.
Carminatti, Graciela. "Entrevista a José Donoso." *Revista de la Universidad de México* 25:5–6 (December 1980-January 1982), 57.
Cirlot, Juan Eduardo. *A Dictionary of Symbols.* trans. Jack Sage. New York: Philosophical Library, 1962.
Donoso, José. *Casa de campo.* Barcelona: Seix Barral, 1978.
———. "Ithaca: The Impossible Return," *The City College Papers*, 18 (1982).
———. *El jardín de al lado.* Barcelona: Seix Barral, 1981.
———. *Tres novelitas burguesas.* Barcelona: Seix Barral, 1973.
Gutiérrez Mouat, Ricardo. *José Donoso: Impostura e impostación (La modelización lúdica y carnavalesca de una producción literaria).* Gaithersburg, MD: Ediciones Hispamerica, undated (ca. 1980).
Rodríguez Monegal, Emir. "José Donoso: La novela come Happening." *Revista Iberioamericana* 76–77 (July-December 1971).
Schwartz, Ronald. *Nomads, Exiles and Emigres (The Rebirth of the Latin American Narrative, 1960–80).* Metuchen, NJ:Scarecrow Press, 1980.

The Bitter Air of Exile: Russian Émigrés and the Berlin Experience
Shoshanah Dietz

The Bolshevik Revolution of 1917 initiated not only many political and social changes in Russia, but had a profound impact on Russian culture. Some Russian artists accepted the changes eagerly and conformed to new demands; others, ambivalent about the Communist government, remained in Russia and attempted to find a compromise. Artists who could not agree to the new demands and would not compromise left Russia for the West, particularly Germany, although they often did not realize that they were leaving their homeland for permanent exile. Russian émigré life in the Berlin of the early 1920s represents a period of transition for many Russian émigré poets, as this was to be only the first stage in their long journey as émigrés.

This third group left either for cities within the Slavic world—Prague, Belgrad, Warsaw—or more often for the West and, during the first years of exile, particularly Germany. In addition to the Russian intelligentsia's traditional attachment to German philosophy, culture, and education, many fled to Germany because it was close, cheap, and generous in issuing residence visas. Berlin was also one of the most exciting, cosmopolitan centers of theater, art, literature, and film in Europe. During the early 1920s, Berlin was particularly attractive for Russian writers for several reasons. Many Russian-language dailies and weeklies appeared in Berlin. The book-publishing industry in Germany was one of the best organized in the world; costs were low and German interest in Russian literature was high. Berlin soon became the most important center of Russian publishing—more important than Russia itself. Many émigrés, living in Germany and elsewhere, published their work with German publishing houses, and after 1921, even Soviet writers published in Berlin. Dmitrii Merezhkovskii, Zinaida Hippius, Marina Tsvetaeva, Andrei Belyi, Vladislav Khodasevich, and Georgii Ivanov are among the many émigré poets who visited, lived, or published in Berlin. The poet and novelist Andrei Belyi claimed that in Berlin "the Russians feel even more at home than in their homeland" (1987, 250). The émigré poet Khodasevich expressed more ambivalent feelings on adopting Berlin as second home; it was neither a part of the Russian family of cities, nor was it entirely foreign—it was "the stepmother of Russian cities" ("Everything is stone"/"Vse kamennoe").[1] In the beginning many Russians considered Berlin a temporary home, somewhere to wait out the dramatic upheavals in Soviet Russia. It was only after the collapse of the White armies, the end of the civil war, and the consolidation of Bolshevik power in the early 1920s, that members of the émigré community were forced to consider themselves in permanent exile from Russia. Ironically, just as they were coming to accept their identity as permanent émigrés in Berlin, the economic and political conditions in Germany turned chaotic, and many of the émigrés living there began to consider another city in which to settle. By the mid-1920s, the center of Russian émigré intellectual life had gradually shifted from Berlin to Paris. For many Russian émigrés, then, the time in Berlin represented a period of adjustment to life in exile, a transition stage in their identities from Russian to émigré poets.

Émigré poetry during this first wave of exile reveals not so much the interaction with a specific environment, such as Berlin, but rather reaction to the exile experience itself—an experience in which the theme of separation from the homeland as well as alienation from the new environment plays a significant role. The first wave of such poetry reveals this transition period in both the poet's life and work—the former life in Russia is far from forgotten, yet the present, though overwhelming, is unreal. Much of Georgii Ivanov's émigré poetry belongs to this first stage. While his poems may be tributes to the Russia of his memory, he more often reveals his ambivalent feelings toward Russia's existence and his own existence outside Russia. Both Marina Tsvetaeva and Vladislav Khodasevich write about their Russian past, but the alienation and loss of self caused by the émigré experience is revealed particularly in their poetry. Berlin, the first step of emigration, becomes a mere transition in the consciousness of the émigré poet, whose poetry reveals the reluctant abandonment of the homeland and the sense of marginality and alienation of life in exile.

Though the émigré experience may affect an individual in diverse ways, Russian émigré poets responded to this experience with several common motifs, all revealing their sense of alienation and ambivalence toward the émigré experience. In an effort to retain their Russian identity, these poets looked to the past, to life in Russia as they knew it or nostalgically remembered it—a time when life was better or at least when they felt secure of their place in the culture, where, as Khodasevich reminisces in a poem written in exile, "Everyone listened to my verses [Vse slushali stikhi moi]" (Khodasevich, "Petersburg"/ "Peterburg"). Such émigré poets as Ivanov, Tsvetaeva, and Khodasevich continued to write about Russia throughout their lives in exile. Yet émigré poets, earlier nostalgic for the Russian past, begin to reveal a shift of perspective in their obsession: the Russia of their past is now compared to the Russia of the present, or Russia is rejected altogether. Just as the 'new' Russia has denied them a role in its culture, they deny the reality of Russia's very existence for them. In his poem "Russia is happiness. Russia is light" ["Rossiia schastie. Rossiia svet"], Ivanov juxtaposes positive and negative images of Russia, beginning with a Russia of happiness and ending with one of terror. He describes the landscape and cities, yet remains ambivalent about the existence of either.

Rossiia schastie. Rossiia svet.	Russia is happiness. Russian is light.
A, mozhet byt', Rossii vovse net.	And perhaps Russia is not there at all.
I nad Nevoi zakat ne dogoral,	And above the Neva the sunset did not burn,
I Pushkin na snegu ne umiral,	And Pushkin did not die in the snow,
I net ni Peterburga, ni Kremlia —	And there is no Petersburg, no Kremlin—
Odin snega, snega, polia, polia . . .	Only snow, snow, fields, fields . . .
Rossiia tishina. Rossiia prakh.	Russia is silence. Russia is ashes.
I moshet byt' Rossiia-tol'ko strakh.	And perhaps Russia is only terror.

Ivanov expresses not only his ambivalence toward Russia's existence, but also his alienation from his Russian past. He begins to doubt his own memories of its existence: "There is no Petersburg, Kiev, Moscow—Perhaps there were, and I've forgotten. [Netu Peterburga, Kieva, Moskvy,—Mozhet byt'i byli, da zabyl, uvy.]" This ambivalence disappears in his poem "How good it is that there is no tsar" ("Khorosho, chto net Tsaria"), in which he rejoices at this nonexistence: "How good it is that there is no tsar . . . no Russia . . . no God. How good it is that there is nobody . . . nothing. [Khorosho chto net Tsaria . . . net Rossii . . . net Boga . . . Khorosho chto net nikogo . . . net nichego]." Ivanov's absolute denial of Russia's physical existence demonstrates his rejection of and alienation from his former homeland, yet there are signs of transition that indicate an acceptance of a metaphysical Russia within the émigré when Ivanov pronounces that "His Russianness is a matter of heart and mind [Russkii on po serdtsu, russkii po umu]" (In Russia there are not even precious graves" / "Net v Rossii dazhe dorogikh mogil") and no longer a matter of one's mere physical presence in Russia.

Ivanov's alienation from Russia illustrates but one stage in émigré poetry. In the poet's transition into an émigré poet, the gradual realization that one no longer lives and writes in one's native culture, but in a foreign one, becomes a significant issue, and poets often attempt to work out their feelings of confusion, ambivalence, and alienation in poetry. The popular post-Romantic concept of the creative artist, of course, is that an artist never truly belongs to or fits into any society; by definition, the artist is, and must be, always in a kind of self-imposed exile—an outsider, distant and alienated from mainstream society. In her essay "The Poet and Time," Tsvetaeva promotes this belief and declares that "every poet is essentially an émigré, even in Russia" (1982,136). The émigré Georgii Adamovich even considered the condition of émigré life a positive experience: "There is no pain sweeter than to lose everything. / No fate more joyful than to become a wanderer" (Ivask 1972, 69). Yet despite Adamovich's positive attitude concerning the effect of émigré life on the poet, most émigré poets were far from such a positive acceptance of the notion that a poet exists by definition in exile.

As émigré poets moved through various stages of emigration, both spatially and temporally, the émigré experience, both generally and specifically, influenced their work more directly. In "Émigré" ["Emigrant"], a poem written in the early phase of her exile, Tsvetaeva portrays the alienation and loneliness felt in a foreign city. Tsvetaeva recreates the lulling, or even numbing effect of life in a strange environment in her use of alliteration and repetitive case endings in the opening lines: "domami, den'gami, dymami, dumami. . . ." The émigré responds to this condition by comparing it to an experience of anxiety and torture; the emigrant is literally "taken to the rack" ["vziav na dyb"]. Tsvetaeva's final lines sum up the emotional and contradicting responses to the émigré experience: "Superfluous! Divine! Exile! A Challenge! Upwards!/ One never gets used to it . . . The gallows/ Never accepted . . . running around in rags." ["Lishnii! Vyshnii! Vykhodets! Vyzov! Vvys' / Ne otvykshii . . . Viselits / Ne priniavshii . . . V rvani valiut."] The juxtaposition of these positive and negative images of the émigré condition reveals the poet's ambivalence, and these final lines, with their powerful telegraphic style, leave no doubt of the intensity of this experience.

Tsvetaeva's "Émigré" addresses only the general condition of émigré existence. There is no personal "I," and the title refers neither to a specific experience nor city, although the poem was written with Berlin in mind; indeed, Tsvetaeva wanted Boris Pasternak to read this poem while he was in Berlin. Tsvetaeva also wrote poems dedicated to the specific cities—Prague, Paris, and Berlin—where she lived. Her poem "To Berlin" ("Berlinu"), written after spending several months in Berlin in 1922, clearly refers to a specific and personal experience as an émigré. The poetic voice is in the first person singular; the weather, urban images and sounds are specific to her Berlin. Even in this poem, however, one finds much that parallels the generic émigré experience portrayed in "Émigré." The environment once again acts as a hypnotic agent, soothing one into a passive mood: "Rain lulls away the pain./ Below the shutters of a downpour/ I sleep. [Dozhd' ubaiukivaet bol'. / Pod livni opuskaiushchikh staven' / Spliu.]" The atmosphere in Berlin is also hostile; buildings are seen as barracks, and the loneliness and alienation of the 'I' is clearly the predominant sentiment. Despite its title, the uniqueness of the Berlin experience is missing; the setting of Berlin recedes into a mere backdrop for the more overpowering condition of émigré life in general.

Khodasevich also wrote about his émigré experience in Berlin. Unlike Tsvetaeva, who remained in Berlin only several months, Khodasevich lived in Berlin for several years before moving on and eventually settling in Paris. Khodasevich's Berlin poems portray the Berlin experience more specifically than Tsvetaeva, but he too is unable to bring Berlin truly into the foreground. His Berlin, like Tsvetaeva's, is often gray and rainy, projecting a hostile environment for the émigré. In his poem "Berlin Streets [S berlinskoi ulitsy]," the attributes used to portray the city are all ominous, even sinister: Berlin is disturbing, cumbersome, hard and indifferent as stone, shadowy, semi-dark, neither night nor day ("vzvolnovannyi Berlin," "gromozdokogo Berlina," "Vse kamennoe," "ten'," "polutemno," "polumrak"]. In "Berlin Streets" a demonic presence pervades

Doma—kak demony,	The buildings are like demons,
Mezhdu domami—mrak;	Between the buildings is darkness;
Sherengi demonov,	Rows of demons
I mezhdu nikh—skvozniak.	And between them—draughts.

The eerie quality of Berlin is reinforced by the shadowy presence of its people, and the fantastic and inhuman qualities of its inhabitants. In Berlin streets "the human shadow is long," the intersections are filled with darkness and demons. It is a city of "inhuman atmosphere, /[and]

Inhuman speech ["Liudskaia ten' dlinna," "Na perekrestki t'my, / Kak ved'my, po-troe / Togda vykhodim my," "Nechelovecii dukh, / Nechelovech'ia rech'"]. In the many images referring to light and dark, the Berlin experience remains, at best, a shadowy one, where life is neither one nor the other. The ability to distinguish light from dark and reality from fantasy disappears from the émigré's perspective of Berlin.

The dubious existence of reality and the alienating condition of the émigré experience is particularly evident in Khodasevich's "Berlin" ("Berlinskoe"), a poem that challenges, then destroys, the émigré's very sense of self. Khodasevich's poem "Berlin" opens with the almost archetypal scene of the émigré abroad: an émigré sits in a café sipping a drink, watching the outside world go by as the lilac dusk slowly seeps in. From the émigré's perspective, the world beyond the cafe window is unreal and distant:

A tam, za tolstym i ogromnym	And [the world] is over there, beyond the huge,
Otpolirovannym steklom,	Thick, polished café window,
Kak by v akvariume temnom,	As if in a warm aquarium,
V akvariume golubom —	In a blue aquarium —

It is in this transformation of the world outside into a warm, blue aquarium, a world of womb-like warmth and heavenly light that he can never experience, that he realizes his horrifying condition. Staring out into this inaccessible world, he suddenly notices reflections floating by in the streetcar windows and gradually becomes aware that he is watching a double reflection—he is watching a table's reflection in the streetcar window, and in turn, the reflected face is watching him as he sits in the cafe. He then notices that the strange head is severed, totally cut off from its body and environment, moving along at a different pace from the rest of the body and, with a growing sense of horror, he recognizes the distorted head as his very own:

I pronikaia v zhizn' chuzhuiu,	And penetrating into that alien and strange life,
Vdrug s otvrashchen'em uznaiu	Suddenly I recognize with revulsion
Otrublennuiu, nezhivuiu,	The head—severed, lifeless, and
Nocnuiu golovu moiu.	Nocturnal as my very own.

Khodasevich's fantastic image of a severed head floating by illustrates the very essence of the émigré condition: the émigré is forced to recognize and acknowledge his alienation not only from his foreign environment but from his very self.

Despite the increasing years spent outside of Russia and the transition to émigré life in Berlin, neither Tsvetaeva's nor Khodasevich's Berlin poems reflect any shift in consciousness towards creating a positive perspective of their new role as émigré poets or of their integration into life outside of Russia. Their poems reveal a generic, not specific, experience of émigré life and focus on the émigrés' inner life rather than on the external conditions of their existence. Berlin is treated not as unique in itself but as a mere medium through which the poet expresses the ambivalence and alienation of the émigré experience. The spiritual condition of émigré life is the dominant concern in these poems—a condition that reveals the alienation felt in exile, a condition that produces a fragmented sense of self and loss of identity. Berlin is only the first stop on a long journey of emigration for these poets—poets whose poetry reveals the reluctant abandonment of the homeland yet only a marginal acknowledgement of the émigré existence. The harsh influence of the exile experience on the poet's sense of self overrides specific or individual experiences, as Anna Akhmatova, a Russian poet who experienced internal exile herself twenty years later, wrote: "Whether in Tashkent or New York / The air of exile is bitter [Kto v Tashkente, kto v N'iu Iuorke / I izgnaniia vozdukh gor'kii]" (Poem without a hero / Poema bez geroia).

Note

1. All translations are mine and are meant to be literal rather than artistic. All transliterations follow the Library of Congress system.

Works Cited

Andreev, Nikolai. "Ob osobennostiakh i osnobnykh etapov razvitiia russkoi literatury za rubezhom." *Russkaia literatura v emigratsii: Sbornik statei.* Ed. Nikolai P. Poltoratsky. Pittsburgh: Pittsburgh University Press, 1972. 15–38.

France, Peter. *Poets of Modern Russia.* Cambridge: Cambridge University Press, 1982.

Ivask, Iurii [George]. "Poeziia 'staroi' emigratsii." *Russkaia literatura v emigratsii: Sbornik statei.* Ed. Nikolai P. Poltoratsky. Pittsburgh: Pittsburgh University Press, 1972. 45–70.

Karlinsky, Simon and Alfred Appel, Jr., eds. *The Bitter Air of Exile: Russian Writers in the West, 1922–1972.* Berkeley: University of California Press, 1977.

Khodasevich, Vladislav. *Sobranie sochinenii.* Edited by John Malmstad and Robert Huges. Ann Arbor: Ardis, 1983.

Mierau, Fritz, ed. *Russen in Berlin: Literatur, Malerei, Theater, Film, 1918–1933.* Leipzig: Reclam, 1987.

Terapiano, Iurii, ed. *Muza Diaspory: Izbrannye stikhi zarubezhnykh poetov 1920–1960.* Frankfurt: Possev-Verlag, 1960.

Terras, Victor. *Handbook of Russian Literature.* New Haven: Yale University Press, 1985.

Tjalsma, H. W., ed. *Vne Rossii: Antologiia emigrantskoi poezii 1917–1975.* Munich: Wilhelm Fink Verlag, 1979.

Tsvetaeva, Marina. *Sochineniia v dvukh tomakh.* Moscow: Khudozhestvennaia literatura, 1980.

Williams, Robert C. *Culture in Exile: Russian Émigrés in Germany, 1881–1941.* Ithaca: Cornell University Press, 1972.

 Creating the "CanAmerican" Self: The Autobiographies of American Women Immigrants to Canada
Helen M. Buss

The writer, Josef Skvorecky, an immigrant to Canada, describes his feeling of exile, of living in a "land—no matter how hospitable and friendly—where your heart is not, because you landed on these shores too late" (29). His would seem to be a sentiment echoed by many men's accounts from Ovid at Tomis on the Black Sea to Malcolm Lowry at Vancouver on the Pacific Ocean.[1] This dark view of relocating in a new land is not one I have found typical of women (whether they come willingly or not). In account after account of women's relocations, I find female voices attempting an imaginative merging of past and present customs, skills, and values in an attempt to create a gestalt of presence rather than absence. The accounts that have particularly concerned me are the autobiographical writings (diaries, memoirs, letters, etc.) of women immigrating to Canada and among these I find that the women who tell the most optimistic stories of their resettlement are American women.

There are a number of factors to consider in this phenomenon which can be summarized as falling into three categories: the position of the immigration group, the position of the individual immigrant, and the nature of the written account. As Americans, each of the individuals discussed belonged to a favored group. As English speaking, white, well-educated people, they inevitably experience the success of entering a privileged place in Canadian society in which they become part of an "ethnic hegemony [which] perpetuate[s] the power of the dominant ethnic group . . . vis-a-vis other ethnic groups" (Bullivant 1981, 2).

The characteristics that Canadian and American identities share offer these immigrants, to one degree or another, an entry into the "knowledge/power" systems of their new country that no other immigrant group, except perhaps the British, have had.² But the four immigrants I am directly concerned with were women and as such should suffer at least some part of the "double-jeopardy" (McMullen 1981, 53) experienced by other immigrant women in which the individual finds she is disadvantaged by the normal dislocations of the immigrating experience and her adjustment in society is hindered by the fact that her responsibilities as woman make her the conservator of the old traditions rather than an adventurer in a new culture. Instead, what each of these women creates in her autobiography is an account in which the Canadian experience, while allowing them to preserve what is valuable in their American past, permits them to realize aspects of their personalities not permitted full growth in the home country.

It is important to note that each of these women uses the memoir style of writing, that form of writing that allows the autobiographer to join her own life with that of the community, one suitable to persons who see their development as one tied to historicity, interpelated and connected at all times with the significant others of loved ones and community. In this form we see the memoir writer "reconfronting and reappraising ... memories" for the purpose of "bearing witness to them, affirming their significance and meaning for the future" (Billson 1977, 261). With its emphasis on the future, on connectedness, on one's place in the greater community, this form is a fortuitous choice for women, since, as I have found in my research, women most often wish to represent their actual existences, "the personal life of family, relationships, child-rearing, as well as their accomplishments as individuals, in a context that gives meaning to, rather than seeks to transcend, life in the world" (Buss 1988, 60).

Elizabeth Johnston, a woman forced to flee the United States after the Revolutionary War because of her family's tory politics, wrote *Recollections of a Georgia Loyalist* in 1838 at the age of seventy-four. In it she tells the story of her secure childhood as the only child of well-to-do parents, her marriage to a loyalist soldier, the family flight from Georgia, first to Florida, then to Jamaica, their life as a family commuting between the Caribbean and Scotland because of the demands of work and education, and of the final settlement of the family in Nova Scotia, after more than twenty years of exile. She and her family became part of that large immigration of Americans known as the United Empire Loyalists, who have been so influential in the formation of the Canadian nation.

What is interesting about this loyalist account, as far as the phenomenon of the "CanAmerican" Self is concerned, is Johnston's tendency to hold fast to the past self as part of the present self, even though that past self was a product of a country where she and her family are no longer welcome. She does this by avoiding the subject of political or military events whenever possible, except when they directly concern the life of her family. Thus, although her title highlights a very political identity, "Georgia Loyalist," the kind of life Johnston represents tells of the personal qualities imbued in her by the individuals who raised her in Georgia and resulted in the absolute loyalty she gave to her family and friends in exile. In fact, she writes the kind of history, that as Gerda Lerner has pointed out in *The Female Experience: An American Documentary*, is typical of women in that the time periods which are significant in men's histories are muted. For men, participation in the Revolutionary War (on either side) might be considered the shaping event of their lives. Such an experience also implies taking an absolute stand, in which some part of one's past experience is rejected. For women, the shaping was often the period that followed war, when all their resources were called upon to rebuild the damage to family and stability that the great male adventure had caused. In this task, no part of the past can be absolutely rejected as all its skills and values are needed to restructure the self and the family.

Johnston is able to perform the double and often contradictory act of both remaining absolutely loyal to the patriarchal figures (father and husband) who led her into exile (while revealing her own loyalty to female precursors, such as her mother and aunt who shaped her childhood in Georgia) and at the same time showing her own leadership role in settling the family in Canada.[3] The essential act of the Loyalist was to create a new world self while insisting on the reality of the old world self. Johnston is never happy while the family is in Scotland, as this represents forsaking the new world values of her Georgia upbringing. Jamaica is seen as a place that contains the worst of the new and old worlds, a place that corrupts her eldest son and separates the family for long periods because no supportive social institutions such as educational opportunities exist. In this part of her life the family is led by male figures to whom the moral health of the family is a secondary consideration to economic advantages. The move to Nova Scotia, after her husband's death, is seen not in the kind of nationalistic terms in which Canadian histories might represent the loyalist settlement, but in terms of the changes it effects in the family, in which people used to a softer life in the tropics must learn a harder one. She tells us that her daughter, "brought up as she had been in the habits and comforts of a lady" (123) had great difficulty adjusting herself to a largely servantless life in Canada. These personal adjustments are made to stand for all the sacrifices that the Loyalists had to make in choosing the harsher new-world life of Canada where they were nevertheless permitted to remain loyal to old-world values.

Johnston has managed to represent this great change without condemning any country or group, except that she does remark once that during the distressful times of the fighting the "scum rose to the top" (45). But she quickly covers this moment of unpleasantness by adding that even the man sent to arrest her father "was an amiable man, and his turning against my father served to show the spirit of the times and the violence with which civil wars are entered upon" (46). The fact that she has failed to take an adversarial position vis-a-vis her American homeland is indicated by the thirty-six page introduction to the original edition in which the Canadian editor adds information about the actual events of the war and the injustices suffered by Johnston's family and others. For Johnston to have written from such a public stance would have meant to deny the past in a "conversion" strategy typical of traditional male autobiography. Johnston avoids this by concentration on the personal, the domestic and the familial. But because she tells the life-stories of all her significant others, men as well as women, she denies no part of the suffering or the survival of her people.[4]

Martha Black relates in her autobiography, *My Seventy Years*, her beginnings in a prosperous and close-knit Chicago family in the late nineteenth century in which women's roles were narrowly defined by the example of Black's devoted, modest, uncomplaining, and completely subservient mother. Black describes her parents' reaction to her birth. The father complains to his wife: "Susan, I am disappointed. I expected a boy." The mother replies meekly, "Yes, I know, I am so sorry" (17). The recounting of this moment and another in her childhood in which she physically attacks a little girl who is behaving with prescribed feminine submissiveness, as well as Black's obvious admiration for her father who saved the family and their fortunes during the Chicago fire, indicates her desire to be more like the boy her father wanted than the daughter her parents expected her to be.

Black leads a conventional life until her thirties, marrying and having two sons and although she complains of the confining life of young motherhood and the wandering eye of her husband, she accepts her place, since it means being part of a close family life and having the parental approval that she needs. Her rebellion comes when she and her husband arrange to go on the great adventure of their lives, to pan for gold during the Yukon Gold Rush. At the last moment, while in San Francisco, her husband decides he prefers the Hawaiian Islands. It is at this point, far away from family influence, that Black throws off wifely submissiveness and heads for the north without her husband.

The Yukon proves the place where her independent "headstrong" self, the part that emulates her father, can blossom. She not only crosses the Chinook pass in winter and sets up placer claims, but also delivers her own baby in a small shack. The arrival of the child is given the kind of elevated treatment that autobiographers often use, "to turn [the past] into a kind of mythic narrative . . . shot through with Adamic significance" (Porter 505). In Martha Black's writing it is not so much an Adamic significance, but rather one more reminiscent of the Holy Mother that Black seems to be seeking as she describes the "men-folk" gathering around her as she, like the virgin with her divine son, is given gifts by the worshipful sourdoughs, and boasts that her incredibly easy labor is "Mother nature's gift to women who live a natural out-of-door life such as I had done" (130).

Later in her life in Canada, Black marries George Black and becomes the socially correct wife of the Yukon's commissioner (governor) and later his exemplary spouse when he is speaker of the Canadian parliament. This would seem to be a direct refusal of the entrepreneurial spirit that made her a Yukon legend. But for Black it represents the successful harnessing of the opposing selves, the adventurous, individualistic father-defined one not possible in her conventional family life in Chicago, and the ladylike respectability of her mother in which she receives her position and power through her devotion to her husband's interest. This is indicated by the way in which Black chooses to end her autobiography. She considers her crowning achievement to be her election as member of the Canadian parliament after George Black becomes too ill to represent the Yukon. She describes, in dramatic detail, her maiden speech in the house which takes place as the Commons is about to send a message of sympathy to Queen Mary on the death of George V. Her house-leader had declined Black's private suggestion that the sympathies of the women of Canada be added to the telegram. Torn between obeying her male leader's desire to represent only the public Canada and her need to speak on behalf of the private world of women,[5] she finally rises to offer sympathy to "her majesty the Queen [who] has set the women of Canada an example of devotion to family, devotion to business that comes up every day—an example by which we must all profit" (314). The mention of "devotion," her mother's chief quality, and "business" and "profit," her father's preoccupations, joins the significant others that have shaped Black's personality. It is suitable that Black manages this union through the act of praising a conventional mother figure, in a context in which Black has always felt safest (the Canadian parliament in the 1930s being at least as respectably patriarchal as the family she grew up in), and she does so in a moment of rebellion against an authority figure who has just told her in symbolic terms to be the kind of female she has always rebelled against being—the silent, obedient girl. Martha Black creates a self motivated by two contradictory drives: the desire to be an assertive, self-actualizing individual who defines herself separately from family and roots, and the desire to remain connected to all the ideals of feminine submissiveness, loyalty, and conservative values of her American upbringing.

It is ironic that it is her Canadian immigration that allows her to realize fully the contradictions of her American self. Away from the restraints of upbringing, on anonymous grounds (so to speak), she realizes a more androgynous self, but uses that new position to attain a self-definition that is entirely in keeping with her conservative family values.[6] Nowhere in the autobiography is there mention of any difficulty in letting go the republican, anti-monarchist values of her homeland, to become a very public part of a system in which every citizen, especially a member of Parliament, gives her first allegiance to the monarch (and in 1930 that was less a symbolic gesture than it is in Canada today). Indeed, Black seems to take great delight in vice-regal occasions when she must curtsey and defer to the King's representative in Canada.

We have once again the refusal to cast any part of the life in the public terms of national allegiances or social differences (differences which are perhaps greater than these autobiographers would lead us to suspect). Because the development of the double-self of the immigrant is seen as a personal phenomenon by women such as Black (even when it takes place in very public contexts), they are able to hold contradictions in their personalities, indeed to maximize the success of these contrary attributes through their immigration.

But, it might be argued that immigrants such as Martha Black are especially favored, in health, money, and opportunities. Other women have had to come to Canada not as adventurers, or as a result of loyalist convictions, but out of hard economic necessity, at an age and in a state of health which in no way equips them for the hard life of the pioneer, and they experience in Canada, if not failure, then an extremely qualified success. Such a woman is Sarah Ellen Roberts, who was part of the homesteading of the "last best west," the province of Alberta, when the southern part of that province was opened for farming in 1906. Part of her memoir, *Alberta Homestead*, was written by Roberts in the form of an intermittent diary in the first year of her residence in Canada. Since her life became too full of hard work to give attention to her diary, she completed it as a memoir in 1915, after she and her husband, worn out by the homesteading experience, returned to the United States.

Roberts lacked the physical fortitude for pioneering. She was fifty-four, plagued with migraines, timidity, and what amounted at times to a phobia of open spaces and a near obsession with cleanliness. She presents an optimistic face to her readers despite the fact that during her six years in Canada she faced drought, crop failure and prairie fires, and had to leave no wealthier than when she came: "As we look back over the years we spent on the homestead, we remember hardships, of course. But even more vividly, we remember the love we bore each other, we remember the sweet companionship of working together at daily tasks, and of sharing with each other hardship and trial and triumph and sorrow and joy" (264).

In this account we do not see the changes in personality of the young adventurer, or the working out of a personal philosophy of the Loyalist matriarch, but rather we see an identity long ago formed in safe non-rural environments confronted with a reality that threatens the individual with disintegration. Roberts writes of her first experience of the Canadian prairie: "How shall I describe the feeling that then settled down upon me? I had never had it before . . . . It wasn't exactly homesickness or fear or loneliness or awe, although I think that all of these may have entered into it . . . I felt as though I were absolutely alone in the world, and my sense of littleness and helplessness overwhelmed me" (21-22). Roberts does not portray herself as creating a new self equipped to handle the new experience; she remains as ill-equipped at the end of the stay in Alberta as she was at the beginning. Roberts's accomplishment is the written account itself, in which she uses her skills developed as university-trained writer, and her other continuity from her American life, her central place in the lives of her husbands and sons, to recreate the homesteading experience in a texture and depth that is unusual, even in women's accounts of that archetypal American and Canadian experience.

She is an example of the quality noted by John Faragher in other American pioneering women, "who frequently employed a range of stylistic elaborations. They took care to identify names of people and places and specify dates and times. . . . used extended descriptions: colorful adjectives, qualifying phrases, long passages of explanation and summary." Faragher adds that "in general men and women were concerned with different orders of meaning. There was an almost inverse relationship in the way most men wrote about objects and things, most women about people" (130). If Roberts's account is typical, he might have added that such women also recreated the life of the natural world, their personal family's struggles, and the substance of the communities in which they lived. Because her health and age left her unsuited to define the self of her Canadian experience in terms of personal accomplishments, she compensates by recreating a whole era for us. She is driven to encompass in language what she cannot encompass in life. Although constantly doubting her own ability to shape reality with words, using expressions such as "impossible to describe," or "no words can express," or "how can I say," she does indeed "say" a stronger self into being in Canada then she was aware she possessed.

In one passage she describes the coming of a Canadian spring on the prairie after a harsh winter and makes herself subtly a part of the whole natural and human endeavor, not through her activity, but through her place as the central perceiving consciousness offering us the land, the sky, the wildlife, the birds, her husband and sons at work in the field, and culminating with this passage:

> I used to go out to where the men were plowing. It fascinated me to watch the moist earth roll up on the moldboard and turn over, black and cool and sweet smelling. There is nothing quite like that odor. It has in it all the essence of the spring, all the promise of the summer. It is as though the very clods had language and spoke to us of the wealth that lay latent in them. (102–03)

Open, through all her senses and language-making capacities, to all the components of the moment that is spring, she makes an imaginative identification with the land of Canada, whose soil speaks to her in its own language of the "wealth that lay latent" there. Roberts is typical of many women immigrating to Canada in that the moment of feeling a sense of being at home in the new place is not cast in a metaphor of rejection of the other place, but in terms of a positive identification with some aspect of the Canadian scene which realizes the full capacity of the personhood of the immigrant, in this case, the language-making ability of Sarah Ellen Roberts.

The last American woman autobiographer I will discuss, Florence Bird, a Philadelphian, came to Canada with her British husband in an effort to escape what they perceived as the negative influence of conservative, establishment-oriented families in Britain and the United States. Taking the pseudonym, Anne Francis (the name of a maternal ancestor), Bird became a nationally known journalist and media personality who at the height of her career was chosen by then Prime Minister, Lester Pearson, to lead a historic royal commission, one whose final report inspired Anthony Westell of the *Toronto Star* to write:

> At 2.11 p.m. in the House of Commons Monday, the Prime Minister rose, bowed politely to the Speaker and tabled a bomb, already primed and ticking.
>
> The bomb is called the Report of the Royal Commission on the Status of Women in Canada, and it is packed with more explosive potential than any device manufactured by terrorists (Bird 302).

Despite the military metaphor of the journalistic description, it is not in such belligerent language that Bird narrates the progress of her life that led to this historic moment. In fact, what we once again note is the way in which the contentious issues of nationality, difference and contradiction are muted and the values of the merging of self and other, of creating complementariness where one might expect to find contradiction, of creating opportunity where others might find discrimination and inequality, emerge in Bird's account.

In many ways Bird is very similar to her political foremother, Martha Black, in that she writes of her close relationship with an adored father and her feeling of restriction in the role her traditional mother expects of her. Muting her motive for immigration by indicating it was her desire to create an equal relationship with her more internationalist husband that led to coming to Canada, Bird represents herself as a kind of child-wife, working as a journalist under the protection of her more distinguished husband, indulging in her pleasures of horseback riding and travel, feeling unfettered and free in her new Canadian existence and visiting, as little as possible, her troublesome American mother, who advocates a more conservative lifestyle. It is not so much an immigration experience that Bird portrays, as an extended vacation from the serious business of being a traditional woman.

All this ends for Bird during the Second World War, when, like other women, she receives entry into the professional world in a more serious capacity because of the scarcity of males. She becomes a national radio reporter, suddenly responsible for important communications to a nation at war. During this time she is made aware, through the lives of women near her, of the position of women in a patriarchal world. She comes to admire an exiled Englishwoman, raising her family alone while her husband fights overseas. She discovers the fear and humiliation of her housemaid who comes near death in a self-inflicted abortion. The double standards of the community in which she has lived as a privileged woman begin to concern her. Her growing consciousness of women's place in the world and its effect on her public career led to her choice as head of the royal commission and to the moment which Bird dramatizes as the climactic point of her autobiography, when in her capacity as head of the commission traveling in the far north she is able to facilitate one woman's personal goal, an Inuit woman's adoption of children who are under her care, but who could not be legally hers because of her status as a woman. Bird recounts the moment in the iconography of mythic narrative:

> The mother stood up and faced the now silent women in the room. Her face was beautiful with relief and joy as she looked at them. She stretched wide her arms, her

hands open-palmed, in a spontaneous, embracing gesture of happiness. I found that I was weeping. I was poignantly aware of the deep kinship of all women everywhere in all ages (281).

Flora Bird saw her immigration to Canada as an escape from traditional womanhood as taught to her by her American mother. Flora spent half a lifetime shaking off the helplessness and dependence of the traditional woman, yet finds the fulfillment of her selfhood in making an imaginative identification with a very traditional native woman, an identification in which she can make a reconnection with the figure of the mother while becoming "the mother" herself through helping a maternal figure to create a more powerful version of motherhood.[7] In such subtle ways do women return to, and recreate in another context, their maternal heritage and implicitly the values of their mother country.

Recently, Canadians have begun to be aware of an unrecognized immigrant group in their country: the women who accompanied the latest influx of male American citizens to Canada, the conscientious objectors (or draft-dodgers) of the Vietnam era. These women, who as individuals have their American pasts muted by their new Canadian citizenship and their reasons for immigrating muted by their men's more spectacular motivation for immigration, have had a large part in creating and leading the Canadian women's movement. This leadership role does not surprise me. Perhaps, in time, my observations of the contribution and success of American women immigrants to Canada, a success more spectacular than their more favored male compatriots, will be verified statistically.

In the meantime, I would offer some speculation on the reasons for this observed success, and I hasten to affirm that here I offer a suggestive rather than definitive reading of this phenomenon. I would suggest several features that maximize the achievements of these women besides their obvious advantages of language and class. Firstly, they write as women and as women they write of their private and public communities. Theorists of women's autobiography from Mary Mason to Susan Friedman have noted the importance of "connection" in women's self-definition. This need for connection includes the need to reach out to the future, as Elizabeth Johnston and Sarah Roberts do by writing their autobiographies for their personal posterity. A noted Canadian writer, Laura Salverson, who grew up in both Canada and the United States, speaks of her autobiography, *Confessions of an Immigrant's Daughter,* as an attempt "to make of a personal chronicle a more subjective therefore more sensitive record of an age" (5), and this would seem to be a spirit that allows these women to tie self-creation to creation of community, and thus to make themselves integrally a part of the place they live.

This desire for "otherness" often expresses itself in Canadian women's autobiographies as a desire to imaginatively merge some aspect of the individual identity with the land of Canada. I do not mean some concept or idea of the country, or some intellectual, patriotic or nationalistic ideal, but the soil, the rock, the water, the air of Canada. The Canadian poet Daphne Marlatt, on returning from a long stay in the United States, ends her autobiographical long poem, *What Matters*, with the words, "I am here, feel/my weight on the wet/ground" (168). And so it is for Martha Black, who speaks of the Yukon as, "the North Star, my lodestar.... It lured me onward. My whole being cried out to follow it" (92–93). For Sarah Roberts it is the "language" of the prairie soil which speaks to her.

More practically speaking, perhaps Canada has offered a space which is still "open" to these women. As a country that came into being as a political entity one hundred years later than the United States, made up of minimally populated regions only partially defined by centralist tendencies, a country still very actively involved in the process of creating its constitution, Canada perhaps has offered a place where individual women immigrants may be more "open" to a broad range of role definitions. If women, as Patricia Spacks proposes in *The Female Imagination*, have a tendency to complete the self in the imagination, then this quality may indeed make the land of Canada a "lodestar" in the minds of immigrating women.

But many women have figured Canada in their imaginations in much more consciously female images than the "lodestar." For example, the British writer Georgina Binnie-Clark, who farmed and wrote in Canada, called Canada her "virgin mother." Canada is often figured as a female entity in Canadian literary production, not surprising for a country in which the cyclical activity of the land has a great effect on the lives of its people, in a country created under the auspices of that matriarchal figure, Queen Victoria, a country whose people still often figure their relationship with their nearest neighbor, the United States, as that of the richly endowed, but less powerful female confronted with surviving in the same bed (on the same continent) with the powerful, belligerent, appropriating male, who has only recently abandoned his power policy of "manifest destiny."[8] Is it any wonder that individual psyches formed in such a culture might feel less suspicion toward immigrating American females than immigrating American males? The male looks too much like the feared appropriator, the female looks more like oneself. If an American female, raised in a country which teaches its young a more expansionist, more entrepreneurial, more confident mode of being than

Canada generally inculcates, should, upon immigrating, have the savvy to turn those qualities to the service of the communities she enters, then her success is not surprising.

But such speculations take me close to the swampy ground of national stereotypes, not a good ground for literary critics, so I will conclude not with my own speculations, but with the words of Elizabeth Bishop, the American poet who had a Canadian childhood. In "Primer Class," as she looks at the way a flat map of the world enhances the size of northern countries, she has "the general impression that Canada was the same size as the world, which somehow or other fitted into it, or the other way around . . ." (10). This describes, better than any theory, how many women writing of their immigration to Canada have felt, that in Canada they found the whole world, because the vision of the world they brought with them, if it were combined with their desire to connect with the new place, could be successfully "fitted into" their Canadian lives.

Notes

1. Hallvard Dahlie surveys the theme of exile in Canadian fiction, noting the many ways in which writers come to terms with the condition.

2. Bullivant uses the expression "knowledge/power" in the sense that Foucault does to indicate that a society structures itself around certain "discourses," knowledge of which brings power to individuals. In immigrating groups the "knowledge" that is held by those belonging to the ethnic group already in control gives these immigrants access to a privileged position not available to other immigrants. Jean Barman proposes that the large British immigration to British Columbia created such a "migratory elite." Such a position might well have been held by Americans in certain times and locations, e.g., Southern Alberta at the turn of the century.

3. Rachel Blau DuPlessis points out that a "both/and" vision that seeks to end either/or dichotomized views of the world is a female–thinking strategy. The kind of "shifts, contraries, negotiations and contradictions" that she sees women as making in order to construct "a more contextual mode of judgment and a different moral understanding" (276) are similar to the mode I see in the accounts I foreground.

4. Mary Mason traces typical female autobiographical strategies and shows how they differ from the "structure of conversion that we find in Augustine's *Confessions*. . . . [or] the egoistic secular archetype that Rousseau handed down to his romantic brethren in his *Confessions*" (22). Mason sees "alterity" or the "'real' presence of another consciousness" as typical of women's autobiography. Thus, the female autobiographer tells her own story by telling those of her significant others.

5. Susan Stanford Friedman comments on how our patriarchal industrialized society has constructed "highly polarized public and private spheres" (35) and the ways in which this exclusion of the private world disadvantages women.

6. Marion Fowler sees the achievement of a more "androgynous" self as typical of nineteenth-century writing women who come to Canada to travel or settle.

7. Some sense of reunion with the mother is seen as a typical desire in women's accounts of selfhood by critics such as Lynn Bloom, Stephanie Demetrakopoulos, and Bella Brodzki.

8. For a literary discussion of Canada as "female," the United States' as "male," see Evelyn Hinz's suggestion that James Dickey's *Deliverance* and Margaret Atwood's *Surfacing* represents contrasting national imaginations.

Works Cited

Barman, Jean. "Ethnicity in the Pursuit of Status: British Middle and Upper–Class Emigration to British Columbia in the Late Nineteenth and Early Twentieth Centuries." *Canadian Ethnic Studies/Etudes Ethniques au Canada* 13 (1986): 32–51.

Billson, Marcus. Memoirs: "New Perspectives on a Forgotten Genre." *Genre* 2 (Summer 1977): 259–82.

Binnie-Clark, Georgina. *Wheat and Women*. London: Bell and Cockburn, 1914.

Bird, Florence. *Anne Francis, An Autobiography*. Toronto: Clarke, Irwin and Company Ltd. 1974.

Bishop, Elizabeth. "Primer Class." In *The Collected Prose*. Ed. Robert Giroux. New York: Farrar, Straus, Giroux, 1984.

Black, Mrs. George. *My Seventy Years*. As told to Elizabeth Bailey Price. London: Thomas Nelson and Sons Ltd., 1938.

Bloom, Lynn Z. "Heritages: The Tradition of Mother-Daughter Relationships in Women's Autobiographies." *The Lost Tradition: Mother and Daughters in Literature*. Ed. Cathy N. Davidson and E. M. Broner. New York: Frederick Unger Publishing Co., 1980.

Brodzki, Bella. "Mothers, Displacement, and Language in the Autobiographies of Nathalie Sarraute and Christa Wolf." In *Life/Lines: Theorizing Women's Autobiography*. Ed. Bella Brodski and Celeste Schenck. Ithaca: Cornell University Press, 1988.

Bullivant, Brian M. "Multiculturalism—Pluralist Orthodoxy or Ethnic Hegemony." *Canadian Ethnic Studies/Etudes Ethniques au Canada* 13 (1981): 1–22.

Buss, Helen M. "Pioneer Women Memoirs: Preserving the Past/Rescuing the Self." In *Reflections: Autobiography and Canadian Literature*. Ed. K. P. Stich. Ottawa: Ottawa University Press, 1988.

Dahlie, Hallvard. *Varieties of Exile: The Canadian Experience*. Vancouver: British Columbia University Press, 1986.

Demetrokopoulos, Stephanie. "The Metaphysics of Matrilinearism in Women's Autobiography: Studies of Mead's *Blackberry Winter*, Helman's *Pentimento*, Angelou's *I Know Why the Caged Bird Sings* and Kingston's *The Woman Warrior*." *Women's Autobiography: Essays in Criticism*. Ed. Estelle Jelinek. Bloomington: Indiana University Press, 1980.

DuPlessis, Rachel Blau. "For the Etruscans." *The New Feminist Criticism: Essays on Women, Literature and Theory*. Ed. Elaine Showalter. New York: Pantheon Books, 1985.

Faragher, John Mark. *Women and Men on the Overland Trail*. New Haven: Yale University Press, 1979.

Fowler, Marian. *The Embroidered Tent: Five Gentlewomen in Early Canada*. Toronto: Anansi, 1982.

Friedman, Susan Stanford. "Women's Autobiographical Selves: Theory and Practice." *The Private Self: Theory and Practice of Women's Autobiographical Writings*. Ed. Shari Benstock. Chapel Hill: North Carolina University Press, 1988.

Hinz, Evelyn J. "The Masculine/Feminine Psychology of American/Canadian Primitivism: *Deliverance* and *Surfacing*." *Other Voices, Other Views, An International Collection of Essays from the Bicentennial*. Ed. Robin W. Winks. Westport, Conn: Greenwood Press. 1977.

Johnston, Elizabeth Lichtenstein. *Recollections of a Georgia Loyalist.* New York and London. The Bankside Press, 1901.

Lerner, Gerda. *The Female Experience: An American Documentary.* Indianapolis: Bobbs-Merrill Educational Publications, 1977.

Marlatt, Daphne. *What Matters.* Toronto: The Coach House Press, 1980.

Mason, Mary G. "The Other Voice: Autobiographies of Women Writers." In *Life/Lines: Theorizing Women's Autobiography.* Ed. Bella Brodzki and Celeste Schenck. Ithaca: Cornell University Press. 1988.

McMullen, Lorraine. "Ethnicity and Femininity: Double Jeopardy." *Canadian Ethnic Studies/Etudes Ethniques au Canada* 13 (1981):52–62.

Porter, Roger J. "Edwin Muir and Autobiography: Archetype and Redemptive Memory." *The South Atlantic Quarterly,* 77 (1978): 504–23.

Roberts, Sarah Ellen. *Alberta Homestead, Chronicle of a Pioneer Family.* Austin: Texas University Press, 1968.

Salverson, Laura. *Confessions of an Immigrant's Daughter.* 1939. Toronto: University of Toronto Press, 1981.

Skvorecky, Josef. *The Bass Saxophone.* Translated from the Czech by Kaca Polackova-Henley. Toronto: Anson-Cartwright Editions, 1977.

Spacks, Patricia Meyer. *The Female Imagination.* New York: Avon Books, 1972.

 Exile and Intertextuality in Maxine Hong
Kingston's *China Men*
Shu-mei Shih

The theme of exile is one of the principal narrative threads which link the eighteen fragmented segments of *China Men*. It is most prominent in Kingston's depiction of the experiences of the "China Men,"[1] who came to America as sojourners or permanent settlers. She discusses the nature of this exile for three different generations of China Men, from Bak Goong (great-grandfather) who worked on sugar plantations in Hawaii in the mid-nineteenth century, Ah Goong (grandfather) who helped build the transcontinental railroad in the late nineteenth century, to BaBa (father) who owned a laundry business in New York and San Francisco in the early twentieth century. All of them remain nameless, referred to only as the narrator's great-grandfather, grandfather and father, because they represent the collective experience of China Men in America. Kingston reconstructs this experience through historical sources, "talk stories," traditional Chinese fables, various myths and, most importantly, her own narrative imagination. Her reconstruction of Chinese American history has multiple implications regarding the relationship between dominant and marginal discourses, and the problem of representation of ethnic-minority histories in the macrohistory of America. In *China Men*, Kingston explores the consequences of China Men's marginality in the country of their exile, while at the same time mirroring their marginality with that of Chinese women at home in China where patriarchal values predominate. Double commentary is the most frequently used writing strategy in *China Men*.[2]

As defined by Michael Seidel in his *Exile and Narrative* imagination, an exile is "someone who inhabits one place and remembers or projects the reality of another" (1986, ix). In this sense, an exile is one who is capable of invoking or experiencing two realities simultaneously. As actual exiles, Bak Goong, Ah Goong and BaBa's lives show the movement back and forth between the realities of China and America; yet more significantly, exile also defines Kingston's particular kind of imagination. She constantly invokes images from the country which exists vividly only in her imagination;[3] although she is not physically in China, her text is infused with evocations of that land. As the narrator (who seems to be a thinly disguised version of the author herself and similar to the narrator in Kingston's first book *The Woman Warrior*) puts it, China is "a country I made up" (1981, 89). Kingston's ability to recreate the China from her mother's "talk stories" (as she describes them in *The Woman Warrior*), and her desire to dwell on the interplay of cultural codes of both America and China show that she has the sensibilities of an exile. Her America is infused with the memory of China. Her imagination can thus be called an exilic imagination.

The exile experience stimulates the desire to invoke a different reality; an exile always refers back to the reality of his/her past. In like manner, an intertext invokes the reality of other texts. Robert Scholes's succinct definition of the intertext as "a text lurking inside another" (1982, 145) parallels Seidel's definition of an exile who possesses another internal reality. China, for China Men as well as for Kingston, is the dominant intertext to their American reality. In this paper I focus on four sections of *China Men*, each of which is a story based on a famous Chinese fable, and consider their relation to the rest of the text in terms of the exile theme. These sections serve two intertextual functions in the book: 1) they serve as intertexts to the other fourteen sections of the novel, particularly to sections immediately preceding or following them. 2) They also enrich the novel by drawing in the Chinese fables as intertexts to Kingston's own versions. I shall examine them in order to comment not only on the implications of exile for China Men, but also on Kingston's work as the product of a writer with exilic imagination, that is, the relationship between exile and writing.

Exile and Marginality: "On Discovery"

In this first intertext which begins the book, Kingston relates a tale about a certain Tang Ao who finds himself banished to a world where sex roles are reversed, where he is forced to become a woman. This poignant fable about Tang Ao's forced feminization in the Land of Women is taken from the Ch'ing Dynasty novel *Flowers in the Mirror* by Li Ju-chen (c.1763–1830). The book is commonly read as a social and political allegory; the chapters which deal with the trips of the protagonists (Tang

Ao and Lin Chih-yang) to the Land of Women present a satire on social injustice in general and the suppression of women in particular. In Li Ju-chen's version, genders are reversed in the Land of Women: men are called women and play the roles of women, and women are called men, wear men's clothes and act like men. It is a women-centered society. The King (who is a woman) becomes infatuated with Tang Ao's companion, Lin Chih-yang, because of his "face like peach blossoms, waist like slender willows, eyes that contain autumn waters and eyebrows like distant mountains" (1987, 241) and proceeds to make him a concubine. After Lin is subjected to a series of physical tortures normally required of women (his ears are pierced, his feet bound and all the hair on his face plucked out), he is proclaimed ready to become an imperial concubine. But at the crucial moment on the nuptial night, he pretends that he has lost his virility and thus dissuades the King from consummating the marriage. The episode ends with Lin's final rescue by the ingenious Tang Ao and Lin's reunion with his family.

Kingston makes various changes in the original fable. In her version, it is Tang Ao, not Lin Chih-yang, who is taken captive in the Land of Women when he is searching for "the Gold Mountain," which is the name early Chinese immigrants gave to San Francisco. He is put into chains, unlike Lin Chih-yang who is confined to a well-furnished room in *Flowers in the Mirror*, but like early Chinese laborers who were locked below decks in the ships on route to America as described in "The Great Grandfather of the Sandlewood Mountains," another section of the book. Again different from Lin Chih-yang in *Flowers in the Mirror*, Kingston's Tang Ao is turned into a woman to serve meals at the queen's court (1981, 10). In Tang Ao's case, there is no heroic friend to save him, and escape from this woman's land is not feasible at all.

Kingston's fable is an allegorical rendering of the exile situation of China Men in America. Tang Ao is the representative China Man who comes to America in search of the "Gold Mountain" during the Gold Rush in the nineteenth century. But instead of reaching the "Gold Mountain," he is captured and deprived not only of his freedom (enslaved in chains) but also of his manhood (he is turned into a woman and forced to do woman's work—serving meals). Kingston is clearly commenting on the effeminization of China Men by the dominant American culture that has created the stereotype of the Asian man as feminine and submissive, and she thereby echoes the critiques of such stereotypes by male Asian-American writers such as Frank Chin and Jeffery Paul Chan.[4]

Kingston further reinforces her fictional elaboration of China Men's emasculation with historical evidence in "The Laws" section of the book. It is a factual account of Chinese American legal history, a history of segregation and discrimination which witnessed the enactment of such laws as the Chinese Exclusion Act of 1882 and the anti-miscegenation laws of 1924, according to which Chinese men were banned from becoming citizens of the United States and barred from marrying white women. In this way, Chinese men were symbolically castrated and emasculated. They were not allowed to be men since most of them came to America without women. Denied the right to marriage and the legal status of residency, they were relegated to "womanly" professions such as laundry and restaurant work.[5]

Tang Ao's forced effeminization is thus a direct commentary on that of the China Men, simultaneously victimized by the mechanisms of racism and sexism. Social, economic, and legal circumstances beyond their control forced them to do womanly work and in turn they were looked down upon even more because of this involuntary femininity. Sexism saw femininity as a negative quality and racism imposed that negative quality on them.

Alongside Kingston's condemnation of the dominant society's racism and sexism is also her ironic treatment of the issue of sexism in the Chinese context. The physical tortures that Tang Ao must endure are the same ones traditionally suffered by Chinese women in order to enhance their "beauty." Traditional Chinese standards of beauty were defined by men and helped to ensure the subservient position of women in society and the family. The bound feet that epitomized women's imprisonment and subservience in traditional China become the fate of China Men in America. Kingston ironically observes how China Men have become objects of the same kind of sexism which they themselves practiced on their own women at home. Here we see Kingston's characteristic feminist touch. Although she sympathizes with the emasculation of China Men, she at the same time protests against their oppression of Chinese women. In this double-edged criticism, one side turned against racism, the other against traditional patterns of patriarchy, Kingston again operates in a double reality befitting our characterization of her exilic imagination.

Kingston's first book, *The Woman Warrior*, explores the ramifications of female marginality in the male-centered societies of both China and America; but *China Men*, as exemplified by this opening section, investigates the meaning of China Men's marginality in white-centered America, while at the same time retaining a feminist perspective. In the sections that follow, Kingston writes of the various contributions China Men made to the welfare of the country that denied them, and how their blood and sweat enriched the American soil. Arguing against the essentialism of the white-centered discourse which defines China Men as feminine and thus marginalizes them, Kingston complements Julia Kristeva's view that marginality is not a matter of essence, but one of positionality in a given society (Moi 1985, 166). Like Kristeva, Kingston is concerned with the imposed marginality of women in patriarchal societies, but she goes a step further by describing how men of a different race can become victims of the same Center/Margin bifurcation that they themselves perpetuate in their treatment of women. Kingston's appropriation of the fable from *Flowers in the Mirror* drives this point home. By revealing the politics of Center and Margin, Kingston shows how being exiled in America has created a common fate for both Chinese men and women. We may call this the moral of the fable. It is the discovery of a true knowledge of the politics of the self and the Other, and the mechanism of subordination and imprisonment.

Exile and Desire: "The Ghostmate"

Whereas "On Discovery" deals with the relation between exile and marginality on the social level, "The Ghostmate" and its paired section "The Father from China" explore the meaning of exile on the level of personal desire. "The Father from China" depicts the narrator's attempt to understand her father through an imaginary construction of BaBa's past as a scholar and teacher in China as well as his youthful days in New York working as a laundryman. BaBa's life in New York becomes a specific example of what it means to be emasculated and marginalized: BaBa washes other people's clothes and cannot have sexual relationships with white women. There is much parallelism between this section and "The Ghostmate," which depicts a nameless scholar's exile into a fantasy land where he lives with a beautiful ghost. The word "ghost" in Chinese is often used to mean "foreigner," so a "ghostmate" can also mean a "foreign mate."[6] BaBa's exile into the foreign land is not unlike the nameless scholar's exile into the "ghost" land; both are educated as scholars and have taken part in the Civil Service Examinations; both eventually learn skills traditionally considered womanly—Baba washes clothes, the scholar practices embroidery; and both are finally reunited with their wives.

Through this mirroring Kingston continues to explore the issue of men's effeminization in an exiled land, but most importantly, it foregrounds the role of desire. The Chinese genre to which stories like "The Ghostmate" belong, *ch'uan-ch'i* tales (literally "tales that transmit the strange") popular in the T'ang and Sung Dynasties in China, is specifically known for depicting tales of desire. These tales usually have a range of formulaic motifs, the motif of the ghostmate being one of them.

In the highly stratified and hierarchical societies of T'ang and Sung China, scholars' common goal in life was to enter officialdom through passing the many levels of the Civil Service examinations. But the road to success was narrow and difficult. Many scholars frustrated by failure in the examinations turned instead to the writing of supernatural *ch'uan ch'i* tales where the world operated on their own terms. Through writing these tales they gave expression to their desires suppressed by Confucian codes of behavior and to their frustration and disillusionment at their inability to become mainstream figures in the political arena of the time.

Kingston's insertion of this supernatural tale is to show, through parallelism and difference, the nameless scholar's consummation of desire which BaBa is barred from in both China and America. BaBa's job in China as a teacher in a village school is described as obstructing the fulfillment of personal enjoyment:

> The students ruined his eating; they ruined his sleep. They spoiled the songs of birds . . . no time now for his own reading, no time to practice his own writing. Teaching was destroying his literacy. (1981, 42)

Worse yet, in America, his highly treasured literacy is turned into illiteracy—his knowledge of the English language being minimal. Although Kingston depicts the life of Baba in New York with light-hearted humor, the stronger emotion of pathos is prevalent. He starts a laundry business with three friends who later cheat him out of his share of it. He spends his money on expensive clothes to impress blonde girls. Although he is well-liked by them because he is good-looking and is a good dancer, he is rejected when he asks for further intimacy. His ungrammatical spoken invitation "You like come home with me? please?" is answered by "No, honey" (1981, 67). In "The Ghostmate," Kingston provides a traditional Chinese scholar's fantasy to compensate for Baba's frustrations. It is fitting especially because Baba is a scholar himself. The scholar Baba in New York cannot exercise his manhood and cannot quench his desires, while the nameless scholar is able to do so in luxury. The physically and emotionally fulfilling experiences of the nameless scholar in "The Ghostmate" serve as an ironic contrast to Baba's life where desires find no outlet. He's gone fifteen years without a woman.

Although the abundance of pathos in Baba's story reveals Kingston as a sympathetic observer, her specific revision of the Chinese tale once again adds a feminist edge to her sympathy. The nameless scholar, exiled to a world of fantasy and dream where all appetites and desires are satisfied by the seductive ghostmate, finds that he has too much time on his hands. So, like a well-kept wife, he stays indoors doing leisurely work associated with womanhood—embroidering two hundred birds, painting phoenixes, creating beautiful pottery, making intricate shoes, and writing love poetry. This confinement indoors represents a kind of fulfillment, but also imprisonment. The scholar begins to feel the need to go outside of the small world to inhale "air that does not smell feverish with gardenias," and not merely see "window-framed pieces of [the sky]" (1981, 81). We see here again the use of gender reversal: the scholar is put into a woman's shoes and experiences the life of a kept wife. By becoming an insider, he sees the misgivings of womanhood—the life of imprisonment—and wants to escape from it, and he does, literally acting out the role of Ibsen's Nora albeit with gender reversal.

The scholar's successful escape from his confinement again offers a fantastic alternative to BaBa's emotional incarceration. For BaBa, the years of unfulfilled desires, repressed anger, frustrations and fears eventually turn him into a man of silence. He refuses to talk about his past to his family and his silence is often felt by the narrator as a form of punishment. It is this silence that prompts the narrator to try to understand him through her imagination:

> You [BaBa] fix yourself in the present, but I want to hear the stories about the rest of your life, the Chinese stories. I want to know what makes you scream and curse, and what you're thinking when you say nothing . . . I'll tell you what I suppose from your silences and few words, and you can tell me that I'm mistaken. (1981, 18)

Her father's silence motivates the narrator to make conjectures about his life story. Thus she tells much of the story in subjunctives or uncertain terms; for example, she says, "My father was born in a year of the Rabbit, 1891 or 1903 or 1915" (1981, 19). She also gives various versions of his story. For example, there are two different versions of his arrival in America.[7] "The Ghostmate" is also told in subjunctives including "if" and "may have been," self-referentially pointing to its own lack of realism. The results of such conjecturing are multiple versions of a story, which is also the characteristic of the Chinese oral tradition of "talk story," which Kingston consciously appropriates. But most importantly, BaBa's silence serves as the catalyst for the narrator's desire to account for the stories never told her. Writing then becomes the tool with which the narrator combats this silence. In the next three sections of the book, Kingston explores the roots of the silence of China Men and shows how her ancestors combatted it, by going back further to the time of Bak Goong, the great-grandfather, and again by utilizing a Chinese intertext.

Exile and Silence: "On Mortality"

"The Great Grandfather of the Sandalwood Mountains" tells of Bak Goong's arrival in Hawaii to work at a sugar plantation. The Chinese laborers there are under the supervision of white foremen equipped with whips who forbid them to speak during work. Kingston notes how this imposed silence (coupled with the difficult living conditions) makes them ill, and even drives some to suicide. Bak Goong recognizes the source of their illness: "I have diagnosed our illness. It is a congestion from not talking. What we have to do is talk and talk" (1981, 116). He thus tells stories and sings with his fellow laborers after work. During work, he devises ways to speak, ingeniously uttering curses while pretending to cough:

> "Take—that—white—demon. Take—that. Fall—to—the—ground—demon. Cut—you—into—pieces. Chop—off—your—legs. Die—snake. Chop—you—down—stinky—demon." (1981, 115)

When he sees that men are still getting sick, he puts together a "shout party": the men dig a hole in the ground and yell into it all their frustrations, longings and secrets. They have "dug an ear into the world" (1981, 118). Such is their defiance of the law of silence that the white "demons" (foreigners) become afraid of enforcing the law, seeing that the laborers are all "riled up." Bak Goong and his compatriots successfully overcome their oppression, symbolized by the imposed silence.

Kingston here is undermining the stereotype of China Men as passively silent. The mechanism of racism is exposed once more: early Chinese laborers are made to appear less than human by being deprived of the power of speech. She presents their heroic struggle against persecution, and shows how they are the pioneers of the virgin land of Hawaii. The island of Mokoli'i is usually referred to as Chinaman's Hat, which is, Kingston contends, "a tribute to the pioneers to have a living island named after their work hat" (1981, 91).[8] They are also the first people to enter the deep forests of Hawaii where even the local Hawaiians do not dare to go.

On the other hand, in "On Mortality" which follows "The Great Grandfather of the Sandalwood Mountains," Kingston explores the connection between silence and immortality and its negative implications. "On Mortality" is Kingston's version of another Chinese *ch'uan-ch'i* tale by Li Fu-yen: Tu Tzu-ch'un is bestowed with riches three times by a Taoist monk, and the monk requires Tu to do a favor in return. He asks Tu to swallow some pills and tells him: "All that you'll see and feel will be illusions. No matter what happens, don't speak; don't scream" (1981, 120). The monk is to make the elixir for immortality while Tu experiences illusions; Tu's silence will ensure the creation of the right formula. In the world of illusion, Tu finds that he has descended into the nine hells. He sits calmly through his wife's torture and even his own without uttering a word. But after he is reborn as a dumb woman, Tu is unable to overcome the bond of love—the husband Tu marries takes her silence as an insult and kills their son in revenge. As he bashes their son against the rocks, Tu shouts out, "Oh! Oh!" and breaks the law of silence. The spell is broken and the magical elixir is ruined.

Tu's silence can mean immortality for the human race; consequently, the breaking of silence has left men forever subject to mortality. In "On Mortality Again," Kingston illustrates the same theme by using a Hawaiian myth: Maui the Trickster instructs the world to be silent and crawls into Hina's body through her vagina while she is sleeping. He is about to succeed in stealing her heart, which would gain immortality for men and women, when a bird, "at the sight of [Maui's] legs wiggling out of [Hina's] vagina, laughed" (1981, 122). This wakes up Hina, whereupon Maui is shut inside her body where he dies. The bird breaks the code of silence and thus there can be no immortality for the human race. In other words, immortality can be achieved only at the expense of human qualities, especially the faculty of speech. The monk's search for immortality is thus also described by Kingston as negating human attributes: the forsaking of "joy and sorrow, anger, fear, and evil desire," and especially, love (1981, 121). Both Tu's love for her son and the bird's expression of mirth require the breaking of silence; in other words, it is these unique human emotional qualities which obstruct the attainment of immortality. Kingston is thus making the connection between humanity/mortality/speech and inhumanity/ immortality/silence. Kingston subtly reinforces her indictment of the silence imposed upon Chinese plantation workers by establishing the connection between speech and humanity.

However, as characteristic of Kingston's exposure of racist America within which reverberates a critique of Chinese patriarchy, the gender reversal of Tu in the fable is again used to expound a feminist theme. Kingston's condemnation of white America's imposed silence on Chinese workers goes hand in hand with her denunciation of the imposed silence on Chinese women by their own men. Although Kingston basically tells the story of Tu Tzu-ch'un in her own language, she consciously incorporates two sexist quotations from the original Chinese fable as a point of attack. When Tu is being reincarnated, the gods and goddesses decide to have him born a woman because he is "too wicked to be reborn a man" (Kingston 1981, 121; Li 1981, 111). And when Tu, now a woman, grows up to wed her husband-to-be, he says to her parents: "Why does [Tu] need to talk ... to be a good wife? Let her set an example for women" (Kingston 1981, 121; Li 1981, 111). Kingston subtly embeds two rebuttals to these statements within the story. The male Tu, who sits calmly and feelinglessly while watching his wife's body "ground to bloodmeal," is far different from the female Tu who breaks the law of silence out of love for her son. The female Tu's capacity for love is contrasted with the cold male Tu—by being reborn a woman, he in fact changes into a better human being.

Tu's cry comes too late. Her silence costs her own son; silence kills. In the original story though, Tu's silence is not the direct cause of her husband's violent outburst; it is her son's silence that maddens him. He tries to speak to the one-year-old son and when the son does not respond, the husband gets angry and says that the son's silence is his wife's indirect insult on the husband (Li 1981, 111). He does not care whether his wife can speak at all. By making Tu's silence the direct cause of her son's death, Kingston makes the point that silence for women is also deadening after all, as it is for the great grandfathers of Sandalwood Mountains. And this is Kingston's signature of revolt against the agents who impose silence on others, and her assertion of speech and humanity.

Exile and Writing: "The Li Sao: an elegy"

In Chinese literature, Ch'ü Yüan (c. 343–277 B.C.) is the archetypal poet patriot who is unrecognized by his sovereign and sent into exile. As Kingston puts it in "The *Li Sao*, an elegy," he "had to leave the Centre; he roamed in the outer world" (Kingston 1981, 250). Exile has placed him in a position of marginality. In this section, Kingston summarizes Ch'ü Yüan's unhappy life in exile, basing her account on Chinese folklore, Ch'ü Yüan's elegy *Li Sao* ("On Encountering Sorrow"), and other "Songs of the South" written about him.[9] For pronouncing anti-war sentiments, Ch'ü Yüan is banished by the king to southern China, where Chinese culture and civilization have not yet reached. Living among what he calls "savages," Ch'ü Yüan longs to return to the capital and serve the country. But he is never pardoned and called back by the king; he lives his life in gloom, writes his elegy and commits suicide by jumping into a river.

This Chinese intertext is again paired with an American text, "The American Father," in which the narrator continues to relate her father's story from where "The Father From China" left off. BaBa loses his job as a caretaker for a gambling den and becomes completely depressed; he does nothing but lie on the sofa either to sleep or stare into space. The only thing he still does is read Chinese newspapers; the scholar BaBa maintains his love of words despite his despair.

In many ways, Ch'ü Yüan is the literary parallel to BaBa the scholar. They are both in double exile: BaBa from China and from the America in which he can not assimilate, Ch'ü Yüan from the capital and from southern China, where he is "misunderstood by Southern Savages" (Kingston 1981, 251). BaBa sinks deep into depression for seven long years. His wife chides him for his inability to fit in the world:

"You are spoiled and won't go looking for a job. The only thing you're trained for is writing poems," she said. "I know you," she said . . . "You poet. You scholar. You gambler. What use is any of that?

. . . What's the use of a poet and a scholar on the Gold Mountain? You're so skinny. You're not supposed to be so skinny in this country. You have to be tough." (Kingston 1981, 241)

In a similar manner, the poet Ch'ü Yüan mourns his displacement and his incompatibility with the world:

How can the round and the square ever fit together?
How can different ways of life ever be reconciled?

. . . .

Many a heavy sigh I heaved in my despair,
Grieving that I was born in such an unlucky time. (Ch'ü Yüan, l. 99–100, 177–78)

They are both poets in exile and in despair, BaBa over his unsuccessful career in America, Ch'ü Yüan over his political misfortune. Their despair is deep, but they come out differently in the end. While Ch'ü Yüan drowns himself in the river after he completes his *Li Sao,* BaBa somehow stands up from the sofa and regathers his vitality—he opens up a laundry business again and starts to raise animals. Raising animals is a metaphor for his rebirth and the capacity to give life and prosper in this land called America. The sense of displacement is obviously diminished.

Ch'ü Yüan's tragic end, death by drowning, is a result of his overwhelming yearning for the past when he was an official in the king's court. He succumbs to the depth and immensity of his own sorrowful nostalgia. On the other hand, BaBa's rejuvenation stems from an acceptance of his present life in America and the understanding that he and his descendants are here to stay. Through the parallelism of the two poets, Kingston shows how Chinese Americans have had to forsake, to some extent, their Chinese identity and cut their ties to the past so they may reconcile themselves to making America their home. The narrator's brother in "The Brother in Vietnam" is the ultimate symbol of the newfound "Americanness" of Chinese Americans. The brother fights Asians in the war. It is in Taiwan and Hong Kong that he feels estranged.

Ch'u Yuan the poet is, in a different sense, a counterpart to Kingston the writer in that they are both preoccupied by two different realities. Ch'u Yuan's nostalgia for the past has prompted his suicide, and yet it is precisely this nostalgia that has motivated the creation of a masterpiece in literature, the Li Sao. If Ch'ü Yüan had not been banished and his sorrow over that banishment had not been great, the work could not have been written. Exile prompted his writing, which made him immortal: the date of his death has become the official "Poet's Day," commemorated with leaf-wrapped rice balls thrown into rivers so that his spirit will be fed; artistically, his poetry will be forever remembered and celebrated. Kingston also honors his immortality by calling him "Ch'ü Yüan the incorruptible" (251). His imagination owes its richness and intensity to the constant act of looking back to the past; and the nostalgic mood is the major mood of his poetry. In like manner, Kingston looks back at the history of China Men's exile, and reaches toward the source of their nostalgia, examining the tradition of her ancestors, and creatively reinterpreting it for the new reality of Chinese America. To do that, she utilizes not only historical materials, but also Chinese fables and tales, thus presenting herself as one with sensibilities of an exile who juggles multiple realities. The fragmented perspective of an exile is reflected in the fragmented structure of her novel, composed of eighteen segments that interact with each other and with their intertexts outside the book. The multiplicity of texts also requires a multiplication of voices: that of the child narrator, the adult historian, the creative writer and the myth-maker, to name a few. Kingston's work best exemplifies what Mikhail Bakhtin calls the "heteroglossia" of the novel.[10] The multiplication of genres within the text—history, fiction, fable, *ch'uan-ch'i*, myth—is perhaps also the signature of a writer with exilic imagination that foregrounds intertextuality and fragmentation.

When trying to define the relationship between exile and literature, Harry Levin remarks that "the most creative minds are those capable of keeping that other world [where they are exiled from] in sight" (1966, 80). This illustrates the collective significance of exilic imagination for writers. In a more extended sense, Levin also contends that all writers are foreigners or exiles among us (1966, 80) because while they live in this same land that we do, they are forever pursuing that other reality of literary imagination. Kingston is thus an exile in many different senses of the word. As a descendant of her Chinese ancestors, she is an exile who forever looks back to the land of the past, China; or as Proust would put it, she observes the higher laws of "une patrie perdue." She draws on her exilic imagination, merging her American experience with a fantastic literary world of fables and legends from China. And by simply being a writer, she is an exile among us.

Notes

1. "China Men" is the term Kingston uses to counter the racist epithet "Chinamen." She does not completely abandon the latter—both are similar in pronunciation—because it has come to mean the Chinese who live in America, different from "Chinese men" who live in China. What she does is to reinscribe the racist term by separating the words and capitalizing them, thus giving them a sense of dignity. The main project of *China Men,* if one may say so, is exactly to establish the

important contributions of "China Men" to the development of America as they toiled on its land for more than one century. "China Men" are pioneers, as Kingston puts it (see 90–91 and 140–141 for specific references to the term). It is in the same spirit that I use this term here.

2. I would like to thank Professor King-kok Cheung of the University of California, Los Angeles for helping me develop this and some other ideas regarding Kingston's works.

3. Kingston had not yet visited China when this book was written.

4. Frank Chin and Jeffery Paul Chan, along with a few other male writers, have been the Asian American voices of protest against stereotypes and racism. *Aiiieeeee!: An Anthology of Asian-American Writers*, edited by Frank Chin and others and published in 1975, is the manifesto of their creativity which they associate with masculinity. Kingston's treatment, we will see, reveals her more feminist orientation.

5. For a sociological analysis of this issue, see Kim, 982.

6. The subtitle to *The Woman Warrior* is "Memoirs of a Girlhood among Ghosts," where the "ghosts" refer to foreigners, in this case, white Americans. In *China Men*, Kingston also uses "demons" in the same sense. "Ghosts" and "demons" are both translations of the Chinese word, *kuei*.

7. In one version, he is smuggled into New York hidden in a crate aboard ship as an illegal alien; in another version, he comes through Angel Island immigration with legal papers. See pp. 50–60.

8. Kingston explores the same theme in "The Grandfather of the Sierra Nevada Mountains" section as well. The contribution of the Chinese railroad workers is compared to that of Nu Wo, a goddess from a Chinese creation myth. They are "the binding and building ancestors of this place [America]" (Kingston 1981, 144–145).

9. "Songs of the South," *Ch'u-tz'u* in Chinese, are poems written in the so-called *sao* mode from southern China with their peculiar song-like rhythm and meter, often incorporating shamanistic motifs which are allegorized to signify the exiled poets' emotions. Ch'u Yuan himself is the creator of this style.

10. For further reference, see Bakhtin 1981.

Works Cited

Bakhtin, Mikhail. *The Dialogic Imagination*. Edited by Michael Holquist, translated by Michael Holquist and Caryl Emerson. Austin: University of Texas Press, 1981.

Ch'u Yuan. *Li Sao*. In *The Songs of the South*. Translated by David Hawkes. New York: Penguin Books, 1985.

Kim, Elaine. *Asian American Literature: An Introduction to the Writings and Their Social Context*. Philadelphia: Temple University Press, 1982.

Kingston, Maxine Hong. *China Men*. London: Picador, 1981.

Levin, Harry. *Refractions: Essays in Comparative Literature*. Oxford: Oxford University Press, 1966.

Li Fu-yen. "Tu Tzu-chun," in *T'ai-p'ing kuang-chi*. Vol. 1. Ed. Li Fang. Taipei: Wen-shih-che ch'u-pan-she, 1981.

Li Ju-chen. *Ching-hua yuan (Flowers in the Mirror)*. Peking: Jen-min wen-shueh ch'u-pan-she, 1987.

Moi, Toril. *Sexual/Textual Politics: Feminist Literary Theory*. London and New York: Methuen, 1985.

Scholes, Robert. *Semiotics and Interpretation*. New Haven and London: Yale Univ. Press, 1982.

Seidel, Michael. *Exile and the Narrative Imagination*. New Haven: Yale Univ. Press, 1986.

Gender in Exile: Mothers and Daughters in Roberto G. Fernández's *Raining Backwards*
Mary S. Vásquez

"I told her so many times that love goes away but the pain remains" (169), says Mima, a character in *Raining Backwards* (1988), by the U. S. Cuban writer, Roberto G. Fernández. We could perhaps agree that this is hardly a notion that will endear the old ways to the new generation. Some female readers may at once recognize the tenor, if not the precise words, of their mothers' teachings on the subject of relations between the sexes. Yet, what distinguishes the import of Mima's remark from teachings about the male world received at every mother's knee by generations of us women in diverse cultures of the Western world? I believe it is the conditioning context of exile, with its texture of interwoven expectations and refutations, affirmations and denials and its complex code of messages both within the exile group and between it and the encompassing culture. The mother and daughter generations and the relationship between them will be examined primarily here through two mother-daughter pairs in two branches of a Cuban exile family in *Raining Backwards*: María de los Angeles "Mima" López and her daughter Connie Rodríguez, on the one hand, and their relative Emelina and her daughter Linda Lucía, on the other.

The satirical yet loving depiction of exile Cuban life in Dade County, Florida, is a constant in the fiction of Roberto G. Fernández. Born in Sagua la Grande and now a faculty member in Hispanic linguistics at Florida State University, Fernández has published the short-story collections *Cuentos sin rumbos* (1975) and *El jardín de la luna* (limited edition, 1976) as well as the novels *La vida es un special* (1981) and *La montaña rusa* (1985). *Raining Backwards* is Fernández's first novel in English.

Like its predecessors, the novel is a funny, heart-tugging, cacophonous portrayal of the Cuban exile generation centered in south Florida and upon its offspring, the children of exile. Through first- and third-person anecdotes, letters, and personal fantasies, *Raining Backwards* portrays a microcosm of the exile community's extended family to which Mima, Connie, Emelina and Linda Lucía belong.

Of the children of Mima López and Jacinto Rodríguez, dubbed a "war hero" by virtue of his attack on the Presidential palace in Havana from his Miami apartment with grenades carried aloft by balloons, Connie is the only girl; the other offspring of this marriage are Joaquín AKA Quinn, who first becomes the saint of Hialeah, Florida, only to rise to nothing less than the Papacy, and Jacinto, Keith or Kicito, a rebel and drug dealer who later leads an insurrectionary group in the Everglades. This family, or at least its older generation, lives fully within the powerful exile family structure. On the other hand, Emelina, of the second mother-daughter pair to be studied here, lives on the fringes of this group, a kind of self-outcast. She has left Mima's cousin-in-law Clavo after three decades of marriage and has gone off to live in the small community of Kendall, south of Miami, where no one knows her. The circumstances in which these two women raise their daughters, then, are quite different: Mima's context is that of the majority within the minority, the contextual reassurance conferred by group identity, while Emelina lives a kind of double exile, removed from the identity group by course of action and by short, but symbolic, geographical distance.

Of these two mothers, Mima and Emelina, members of the mature exile generation both, one is seen centrally in the novel, the other peripherally. Yet, the two represent different female approaches to the rigors of exile life. As members of the generation that chose what it presumed would be a temporary exile, they left behind their beloved homeland for a short stay in a quite alien culture whose differentness belied the ninety miles of distance from the shores of the martyred island. As temporality hardened into permanence, Mima and Emelina's generation had to battle fully in the state of cultural siege shared by political exiles in a new culture. Theirs was, then, a dual struggle for connectedness—with a past and with a present. The effort to retain a vinculum with a cultural context now carried only within was made more complex by the traumatic nature of the separation from the island and by the chosen conception of its temporality. Their other mirror-image struggle, of course, was for connectedness of the group within a new culture with distinct expectations of its members, different mores, and a different texture of encoded and decoded messages between members. Successful operation within the new code was by no means a given. And should dexterity be achieved, might acquisition of a new code mean surrender of the old, and of identity with it? The novel's characters of the mature generation partake of traditional exile approaches to this problem of connectedness: refuge in group identity; rituals of the homeland; the aggrandizement of it, the product of distance and yearning. For operating through this process is a subtle, ironic game of time, evocatively portrayed in *Raining Backwards*. As the temporality of the island's political aberration has become a fixed reality, and for many mature exiles of an even more immutable judgment of it, the island itself has receded in time, in lived experience, in *memory*, engendering ever more extravagant attempts to court its return. Having envisioned an early return to the island, Fernández's exiles now find themselves trying to summon the island to them. As the rituals of collective memory grow in depth of yearning, they become ever more removed from the island itself. Time, then, carries both the exile and the island away.

A chief actress in the island-courting rituals, Mima López is also the novel's most complete exemplar of the duality of adaptation and separateness which is the exile's negotiation with a new culture. Matriarch of the Rodríguez-López family, Mima is perennial hostess of the clan's Christmas Eve roast pig feast and pageant. It is she who cooks the meal throughout the day, she who worries about rain, she who takes her cousin's telephone inquiry as to how much wine he should bring, knowing full well that he will purchase the cheapest brand, then soak off and replace the labels, as he does every year. And it is Mima who labors to bring together the family's various factions, from the heartbroken and alienated Clavo, the abandoned husband, to her own rebellious Keith, the drug dealer. Furthermore, Jacinto's recounting to an unheard and probably majority listener of Mima's reaction when her adolescent children wanted to get an apartment describes an alarm quite culturally appropriate to Mima's matriarchal status. Yet, there is systematic narrative subversion of *Raining Backwards*'s portrayal of a cultural icon: the self-abnegating Latin grandmother, family counselor, repository of family values. Preparing the garnishes for the roast pig, Mima deliberately cuts herself six times in hopes of an exit from the meal preparation and, indeed, from the entire event. It is also revealed tht she detests making mango marmalade, a fact of which even her husband is unaware.

What Mima appears to find infinitely more satisfying is cooking for profit. She establishes in her home a plantain chip business which turns into a multi-million-dollar enterprise. In embodying this classic American ideal of the self-made (wo)man, Mima proves herself a clever and skillful negotiator with the encompassing majority culture. Of the members of the mature Cuban exile generation portrayed in *Raining*

Backwards, Mima López is, in fact, the one who most skillfully—and, it seems, most happily—performs the difficult navigation in majority waters. Indeed, so good does Mima become at placing her very considerable Cuban talents and business acumen within the expectations and judgments of the framing majority culture that Mima takes control of a portion of those majority waters. Is it not her son Quinn, the saint of Hialeah, who becomes Pope after years as the head of an international cult centered—where else?—in south Florida? It is no accident that Quinn is the child to whom Mima is obviously closest. His improbable rise to the Papacy is far less a religious phenomenon than another American success story made possible by the lessons Quinn learned from the master teacher and consummate survivor of them all, Mima herself.

The degree of Mima's skill in spontaneous cultural translation (conducting of herself in two codes) is revealed when a local talk-show host tapes a broadcast interview at her home. Mima has clearly staged the event for majority consumption. Women wearing mantillas play castanets in the background and break into a chorus of "God Bless America" as Mima explains the vital role of *dueñas* and strict seclusion in the bringing up of Cuban *señoritas* and entones the praises of life in the USA.

> "I just want to say how much I love it here. When you have freedom, you can be whatever you want to be. When my deceased husband died, I didn't know what to do. I tried praying to Our Lady of the Macarena . . . but there was no answer. Then something wonderful happened to me . . . Now there is no doubt in my mind, God must be from the United States . . . ."(139)

Mima's adeptness does, however, exact its price. At the Christmas feast, her cousin Barbara is unwilling to lend Mima a hand with the preparations. "'You don't want me to end up like her, having lovers and my own business, do you?'"(44) she demands of her husband. In addition to this partial ostracism by a fellow woman, there are signs that in Mima the native's semi-automatic encoding and decoding in her own cultural terms may have begun to weaken. Her husband Jacinto may well sense this change in his own insistence upon his tradition-consecrated gender views and roles. Speaking with an unidentified majority person, Jacinto offers the most timeworn of perspectives on womankind. On the subject of religion, "'Those are things for women, after all'" (79), Jacinto comments, and on hysteria: "'You know women'" (79). A solicitous host, he asks and exclaims, "'You like more rum? Mima, Mima, bring us some more rum and limes! Hurry up, woman!'" (80). The gap in cultural response between husband and wife becomes fully evident to Jacinto during an odd incident: the family dog spends six hours trying to eat its tail. An unquestioningly superstitious, aging

Cuban, Jacinto interprets this occurrence as confirmation of his fears that their daughter Connie is no longer a virgin. He endeavors to relay this news to his wife.

> I guess Mima noticed the look of despair on my face. "What is the matter? Que pasa? she said." "The damage is done," I answered. "I knew it," Mima said. "You shouldn't have lent Connie the Falcon. I am sure she rammed the car against some telephone pole." She thought it was the car. I guess Mima was becoming a real American. She was more interested in the car than in anything else. Then she knelt and prayed, cried and gave blows to her chest, begging the angels to come at night and repair the damage. She hated taking the bus.(76–77)

Mima misreads Jacinto's distress; she misses the cultural cue. Her response to the damage she *thinks* has occurred is "culturally correct," but she mistakes the cause in a displacement of cultural automatism and a replacement of cultural icons. Her confusion would be unlikely outside the exile experience with its attendant bombardment of conflicting signals and the majority culture's expectation of differing responses.

For the object of Jacinto's concern, the question is, of course, very different. She is a member of what critic Eliana Rivero, following sociologists' leads, terms the ethnics, the children of exile, those who passed into exile as young children and who, hence, did not choose their departure and have grown to maturity in the new land (1989, 189–200). This generation does not carry the same emotional cargo of nostalgia, regret, conviction of right and, some might say, intransigence, which characterizes their parents. A number of Connie's cousins have chosen majority mates, and most of these unions have failed. Connie herself pines for the crude and faithless Billy Cloonan and becomes locked in a no-win spiral which ultimately ends her life; Connie proves to be the mystery girl found hanging upside down from the branch of a ceiba tree. Connie and her mother apparently are not close. In favoring Quinn, the one who is most like her, Mima distances herself from her other son, Keith. And Connie is, after all, a fellow female and, hence, expected to follow most closely Mima's lead, yet one who has departed considerably from the essence of Mima's lament that, "... when we started courting it was beautiful back then. There was no sex, nor all the indecencies there are now" (67). Significantly, it is *Jacinto*, not the girl's mother, who discovers the loss of Connie's virginity—well after the reader has done so. Mima is not only "officially" unaware, telling the police captain that her daughter was "'very different from today's youth . . . [and] never expressed any interest in the opposite sex'" (169), but also clearly fails to read signs in the mother-daughter code. Then, too, the mother may be shielding herself with distance from what she chooses not to see. Though she herself has negotiated so successfully a place within, if not totally in relation to, the majority culture, she may well be unable to accept an alteration of the inviolable—the code of female sexual conduct.

Jacinto's concern with his daughter's virginity is also Emelina's for that of her daughter Linda Lucía. Yet, for this peripherally-seen female character, concern has left the realm of rationality to become a maniacal obsession with what Emelina must see as the source of woman's ruination: the onset of menstruation. Emelina refuses to allow her daughter to menstruate, applying needle and thread to halt the flow of natural development, then, when this measure fails, begging her daughter to hold back the unmentionable. Emelina is, thus, at the pathetic and ridiculous extreme of stereotypical motherly protection of her daughter's innocence in a denial of womanhood itself, her attitude and actions implying a pronounced hatred of her own womanliness. Yet, this woman at the far extreme of at least one Hispanic code of womanliness is at a quite opposite extreme as well. In divorcing Clavo and going off to Kendall, Emelina has rebelled, breaking the clan's codes. For it is she for whom Clavo weeps, the wife who abandoned him after more than thirty years of marriage and moved away. In reality, of course, these opposites are not so opposed; they are two expressions of denial, first of culturally-defined womanly duty, raising an expectation of that most medieval of distinctions, the dichotomy of the exemplar and the hussy, then a denial of the passionate essence that pole implies, much as the medieval code of womanly conduct which is parodied in Emelina's attitudes stands in tacit awe of the forces it pretends to control.

Emelina's attitude toward her daughter, like Mima's, probably has much to do with her experience of exile. Her removal from the majority of the minority functions as a metaphor for exile from the homeland and, incidentally, from its courting rituals. The fact that this character is presented to us with no surname is suggestive of her removal—a separation both by choice and by circumstance, like that of the exile generation itself. Her greatly hyperbolic attempts to apply her birth culture's codes of womanliness are perhaps acts of atonement for her own departure from these codes in her divorce from Clavo, expiatory declarations and displays of the fact that she is indeed a member of her clan, and then some. Her daughter's menstruation becomes a metaphor for the conflictive relationship with both cultures of this character, last seen chronologically trying to join a band, like her boyfriend. Emelina's mad efforts may also be suggestive of her generation's attempts to conjure memories of the beloved island left behind. As for her daughter, Linda Lucía is obliged by her mother to dress in, or *as*, the Cuban flag, her appearance at the culmination of Cuban social events serving as an ever-repeated declaration of an essential and intact Cubanness and a tacit reminder of the enveloping non-Cuban context—again the measure of distance—even as it functions for Emelina as a highly personal expiatory ritual. Family gossip reports that mother and daughter do not get along can surprise no one.

A sometimes unrecoverable past must contend in exile life with a hybrid present and future. It is in that forge of the exilic experience that an amalgam of past and present, the remembered and the immediate, must be wrought, here that gain must negotiate with loss, memory with forgetting, perpetuation with surrender. In this amalgam, Mima may be viewed as an exile successful in achieving her own balance between exile and majority cultures, while Emelina may be seen to fail, taking refuge in physical removal—pure denial—and in aberrant practices which give the lie to any real adaptation. Yet, Mima seems unable to transmit her own expertise to a daughter, lacking, perhaps, the kinds of womanly knowledge about the new culture that Connie needs most, while Connie rejects the lessons of the old. We see Connie alone in her struggles with her boyfriend, with jealousy, and with her rival. Ultimately, Connie literally perishes. As for Emelina and Linda Lucía, both are silenced in the text once the moment of ruination has definitely arrived. Rumors of Emelina suggest continued irresolution. The mother's training cannot have equipped Linda Lucía for life in *any* culture, and if this recurring Fernández character could speak, her indictment would probably be a powerful one indeed.

Works Cited

Fernández, Roberto G. *Cuentos sin rumbo.* Miami: Ediciones Universal, 1975.
———. *El Jardín de la luna.* Miami: Ediciones Universal, 1976.
———. *La montaña rusa.* Arte Público Press, 1985.
———. *La vida es un special.* Miami: Ediciones Universal, 1981.
———. *Raining Backwards.* Houston: Arte Público Press, 1988.
Rivero, Eliana. "From Immigrants to Ethnics: Cuban Women Writers in the U. S." In *Breaking Boundaries: Latina Writing and Critical Readings*, ed. Asunción Horno-Delgado et al. Amherst: University of Massachusetts Press, 1989.

The Reader of Exile: Skvorecky's *Engineer of Human Souls*
Robert S. Newman

I think it safe to say that we normally expect exile or refugee literature to be transparent. That is, we assume that those who encounter it will accept it at face value and perhaps even understand its subtextual implications.

But the varying reception of exiles and refugees over the years should make us wonder about this model of transparency. In this connection, consider the inconsistent sympathies of even intellectuals to German refugees in the 1930s (Muresianu 1988), the disbelief in England and the United States during WWII as to the reality of death camps, the quarrels over post-1945 DP's by both the Left (who saw them as fascists) and the Right (who saw them as Communists), and the rejection by influential segments of the Left of Vietnamese refugees (Jane Fonda's attacks on Van Thoai in *The New York Times*). With examples like these, I suggest that we abandon—if indeed we ever held it—the simple idea that refugee or exile literature is immediately honored as soon as encountered.

We can take a cue here from recent literary criticism, which has emphasized the difficulties inherent in reader response and reception: a text is not complete in itself but must be completed by the reader. (For a recent survey of the literature, see 1989, 29–53.) On a personal basis, readers read only what is important to them (1978); on a social basis—more importantly—the reader's own "horizon of expectations" (Hans Robert Jauss's term)—a social and cultural matter of previous encounters with genres or traditions—may determine the ability to read a text.

When, for example, a liberal western reader of Skvorecky's *The Engineer of Human Souls* encounters the encomium of a Czech émigré as someone who both "represents the extreme right" and yet "is probably the most decent person in the émigré community" (138), the clash between the reader's own liberal sensitivities and that "extreme right" label must lead to sheer cognitive dissonance. Only when we crack Skvorecky's code do we realize that behind the dissonance lies Skvorecky's satiric sense that: a) liberals—like Communists, Nazi's, etc.—judge holistically, deterministrically, and refuse to acknowledge the contradictoriness of real human beings (the personal may not be the political); and b) that liberals are far more comfortable assailing the extreme right rather than the extreme left. A similar litmus test of response can be found in one of Skvorecky's *Lieutenant Boruvka* stories, where a witness to a murder is described as watching on TV "four politicians of the social democratic persuasion [who] were discussing the advantages of violent revolution"(83). Depending on how attuned one is (or was) to Eastern European disenchantment with pre-Glasnost Communism and how cognizant one is about the danger of intellectual praise for totalistic restructuring of society, the joke will either be appreciated or missed.

It has been said, in fact, that what we get in exile literature is often a 'natural' kind of reception esthetic, one inspired not by literary theory but rather by actual encounters between exiles and their new audiences. As Marilyn Fries has pointed out in regard to East Germans, the exile is forced to develop a reception-esthetic of some rough and ready sort when he or she realizes, to use the words of one of Skvorecky's characters, that "you know nothing about me ... about *anything!*"(445). The barbs about right-wingers and Social Democrats should also be understood in the context of what Skvorecky has called a typical Central European mixture of "cynicism" and "humor," born—he says—out of the "schizophrenic" conditions of Eastern Europe where people have been forced to say one thing and think another in deference to ideology. In addition, these barbs are paradoxes, and paradox—as Skvorecky also notes—is a marvelous way of both sharpening one's intellect and maintaining an oppositional stance towards the demands of orthodoxy. What hurts, as Skvorecky well knows, is that one must learn to doubt even one's own orthodoxies.

Facing West/Writing East

In Czech terms, Skvorecky is an Americanist: his novels are filled with allusions to American popular genres, literature, and culture; in North American terms, however, Skvorecky is a Czech bringing word about the disasters of the Nazis and the Communists to an audience innocent of such historical experience.

Skvorecky's double glance, nicely caught in Sam Solecki's title above, is also applicable to Skvorecky's position as an exile, looking backward to his past under the Nazis and Communists and forward to his present life in Canada ("that decadently anti-police democracy"). *Engineer* is especially concerned with that double glance backwards and forwards: on the basis of his experience in Czechoslovakia, and later as an émigré in Canada after the Russian invasion of 1968, Skvorecky attempts to persuade his western readers that there is something naive about their attitudes towards totalitarianism. Using a jumbled retrospective narrative and epistolary correspondence from the Czech diaspora, Skvorecky presents innumerable anecdotes about life under the Nazis and Communists and the attempts of émigrés to cope with the non-comprehension of friends, lovers, and colleagues in the west. In addition, through the semi-autobiographical Professor Danny Smiricky at "Edenvale" College, Skvorecky extends his historical critique to literature by showing how one might instruct Canadian naifs and American draft-dodgers in the art of genuinely "relevant" reading—e.g., how Conrad might be read as an anticipation of Stalin's gulags.

Skvorecky's satire, though it deals with both the Nazi and Soviet experiences, does have a particular political bite to it: Skvorecky wants his readers to understand that the West has traditionally been more upset by the totalitarianism of the Right than that of the Left. Thus, Danny observes of his students that they have always been more upset by Fascism than Communism:

> Fascism holds an attraction for these innocents; Communism does not, hence the drop in attendance. Fascism was one of the great disgraces of their world whereas Communism, they feel, has nothing to do with them. (64)

Skvorecky developed this critique quite explicitly in a blistering article in *Canadian Literature*, "Are Canadians Politically Naive?" In it, Skvorecky excoriates a Canadian peace activist who journeyed to post-68 Prague, saw some rock musicians, and concluded that all was well. Skvorecky attacks her failure to attend to history, read the "pertinent literature," and acknowledge the hidden but almost total suppression of freedom by the Communist regime. Skvorecky's basic attitude is that of Czelaw Milosz, who said (as reported by Peter Esterhazy) that "the difference between Eastern and Western intellectuals is that Western intellectuals have never been kicked in the ass properly" (1990, 274). Skvorecky's *Engineer* may be regarded in part as an attempt to remedy that deficiency.

Reading Exile

In her recent study, *Timely Reading*, Susan Noakes argues that "reading must be understood as the constantly transformed product of historical change, not a timeless process focused on timeless texts but rather a '"timely' activity." She exemplifies her argument by showing how reading itself has been imaged differently over various historical periods—how actual readers embedded in texts have been portrayed by various writers. Such historicized readers reveal different, timebound aspects of the reading process and of the texts they read.

This is a useful approach for Skvorecky because he has made his readers quite historically specific both in the way they read particular texts (right down to the fine teacherly reference to "Norton's Critical Edition, p. 122") and as well in the way they "read" political issues and icons such as the Vietnam War and Angela Davis. Skvorecky has in mind four quite specific kinds of audiences—the exile community itself, the apparatchiks (Communist party members) and censors of the homeland, the inner exiles and dissidents of Czechoslovakia, and, especially, those of us in the West. In dealing with these varied kinds of readers, Skvorecky challenges us to understand more empathetically what exile politics amounts to and what bitter experience it derives from.

Émigrés and Émigré Readers: "I've been there before."

Danny Smiricky is an exile from the period of Prague Spring, 1968; he is an old stand-in for Skvorecky, figuring in much of his fiction. In *The Cowards* (1958), Danny was a youth at the close of WWII, more interested in girls and swing than in the Resistance; hence the irony of the title and one reason the Communists banned the novel. At the end of *The Cowards*, Danny also makes an unsettling discovery: the Communists, whom he had always thought of as Social Democrats like himself, are now circulating inflammatory pamphlets (their rhetoric amply parodied by Skvorecky) about getting rid of the "bourgeois" once they come to power; Danny thinks to himself that this must mean people like the tobacconist down the block and even his own father, who manages the local movie-house. He is disturbed. And of course the Communists do come to power in 1948, and do exactly what they said they would do—get rid of everyone but themselves, despite their promises. Coalitions with Communists are dangerous and Communists are secret totalitarians. Exiles know this; the West doesn't.

In *Engineer*, Danny is no longer the callow adolescent of *Cowards*. What he suffers from now in Canada, however, is the psychological problem of identity and continuity. Robert Edwards suggests that "exile attacks identity by threatening continuity and one's ability to project a self located in time and space confidently toward the future" (20). In *Engineer* a sense of discontinuity is ever present. Danny narrates his story in a loosely associative way in which events in the present or letters from abroad trigger memories of the past. In fact, all that he has of his homeland is memory. There is a reiterative sense of a lost homeland, a lost language. A minor character, Veronika, provides a neat encapsulization of this psychic fracturing as she says to a new émigré "I guess we need them both, Prague and freedom. But the way things are, we can't have them both. It's either-or" (455). Veronika plays out a typical émigré wish to annihilate such discontinuity by returning to her homeland, although once there she realizes how miserable a place it is and returns again to Canada. Danny is under no such illusions but he does speculate on the loss involved in his very use of Czech, a language now useful only for recording memories and playing with puns that only a limited readership will understand (cp. Nadia, Nadezdha, 'hope' in Russian).

On the other hand, discontinuity doesn't arouse uniform pain and loss. Danny opens his narrative with a joyous salute to the Toronto skyline as "more beautiful to me than the familiar silhouette of Prague Castle. There is beauty everywhere on earth, but there is greater beauty in those places where one feels that sense of ease which comes from no longer having to put off one's dreams until some probable future, where the fear which has pervaded one's life suddenly vanishes because there is nothing to be afraid of" (4).

Even here, though, appearances are deceiving. Though Danny can travel through upper New York State and be reminded of the hills of his native Bohemia, it's obviously not the same thing, and equally important if we consider the novel's overall trajectory, the sense of loss is a deepening one. Towards its penultimate point, Danny is in Paris with his now-mistress, Irene, and takes her to the Deux Magots where he, Kundera and Forman speculated in 1968 about what was happening in Prague as the Russians took over. The sense that we get here is of persistent breaks in identity, of memories floating back, of loss, of what might have been, and of an overall sense of despair characterized by existential gloominess and scatological ironies.

According to Maria-Ines Lagos-Pope, quoting the Chilean Hernan Valdes, exile writing has two key functions for the exile community: 1) to "incite the reader to rebellion, [and] stir up his solidarity with respect to concrete fact" (i.e., before corrupt newspapers at home print falsehoods); and 2) to deal with memories as a means of transmitting stories for future generations and thus ensure the survival of a "collective identity" (123–4).

One caveat should be made, however, about inciting the reader to rebellion because, in Skvorecky's case, that's not exactly what he wants to do: violent revolution just breeds more misery, as he told a Toronto Conference on Human Rights in 1983 ("Why Revolution is Usually the Worst Solution"). Of course, reform is slow and radicals in the West detest slow change even though they have the mechanisms for it, but as Veronika puts it ironically, "All it takes is time. That's all. Over there, you need the courage of a test pilot if you want to change things" (441).

But certainly Skvorecky is concerned with the idea of "solidarity" as to "concrete fact" as a way of ensuring the survival of collective identity. This is the purpose of writing, publishing (see Skvorecky on his own "68 Publishers"), and reading. Thus he tells endless stories about life under Nazi and Soviet rule and has his various correspondents in the Czech diaspora tell their stories as well.

What we get from the Nazi period is the great ésprit of the Resistance and yet also the reality that people sometimes have to be dragged into it against their will. Danny is driven to action by Nadia only because she forces the issue of conscience on him by never letting him forget how both her own father and Rebecca's died in the death camps.

Analogously, Danny tells stories about life under Soviet rule and it's the same old business with one tyranny merely replacing another: tragedy repeated—we are told—becomes farce. Again, people talk in whispered tones in the toilets, where some freedom remains; or they write scathing scatological satires—immediately banned—about Stakhanovite fecal productivity. No one can take a joke.

Much of the resistance activity in the novel takes the form of the classic Czech statement in Hasek's *Good Soldier Schweik*—the smilingly passive outward appearance, the inner subversion. (In the Messerschmidt plant, an old geezer fools the foreman by pushing the same barrel around from one end of the plant to the other. "Get your own barrel," he warns Danny.) Interestingly, Skvorecky has said that he hadn't read *Schweik* until adulthood, but that such Schweikian resistance had so permeated Czech culture that you needn't have read Hasek to enact Schweikian gestures. It is precisely this kind of collective resistance to tyranny that Skvorecky wishes to preserve for his Czech readers, and perhaps for us as well.

Skvorecky does not, however, gloss over the fact that there are conflicting attitudes, both generational and ethnic, within the émigré community. Of the former, there are amused references to the way the pre-WWII émigrés are horrified at the ostensible pornography of Mrs. Santner and her husband (cp. Skvorecky and his wife and "68 Publishers"): they don't understand that mores have changed and that sexual (cp. Kundera, published by "68") or scatological themes (Skvorecky's own novel here) represent a last bastion in the fight against totalitarian deadness.

Ethnic conflicts also persist, and Skvorecky is intensely honorable in depicting these and in urging his readers to put them in perspective. Much of this revolves around fears of a Jewish conspiracy at work to torpedo the Czechs even in Canada. Skvorecky suggests that if we are to 'read' such anti-Semitism correctly, we must see it as an expression of a much larger feeling aroused by the memories of secret police and the real presence, here and now, of Czech agents, putting pressure on émigrés in places like the Empire State Building Observation Deck. (Skvorecky's review of the Canadian spy novel, *The Red Fox*, shows that he finds the spy trope quite meaningful and real.) Finally, too, Skvorecky draws continuity between past and present to suggest that the real undercurrents of anti-Semitism which must be resisted involved the Nazis, obviously, but also the Communists, who falsely executed the Jewish Rudolf Slansky in the celebrated show trials of an earlier era.

In a memorable scene celebrating Czech Independence Day, Skvorecky pulls together the varied threads of identity, memory, and conflict, and offers them as parts of an ultimately joyous moment. Danny notices the discontinuities of identity—the "second-generation Mississauga Czech accent," the Czech dancers doing a Highland Fling—but he also notices that all the fractious groups are here singing the Czech national anthem together, and that their patriotism is not ideologically forced or manufactured—it is the genuine product. Moreover, even though Danny is a somewhat distanced observer, he is nevertheless happy and proud to be a part of this kind of celebration. One cannot help but feel that Skvorecky, thinking not so much of his émigré audience but of his Western liberal audience, sees this scene as a challenge to the conventionally anti-patriotic ethos of liberals, radicals, and intellectuals.

Apparatchiks and Censors

Paul Tabori reminds us that the "successes" of the exile "are likely to be envied or derided" in his homeland, presumably by the true believers, apparatchiks, and assorted defenders of the faith. Interestingly, he points to how "in the case of small nations" the exile "may undergo the curious process of transformation from American/Russian/Fascist/Communist . . . . hireling" into "our compatriot who lives abroad" and finally into "our distinguished former fellow-citizen" (38). There is considerable interchange and communication between émigrés and those in the homeland who, even if they are part of the regime, must keep track of what the émigrés are saying and doing.

Skvorecky touches on this process in several ways. First, there are those travellers who come to Danny from Prague bearing gifts: this arouses genuine fear because as an émigré you don't know what kind of a Mr. Novak has left a message for you—the police-state kind (who else would get permission to travel?) or the dissident and ordinary well-wisher kind?

Secondly, Skvorecky provides damning portraits of two characters who represent apparatchik ideals—the party boss Uher and the peasant Losja. Uher keeps coming back into the action, meeting Danny in New York, once at the Empire State Building, another at a jazz club to hear Earl Garner (at least he retains his good taste from the 40s). He tries to force Danny—and to some extent succeeds—into pressuring another émigré to maintain a political silence on a crucial matter. Uher is a former priest, thus fitting Danny's view that tyrannies are created by "perverted saints." Uher was hard-hearted as a priest, refusing to hide Danny from the Nazis after a blown sabotage effort, and he's just as hardened, in the Hawthorne sense, now, under the Communists; in fact he's gone from a kind of resistance to the Nazis to becoming the oppressor under the Soviets: the ends do justify the means, there is indeed only a single truth and the Party has it, Dubcek was a fool trying to exact revenge for political slights he had received and so on.

Losja, a childhood buddy of Danny's from Kostelec, is treated differently from Uher. He is a comic lout, a fool, an idiot who can barely spell, a believer first in the Nazis and then in the Soviets, but he is also something of an innocent and for that reason still seems to get Danny's sympathy—at least he keeps writing letters to Danny from the beginning of the novel to the end, suggesting that perhaps Danny doesn't discourage such news from his old buddy even if he ridicules and rejects what he now stands for. Losja has prospered and goes on official trips to the Soviet Union and East Germany, where he sends back enthusiastic "articals" for the collective farm's newspaper. He is crudely anti-Semitic, was crudely sympathetic to the Nazis before and is crudely enthusiastic about the Communists now. In this pre-Glasnost moment, Losja does have the last word in the novel, thus giving us a despairing image of the fate of the Czech nation. Here too it would seem that personal communication through letter-writing does not represent any kind of self-examining consciousness. Losja never for one moment doubts anything and is blissfully stupid from beginning to end, and from one regime to the next. He is an image for all to see of a man totally devoid of conscience.

Inner-Exiles

In a fine discussion of Heinrich Boll's *Billiards at Half-Past Nine*, Rosemarie Morewedge emphasizes the idea of "inner exile"—the condition of hidden dissidence in those who find a regime intolerable but who cannot escape it. Though controversy over whether the term's significance exists, *Engineer*'s homeland Czech portraits would seem to make it a meaningful concept for Skvorecky.

With the true Mr. Novak who brings a recording from Prague as testimony to his devotion to Danny's writings, we have an indication of such inner exile, and presumably of how "tamizdat" writing—émigré writings from abroad, smuggled back into the country and circulated there—has an effect on those who cannot or will not emigrate. In an essay on "68 Publishers," Skvorecky himself notes how his and his wife's company published dissidents like Havel, Klima and Vaculik whose work would otherwise have been lost. We might guess that such writers' works would be among those *samizdat* publications smuggled back into Czechoslovakia. Jiri Pehe, summarizing Havel's essay "Power of the Powerless," supplies a further increment by suggesting that the essay's message is a supremely appropriate one for those still in Czechoslovakia, i.e., to guard against passivity and the surrender of one's conscience. Through the epistolary materials of the novel, Skvorecky does show us what conditions are like for Czech writers who either do not emigrate or who attempt for the longest period to resist imigration. The two polar positions are exemplified by Vrata and Jan. Vrata writes sardonic letters on his various attempts to keep his psyche together under the Communist regime, though eventually he does emigrate to West Germany and prospers. Jan, the tragic case, writes long and earnest letters about trying to fit in with the regime, emulates the advice of the socialist poet Neumann, and conducts critiques of both extreme avant-gardism (c. 1966) and socialist-realism (his ideal is that "mimesis" whereby ordinary people can "recognize" themselves). In the euphoria of 1968, Jan progresses to hopes of a socialist literature with a "human" face, and then finally, enigmatically, commits suicide.

Skvorecky's point is a simple one: if you want to write freely you can't very easily stay at home unless, like a would-be reformer (or like Havel himself), you have the courage of a test pilot. Thus Jan on the self–censorship of inner exile:

> The familiar merry-go-round has started up again: the ascendant generation of compulsive young writers willing to make the required omissions if only they are allowed to see themselves in print. Dan, I have finally reached the conclusion that there are all kinds of risks that are involved in freedom—but the risks of unfreedom are unbearable. (497)

Much earlier, Danny gives us a version of what might have happened if he himself had stayed in Czechoslovakia, writing "miniromances uncomplicated by the larger dramas of life":

> People would read my books and would perhaps even like them, for once upon another less orthodox time my stories gave form to their unscientific feelings. They would remain faithful readers even if I were brought to heel. People in that country are forgiving. Sometimes I might even enjoy the satisfaction of feeling useful, of giving moments of pleasure to others. And I would avoid altogether themes that could not be written about with those eliminations. (131)

Danny, though, finally adds:

> But such things cannot be eliminated from the mind. Only from the page. And from time to time—after writing books full of cautious, utilitarian games, after all those winsome, tranquilizing little books—I would have to put together a book made up of the eliminations. (131)

We should note, however, that at the beginning of *Engineer*, Danny does call attention to three writers still in Czechoslovakia: two men of conscience—Vaclev Havel and Bohumil Hrabal—and one hypocrite—Pavel Kohout, who, "given his enthusiastically socialist past . . . is a sitting duck for satire" (43).

Host-country Readers: "You know nothing about me"

It is clear that liberals and radicals in Canada and the United States are of primary concern to Skvorecky: he wants to bring his experience in Czechoslovakia to bear on their assumptions about ideology and revolutionary politics. In the novel's repeated and varied struggles over such politics, Skvorecky also does what exiles like Conrad and Nabokov had done before him—takes constant measure of the reader, interrogating him by proxy through the discomforting and satiric agonies between the major characters to make sure that the exile experience is understood. Veronika's exasperated outburst to her Canadian boyfriend Percy as he blathers on about the unfortunate difficulties of Angela Davis will serve as the archetypal moment here. Angela Davis, she yells at him, is "a Communist. She represents a system that destroyed my father. How can you expect me to sympathize with her? You know nothing about me" (445). And with that, she breaks off with Percy. (See Skvorecky's own critique of Davis in "Are Canadians Politically Naive" and in "A Judgment of Political Judgments.")

Basically, there are two types of readers that Skvorecky has in mind for this novel and that he directly images for. First, there are the naifs and innocents of the West, Danny's Edenvale students for the most part. They are sometimes uninterested in hearing about literature or war; they lack almost any historical knowledge of the past, whether Nazi or Soviet but especially the latter; and they lack any real possibility of that "recognition" which Danny's friend Jan thinks is crucial to literary "mimesis." (When they hear about horror, they think of Steven King, not Poe, not Lovecraft, and certainly not Conrad.) In this respect, the whole novel—its narrative by Danny, its epistolary reports from others—is an attempt to remedy the lack of history among students (and others, peace-types included) by giving them stories about what it was like to live actually under the two great totalitarianisms of the twentieth century.

The second type of Western reader that Skvorecky has in mind is the more difficult and intractable type, the committed left-of-center radical. This includes especially the somewhat buffoonish O'Reilly and the more serious Hakim, both American draft dodgers; in addition, there is the Marxist Study Group among the Edenvale faculty. Invited to join their discussions, Danny is sardonic in responding to their invitation with Huck's last words: "I been there before."

The political situation Skvorecky has posed for himself in *Engineer* may be said to involve conflict between members of the same political family. Skvorecky has described himself as a "Christian Socialist," and he addresses a culture that has much in common with the Left in terms of domestic social policies. Where he parts company with it is on the Vietnam War and more generally on the admiration in the adversary culture for totalistic restructurings of society and for liberation movements which wind up advocating suppression of freedom in the name of the revolution. Skvorecky is aware that he would be classified by other members of the family as "reactionary" but he, nevertheless, wants to insist that on the basis of his own lived experience under the totalitarian rule of both the Nazi and (especially) Communist kind, and on the basis of the literature he knows so well, one ought to be deeply suspicious of all revolutionary ideologies. (He cites a history of "eye-openers" in "Are Canadians Politically Naive"—"the Hitler-Stalin pact, the East Berlin worker's uprising, Gulag revelations, oppression in Hungary, Czechoslovakia, and Poland, in Cambodia, Afghanistan and Ethiopia . . . .") As Danny suggests towards the novel's end, "Every violent revolution ends with mass exodus back to the ideals that have been violated by the revolution itself" (506).

Danny's theory of literature involves relevance—he praises a student for reading Fitzgerald "as novelists ought to be read, thoroughly. She relates his book to the world around her" (279). No French-fried structuralism for Danny! It also involves awareness that while the "message" of literature is always the same, as in the Terence apothegm "Homo sum" ("Nothing human is alien to me"), "so much that is human," Danny continues, "is still alien to so many people." Hakim, however, chimes in with a mocking comment that these are nothing but "wisecracks" and that the merely "human" isn't a good test of the literary because, for example, a "reactionary" is also "human" but unpalatable.

In answering Hakim, Danny establishes a key aspect to his narrative and to his creator's own sensibility," the idea of opposition, paradox, skepticism and self-doubt. "Once," he tells Hakim, "they asked Evelyn Waugh if a good artist can be a reactionary" but Hakim cuts him off, asking "Another wisecrack?" Danny replies with a defense, really, of all satire and irony:

> Haven't you noticed that all good wisecracks are based on dialectics? They are. And Waugh replies, "An artist must be a reactionary. He has to stand out against the tenor of the age and not go flopping along; he must offer some little opposition." Some little opposition, Hakim.... (291–2)

Later still, Danny offers a defense of paradox, another essential aspect of his procedure: "Am I right? Perhaps. I am speaking in paradoxes, and they are only partially true I know, but they rouse the intellect out of its winter's sleep of adaptation" (508). After attacking "established scholars" who join "great movements of simplifications, which then radically shake the world" (having left their "intellect behind"), and then belatedly realize (or is it only these scholars' children who realize) that a scholar ought to be "scientific, indifferent to the ways of the trigger, but active in the search"—after all this attack on radical intellectuals, committed intellectuals, Danny sums everything up about his own position by saying that the true scholar has "beaverlike teeth" and doubts everything: "de omnibus dubitare—the only thing antagonistic to man is the absence of antagonism—of contradictions perhaps not antagonistic, but of contradictions..." (508). It is in this spirit that *Engineer*'s narrative structure itself proceeds.

In keeping with Noakes's hypothesis, Danny is a historical reader and can't help but choose his students' reading from the vantage point of his own experience. Essentially he offers a conservative reading of American literature by selecting Hawthorne (along with Conrad) who in contrast to Melville (perhaps) and Whitman or Thoreau (certainly) emphasize the dangers of the ego rather than the defects of society. Danny reads these texts tendentiously, "paradoxically," though defensibly. In some cases, the choices are less than political—Poe seems to be there for his melancholy and celebration of the lost "Lenore" (like the Czech Irene?—Skvorecky throws in an atrocious pun, allowing us to hear "'Goodnight,' Irene said"). In other cases, the choices are political: Hawthorne and Conrad, certainly, Twain for his pessimism and samples of the cruelty men can perform on each other, Crane for the concreteness of war and violence, Lovecraft at the end as Poe at the beginning, for the "Mountains of Madness" and the closeness of "madness" to reality.

It is important for us to understand why Skvorecky has created a whole novel in which the sections are labeled with major authors—Poe, Hawthorne, Twain, et al.—and especially why Hawthorne and Conrad are so essential to his political reading of literature. That is, were it not for the classroom analyses of Hawthorne and Conrad depicted in the novel, it would be easy to assign the novel's politics to the realm of the anti-Stalinist and let it go at that. Everyone agrees now: Stalin was bad. But Skvorecky, through Hawthorne and Conrad especially, wants to attack ideological and revolutionary thinking at its roots—the conviction that the idealist can enforce his values on others by sheer power because his conception is the only true and virtuous one. Skvorecky quotes Hawthorne as saying, "Is there no virtue save what springs from a wholesome fear of the gallows?" This is Orwellian "goose-flesh justice," linked explicitly to the "kingdom of Mao or Fidel," and, by a terrifying allusion, to the Nazis: "[Hakim] does not know of the only final solution to the social problem, the one that Sinclair Lewis knew about. That there is no such solution" (126). Likewise, Danny quotes Hawthorne on exclusivity and the idea of a vanguard party to Hakim: "Cannot you conceive that a man may wish well to the world, and struggle for its good, on some other plan than precisely that which you have laid down?" (72). Later, Smiricky quotes from *The Scarlet Letter* on Dimmesdale's having stayed "within the limits of what their church defends as orthodoxy," and, whether Hakim gets the point or not, thinks to himself "I am sustained by the mystical sensation that my spirit and Hawthorne's have touched, and together we are making fun of that serious-minded comrade, Mr. Hollingsworth of Brook Farm" (118). Danny enlarges his point with further quotations on the "love of justice" being a perilous one for its running in a single "exclusive" channel, thus distilling out from it "the true juices of the heart." Skvorecky sees a link to Bunyan here, and thus ties the noose around revolutionary schemes which lead to their very opposite: "I see in Hollingsworth the exemplification of the most awful truth in Bunyan's book of such; from the very gate of heaven there is a by-way to the pit!" (118).

"Hardness of heart," the centerpiece of Hawthorne's ethic, is not only something that Danny applies to revolutionary types like Hakim but also, ironically, self-doubtingly, to himself: "My heart hardens. I am ashamed. I ought to understand him, an American Arab who did not want to go to Vietnam just as I did not want to go to a concentration camp, nor later to the Gulag" (117). Nevertheless, despite his awareness, Danny seem to blame Hakim for indiscriminately accepting the nostrums of the radical Left. In a heavily ironic passage which must be read carefully, Danny notes Hakim's great "intellectual hunger" but also, sardonically, how the university is "grown hypertrophic with freedom, can only offer him alternatives, not clear answers" (117). Hakim's trouble, like that of all ideologues, is a "hunger for certainties." He finds those, says Danny, "in the familiar soup-kitchens" [i.e., the Marxist study groups and pamphlets], where he is offered "single-minded truths." Though of all the male students, Hakim is most like Smiricky himself, Danny nevertheless rejects Hakim's politics: "But I too carry within me my own irrational Vietnam and I feel an irrational distaste for this deserter" (117). It would seem too that Hakim's P.L.O. sympathies have energized Danny's memories of the Jews in Czechoslovakia, and the present-day business reported by Rebecca from Israel—of P.L.O. bombs killing Rebecca's only son.

Even more than Hawthorne, Conrad provides Skvorecky with a powerful and conservative critique of revolution. Kurtz' plans for ridding Africa of slavery had ended up—as Hawthorne in effect prophesied—in the Bunyanesque "pit" where "extermination of the brutes" is the final solution. Danny has great fun with his class, telling them as well that *Heart of Darkness* isn't a "novel" but a "prophecy" of Stalin and the gulags. Danny also reads an attack on "real revolution" from *Under Western Eyes*, in which the "best" do not come forward, only "fanatics" and "intellectual failures"; the rest become mere "victims," with their hopes grotesquely betrayed, their ideals caricatured: "that is the definition of revolutionary success." Danny urges Hakim not to be such a victim, but Hakim thinks this is all nonsense (424). For him *Heart of Darkness* is a critique of "imperialism" and not a horrifying journey of the soul; "exterminate the brutes" he sees only as the motto of imperialists, though he tacitly adopts it himself when he contemplates getting rid of a resistant older generation in one fell swoop. And he mocks Conrad ultimately as hopelessly "idealistic, decadent, vague."

Apart from these readings of literary classics, Skvorecky takes up a variety of late twentieth-century revolutionary movements and the way they are read. It would seem that Skvorecky has pretty well covered the map of the late 70s in this respect, right down to the Dene Nation protests in Canada. At the center of all these is the Vietnam war and its draft-dodgers, including both Hakim and O'Reilly (who is married to a Czech émigré).

There is a certain irony in the way O'Reilly's support for the Viet Cong and his draft-dodging in Canada is handled. The Czechs taunt him repeatedly for being a coward, for refusing to defend the principles of his own country, but of course the title of Skvorecky's first novel was

The Cowards and so one can see a minimal sympathy (as with Hakim) for O'Reilly's position. But when O'Reilly throws up attacks on fortress America—racial discrimination, class-justice, Sacco-Vanzetti, the Rosenbergs, Danny draws the line. The crucial interchange comes when O'Reilly cites Angela Davis's imprisonment as the key example of American injustice, as bad, he says, as the hanging of Rudolf Slansky. Here we have the equivalence doctrine—i.e., the argument that America and Russia (or its satellites) are equivalent in injustice with nothing to choose between them. "But," says Danny, "the cellist does not appreciate the qualitative equivalence of poor eyesight and a broken neck"—Davis in prison, Slansky hung (413).

Many of these themes come together in what is perhaps the most extraordinary argument in the novel, that between Danny and Allen Ginsberg, on the latter's commune outside Albany. (As with Skvorecky himself, Danny is repaying a visit that Ginsberg made to Prague a few years earlier, as a consequence of Danny's having translated portions of "Howl" for a magazine he edited.) At three in the morning, in the tent where Danny is sleeping—just next to the outhouse—Ginsberg comes to Danny with a joint and invites him to partake. Eventually, Ginsberg gets to shedding crocodile tears over his own comfortable state as against the miseries of Vietnam ("I'm so happy here," said Allen, "so happy that I feel selfish").

> But as the sun comes up and the joint burns down, the stench from the toilet exploded forcefully into the air, and it seemed to me that I was dreaming a dream, my bladder full, about a shithouse all choked up with shit, pissed upon, fecalized until it could hold no more, and suddenly I felt as though Allen were unabashedly enthroned on an enormous shithouse world, and meditating thus: You see? America! Isn't it marvelous. ... I always think to myself that the general idea of revolution against American idiocy is good and I guess it's a good thing, like in Cuba, and obviously in Vietnam. But what's gonna follow? the dogmatism that follows is a big drag. And everyone apologizes for the dogmatism by saying, well, it's an inevitable consequence of the struggle against American repression. And that may be true too, meditated Allen on his enormous shithouse of the West. (293)

After this parodic meditation of Ginsberg, Danny offers his own silent comments:

> That may be true, Allen, yes, except for the fact that in my little country over there, there was no American repression, and all the same dogmatism came, and it was terrible, you're right, we even had the gallows, you kind, considerate king of the shithouse in Upper New York State. A writer must be a reactionary . . . offer some little opposition. (293)

Skvorecky catches the rhetoric of the Left here—its self-satisfaction, its pomposity, its Orwellian defense of the indefensible ("dogmatism," "a big drag"). The rhetoric is crucial because it exemplifies perfectly the process described by Hawthorne and Conrad—the descent from the ideal to the terrifying, following on the conviction of total self-righteousness. And just as with the Nazis—the foreman getting a direct shot of Ponykil's cosmic diarrhea—so here too "this kind considerate king of the shithouse" is given a terrible razzing for his stenching commune (shades of Brook Farm), empty verbiage, and, worst of all, ignoring of the enormous difference between American behavior in Vietnam and Russian behavior in Czechoslovakia. (Earlier in the novel, Danny tells a student—in opposition to the cliche that all wars are bad—that some wars are just; WWII was such a war. And it might be that American involvement in Vietnam, for Skvorecky, would also represent such a just war.)

With the word "reactionary," Danny takes up the epithet often used by the Left to attack precisely the kind of testimony an escapee from Prague would bring to the West about the nature of Russian tanks. Émigrés, in this view, are untrustworthy, perhaps "fascists," certainly bourgeois" and middle-class, and hence untrustworthy. (These have also been the labels used to attack Vietnamese boat-people.) Danny had joked earlier about being in "opposition": what he means is that there is now a kind of Left-of-Center adversary culture that is in a certain sense dominant and so in need of precisely the opposition that émigrés like Skvorecky supply.

Since my subject here is the reader of exile, we should consider one final example of such a reader and his fate. This is Mr. Pohorsky, who all through the novel has been engaged in what is, from Skvorecky's point of view, a seriocomic version of all the "Liberation Army," struggles that he's heard about in the world news. Mr. Pohorsky wants a "Czech Liberation Army" and he has other ingenious ideas of a Schweikian nature too—e.g., sending postcards to Prague in such a way as to somehow bankrupt the Communist regime. But toward the end of the novel we learn in a newspaper article that Mr. Pohorsky has suddenly died, apparently in the process of trying to build a letter-bomb. Near his body are the instructions for the bomb, from a radical-left American group in New Jersey. Quite literally, Mr. Pohorsky has read the wrong literature and certainly in the wrong way. He has ironically emulated all the violent revolutionary movements in his despair and hatred of a regime that destroyed his homeland. To choose violence is to be simply self-destructive. While Skvorecky would seem to reserve the right to enter into a "just war," he does make a crucial distinction between that and a kind of revolutionary idealism that only ends up by destroying itself, even in the noble cause of trying to overthrow tyranny in one's native land.

It may seem with Glasnost, with Havel installed as President of the new Czech republic, and Dubcek returned in glory as speaker of the Czech parliament, that Skvorecky's satire and commentary in *Engineer* have only historical relevance, but this would be to miss the deepest aspect of his ironic address to himself ("irrationally hardened") and the ironic critique of human hunger for power. So long as we are human beings, Skvorecky warns us, that desire for power can reappear; *glasnost* can be undone not only by Soviet tanks but also by our very egoism and the belief that we alone are right. Huck Finn's words ("I been there before"), directed at the Marxist study Group of Edenvale in this instance, suggest the repeated possibilities of such egoism and ideology. Skvorecky's ironic motto, appropriated from Evelyn Waugh, is perhaps the only and ultimate antidote that Skvorecky wants his readers to see: "opposition, a little opposition, is necessary; the artist must always be . . . a 'reactionary.'" He must in effect—so we learn—oppose even the opposition that had seemed too ideal and idealistic. ("*Omnibus dubitare.*") This will be the lesson Skvorecky wants us to take from a novel which may have been rooted in his personal experience and historical consciousness but which has permanent value for us in circumstances quite unlike his. To understand this lesson is also, perhaps, to avoid the mistake of transparent reading—that is, to avoid reading the exile experience from our own limited perspective without any sense of the exile's ironic and often ambivalent attitude towards his readers themselves

Works Cited

Bleich, David. *Subjective Criticism.* Baltimore: Johns Hopkins University Press, 1978.
Edwards, Robert. "Exile, Self and Society." In *Exile in Literature*, ed. Maria-Ines Lagos-Pope. Lehigh, Pa.: Bucknell University Press, 1988. 15–31.
Esterhazy, Peter. "On Hungarian Contemporary Literature." in *Cross Currents* 9 (1990): 273–279.
Fries, Marilyn Sibley. "Problems of Narratizing the Heimat, Christa Wolf and Johannes Bobowski." In *Cross Currents* 9 (1990). 219–32.
Goldie, Terry. "Political Judgments." *Canadian Literature* 104 (Spring 1985): 165–67.
Jauss, Hans Robert. *Toward an Aesthetic of Reception*, tr. Timothy Bahti. Minneapolis: University of Minnesota Press, 1982.
Lagos-Pope, Maria-Ines. "Testimonies from Exile." In *Exile in Literature*, ed. Maria-Ines Lagos-Pope. Lehigh, Pa.: Bucknell University Press, 1988.
Mailloux, Steven. *Rhetorical Power.* Ithaca: Cornell University Press, 1989.
Morewedge, Rosemarie T. "Exile in Heinrich Boell's Novel *Billiards at Half Past Nine.*" In *Exile in Literature*, ed. Maria-Ines Lagos-Pope. Lehigh, Pa.: Bucknell University Press, 1988. 102–120.
Muresianu, John F. *War of Ideas, American Intellectuals and the World Crisis, 1938–1945.* New York: Garland, 1988.
Noakes, Susan. *Timely Reading, Between Exegesis and Interpretation.* Ithaca: Cornell University Press, 1988.

Pehe, Jiri. "The Dissident Writers: What Are They Saying?" In *The Prague Spring: A Mixed Legacy*, ed. Jiri Pehe. New York: Freedom House, 1988.

Skvorecky, Josef. "A Judgment of Political Judgments." *Canadian Literature* 110 (Fall, 1986):171–76.

——. "Are Canadians Politically Naive?" *Canadian Literature* 100 (1984): 287–311.

——. "A Revolution is Usually the Worst Solution." In *The Writer and Human Rights*, ed. Toronto Arts Group for Human Rights. Garden City, N.Y. Anchor Press/Doubleday, 1983, 115–20.

——. "On the Scent of Treason" [review of *The Red Fox*, by Anthony Hyde.] *New York Times Book Review* 1 Sept. 1985: 8.

——. "Sixty Eight Publishers Corp." In *The Prague Spring: A Mixed Legacy*, ed. Jiri Pehe. New York: Freedom House, 1988.

——. *The Cowards*. Translated by Jeanne Nemcova. New York: Grove, 1970.

——. *The Engineer of Human Souls*. Translated by Paul Wilson. Toronto: Lester and Orpen Dennys, 1984.

——. *The Mournful Demeanour of Lt. Boruvka*. Translated by Jeanne Nemcova. New York: Norton, 1986.

Solecki, Sam. "Writing West/Looking East: The Fiction of Josef Skvorecky." In *Cross Currents* 9 (1990). Tabori, Paul. *The Anatomy of Exile*. London: Harrap, 1972. 163–72.

 "Home is a Place Where You Have Never Been": The Exile Motif in the Hainish Novels of Ursula K. Le Guin
Frank Dietz

Ursula K. Le Guin has been recognized as the most important contemporary author of science fiction and fantasy in the USA. Her work by now includes sixteen novels, as well as several collections of poetry, short stories, and essays. Two groups of novels form the center of her work: the Earthsea trilogy of fantasy novels (which she expanded to a tetralogy in 1990) and the five Hainish novels: *Rocannon's World* (1966), *Planet of Exile* (1966), *City of Illusions* (1967), *The Left Hand of Darkness* (1969), and *The Dispossessed* (1974). These five science fiction novels, as well as a number of related short stories, are set in the same world, a future universe populated by humanoid races descended from the ancient civilization of Hain. While this kind of world-building is not uncommon in science fiction, the Hainish cycle is unique in its relation to the mode of utopian literature. Le Guin's Hainish cycle forms a meta-utopian construct which problematizes the very possibility of imagining utopia. It uses utopian motifs to criticize the stasis of traditional utopianism and to envision a dynamic utopia which must always remain incomplete, thus challenging the reader to complete it. These ambiguous utopias or "heterotopias," as Samuel Delany calls them, intentionally avoid the escapist pleasure of utopian felicity, while preserving the genre's critical stance. These texts, as Peter Ruppert wrote in his reader–response–oriented study of recent utopias, "inspire us not with derision and a sense of futility but with the desire to envision social and political arrangements that can correct the flaws, illuminate the blind spots" (1986, x). The figure of the expatriate plays a crucial role in these novels and stories because he acts out the transition from the static utopian locus to the ever-present utopian horizon, a development that we also find in other recent utopian fiction (cf. Dietz 1987, 146–160). The expatriate thus acts as an analogue of the readers who are also called on to transcend the utopian locus. The term "utopian locus," as Bulent Somay has defined it, expresses the utopian longings of a particular period in a finite, static form: "What the utopographer did was to verbalize and enclose the utopian horizon of an age, which was itself non-discursive, infinite, and open-ended" (25).

Le Guin herself has stated that she considers the term "utopia" to be inadequate for contemporary works such as Russ's *The Female Man* or her own *Always Coming Home:*

> Some people have been writing utopian novels which get called utopian; but the word would fit them only if we totally redefined it and could ignore its connotations, such as didacticism, unrealism, and unreadability. (Le Guin 1989, 8)

This statement marks the culmination of a long process in which Le Guin has challenged and revised the utopian genre. The static quality that Le Guin objects to has been a characteristic of traditional utopian literature from More's eponymous work to twentieth-century representatives of the genre. These works depict a particular society, in which, to quote a well-known definition by Darko Suvin,

> sociopolitical institutions, norms, and individual relationships are organized according to a more perfect principle than in the author's community, this construction being based on estrangement arising out of an alternative historical hypothesis. (49)

The utopian locus itself necessarily contains contradictions, as it attempts to reconcile opposing forces of contemporary society in a static image (cf. Marin *passim*). Writers of more recent utopias, such as Robert Graves, Joanna Russ, Samuel Delany, Marge Piercy, John Varley, and Le Guin, have therefore foregrounded the inadequacy of the utopian locus. While H. G. Wells already called for a "kinetic utopia" in his 1905 novel *A Modern Utopia* (5), it was only in these recent utopian novels, notably Le Guin's own, that this problem becomes a central one. Le Guin's Hainish novels move from a portrayal of the conflict between pastoral and technological utopias to a depiction of a world of eternal flux in which the only form of utopia is an ambiguous one, as she expressed it in the subtitle to *The Dispossessed.*

Le Guin's metautopian critique stands in the tradition of other works that employ self-reflexive strategies, including Wells's *A Modern Utopia* (cf. Parrinder, 115) and even More's *Utopia* itself, which as one critic has claimed, "parodies utopia in advance." (1981, 171). What is unique about the Hainish cycle is the extent in which the metautopian element dominates the later novels, and the acerbity with which they attack the notion of a stable utopian society. While Le Guin's first three novels still employ these genre conventions (though in an ironic way which undermines the closure offered by traditonal utopias), her later works in the Hainish cycle subvert the illusion of idyllic happiness and suggest that the price for utopia may be too high. The figure who challenges the utopian status quo, who introduces change, and who acts as a social catalyst, is always that of the expatriate.

Exile, then, becomes much more than a plot device for Le Guin. In these novels, the tension between home and exile, familiarity and isolation finally emerges as a positive force. Being in exile represents not only a metaphor for mankind's spiritual condition, but also offers the hope of eternal renewal. Only the exiled individual can gain enough distance from society to be truly creative, to envision alternatives. The figure of the expatriate introduces a dynamic factor into the world of the novels that counteracts dystopian dogmatism and stagnation. All of Le Guin's expatriates eventually return home, but they are forced to recognize that the exile experience had changed them profoundly. The experience of exile thus symbolizes a world of eternal flux, and exile and return complement each other in a paradoxical way: "You can go home again," as one of Le Guin's protagonists remarks, "so long as you understand that home is a place where you have never been" (TD 44).[1]

Le Guin's first two novels, *Rocannon's World* and *Planet of Exile* explore utopian motifs on several levels. First, they both portray harmonious societies isolated in space and separated from the flux of history. Thus, they connect to the tradition of pastoral utopianism that stretches from Diderot's *Supplement to Bougainville's Voyage* to William Morris's *News from Nowhere* and such contemporary works as Robert Graves's *Watch the North Wind Rise* and Ernest Callenbach's *Ecotopia* and *Ecotopia Emerging*. This pastoral world is threatened by the encounter with a technological society which attempts to set up a technocratic utopia (a theme Le Guin repeated in her novel *The Word for World is Forest*). Besides the pastoral and the technocratic vision, there is the utopia represented by the League of All Worlds. While the League sometimes acts as an instrument of technocracy (particularly in *Rocannon's World*), it already anticipates the eventual utopia of intercultural communication represented by the Ekumen of Known Worlds.

The pastoral societies described in the first two novels (the Fia and the Tevar) are as harmonious, isolated, and static as most traditional utopian societies. The expatriate protagonists, Rocannon and Jacob, destroy this isolation and thus initiate a period of change. As I have shown elsewhere in reference to Robert Graves's utopia, this type of character represents a reversal of the traditional utopian traveler (cf. Dietz 1990, 1). The expatriate in utopia initiates a series of changes which will transform the static felicity of traditional utopianism into a kinetic utopia that always reopens the gap between utopian locus and utopian horizon. Thus, Jacob in *Planet of Exile* initiates a process that will eventually transform both the pastoral Tevar society and the technological enclave of the Terrans, resulting in an open-ended social evolution that might eventually merge pastoralism and technocracy.

Falk, the protagonist of *City of Illusion*, encounters a seemingly utopian society that (like the future World of Wells's *The Time Machine*, which appears to have influenced Le Guin's first three novels) turns out to be a dystopian nightmare. When Falk first sees Es-Toch, the city of the Shing, he perceives it as the embodiment of perfection:

> The City of the Lords of the Earth was built on the two rims of a canyon, a tremendous cleft through the mountain, narrow, fantastic, its black walls striped with green plunging terrifically down half a mile to the silver tinsel strip of a river. On the very edges of the facing cliffs the towers of the city jutted up, hardly based on earth, linked across the chasm by delicate bridgespans. (248)

Soon, however, Falk finds out that the Shing are despots, and that the technological dream city is a "city of illusions." This contradicts one of the basic conventions of utopian literature, namely that social perfection expresses itself in spatial symmetry. Falk reacts with an action typical for the protagonists of the later part of the Hainish cycle: he flees to his home planet. Thus, exile (which is simultaneously return) symbolizes both the rejection of dystopian repression and the elusive hope of finding a true utopia.

Several of Le Guin's stories are related to the Hainish novels, and—not surprisingly—the motif of exile appears here as well. The story "The Ones Who Walk Away from Omelas" marks a transition to a more ambiguous view of utopia. Le Guin herself has established the connection between the story and the Hainish cycle in her foreword to "The Day Before the Revolution." She presents this story about the life of Odo (the founder of the anarchist movement in *The Dispossessed*) as a preamble to her novel, and remarks; "This story is about the ones who walk away from Omelas" (268). Omelas is a utopian city with a sinister secret: a child imprisoned in a dark cellar. The suffering of the child is (in some mysterious way) the precondition for the happiness of the community. Most of the inhabitants of Omelas repress this knowledge, but some cannot accept the suffering of even a single individual and walk away from Omelas. The ending of the story, one of the most moving passages in Le Guin's fiction, emphasizes the finality of their exile:

They go on. They leave Omelas, they walk ahead into the darkness, and they do not come back. The place they go towards is a place even less imaginable to most of us than the city of happiness. I cannot describe it at all. It is possible that it does not exist. But they seem to know where they are going, the ones who walk away from Omelas. (WTQ, 284)

Fredric Jameson's denunciation of the story as a "nasty little fable" expressing "counterrevolutionary antiutopianism" (251) misses the point. "The Ones Who Walk Away From Omelas" is only antiutopian in the sense that it refuses to let utopia be limited to a particular place. The "good place" always remains "noplace."

Whereas going into exile is presented as a pragmatically necessary action in the early Hainish novels, it becomes a moral action in the last two books. The expatriate not only can leave an oppressive society behind, he may also find his own identity in the process. Le Guin never romanticizes the figure of the exile, and she always emphasizes the price that the individual has to pay. Overall, however, exile also opens new possibilities and insights. The dual nature of exile appears quite clearly in *The Left Hand of Darkness*, the novel which first brought Le Guin's work to the attention of mainstream critics.

Le Guin has structured *The Left Hand of Darkness* around the dichotomies of male/female, familiar/strange and home/exile, but she subverts these oppositions in the course of the narrative. Genly Ai, a diplomat and anthropologist representing the Ekumen of Known Worlds (an organization succeeding the more expansionist League of All World's in Le Guin's earlier Hainish novels) is the only Terran on the icy planet Gethen or Winter. Ai's alienation from his environment is worsened by the fact that he is the only heterosexual person on a planet whose inhabitants are sexually dormant except for brief periods (the kemmer), when they can become either male or female. Naturally, the Gethenians regard Ai as a pervert. In what he himself calls an "access of self-alienation," Ai states: "I was alone, with a stranger, inside the walls of a dark palace, in a strange snow-changed city, in the heart of the Ice Age of an alien world" (LHD 327). Ai's fate becomes entangled with that of a Gethenian outsider, the courtier Estraven, who has been sentenced to exile for his alleged disloyalty to the king of Karhide.

The Left Hand of Darkness might seem an unlikely utopia at first, describing an icebound world of material scarcity. However, the narrator emphasizes that the language of Karhide knows no word for war, that there is no gender stereotyping, and that he never saw a child mistreated. This idyllic, if spartan, world is threatened by the border conflict between the feudal country of Karhide and the stalinist Orgoreyn. While both countries exhibit more and more signs of totalitarianism, two expatriates cross the literal and metaphorical borders between these countries.

Genly Ai also has to cross borders before he can fulfill his role as an envoy of the Ekumen of Known Worlds, an organization dedicated to utopian goals:

> Increase of knowledge. The augmentation of the complexity and intensity of the field of intelligent life. The enrichment of harmony and the greater glory of God. Curiosity. Adventure. (335)

In the beginning Ai rejects the utopian potential of a society free of gender roles by regarding himself as "normal" as opposed to the ambisexual Gethenians. Even though he is supposed to be a neutral observer, he is aware that his perspective is distorted by his own views on gender and sexuality:

> Though I had been nearly two years on Winter I was still far from being able to see the people of the planet through their own eyes. I tried to, but my efforts took the form of self-consciously seeing a Gethenian first as a man, then as a woman, forcing him into those categories so irrelevant to his nature and so essential to my own.(LHD 323)

Conversely, Estraven, unlike other Gethenians, believes Ai's claim to be an envoy from a foreign world, but is constrained in his relationship with Ai by the rules of his society. It is only after both Ai and Estraven have been gone into exile that true communication becomes possible. The experience of exile literally strips everything away, until, at the climax of the novel, pure humanity emerges.

During this dangerous journey Ai gradually sheds the last vestige of his former prejudices by recognizing Estraven as what "he" really is:

> And I saw then again, and for good, what I had always been afraid to see, and had pretended not to see in him: that he was a woman as well as a man. (LHD 457)

On their return to Karhide, Estraven is killed by a border guard. The story narrated in *The Left Hand of Darkness* is an attempt by Genly Ai—who knows that "Truth is a matter of the imagination" (LHD 317)—to share the communion he experienced with Estraven. He has reached this goal when Estraven's son asks him: "Will you tell us how he died?—Will you tell us about the other worlds out among the stars—the other kinds of men, the other lives?" (LHD 488). The severe exile, the most extreme isolation, finally leads to a communication which, as Ai has heard from the Handdarata mystics, will cause the planet Gethen to join the Ekumen.

The dichotomies of utopia and exile are also central in the novel *The Dispossessed*. This complex novel, which Le Guin subtitled *An Ambiguous Utopia*, is dominated by the image of the wall. "There was a wall. It did not look important" Le Guin writes in chapter 1, only to state shortly afterwards that "the idea of the wall" was important and that for "seven generations there had been nothing in the world more important than that wall" (TD 1). This wall, which encloses the spaceport of the arid planet Anarres (or, as the narrator points out, the rest of Anarres, as all walls are ambiguous), becomes the central metaphor of the book. The entire Annaresti society is in exile, as the Odonians, a group of socialists, were dispossessed when they were forced to leave the planet Urras 150 years earlier. Odo herself, the founder of the movement, never reached Anarres and stayed in a hostile world "an alien: an exile" (TD 82).

Shevek, the protagonist of *The Dispossessed*, grows up in the Odonian utopia Anarres, but soon finds himself at odds with his environment. Anarres, though nominally a decentralized and anarchist society, has gradually developed new power structures. Shevek's research in unorthodox fields of physics brings him into conflict with the aggressive bureaucrat Sabul and eventually leads him into exile on the planet Urras. His voyage to Urras in a spaceship, though, is not associated with feelings of liberation: "He was clearly aware of only one thing, his own total isolation. The world had fallen out from under him, and he was left alone" (TD 5).

In his exile on Urras, a world very much resembling our present one, Shevek finds himself isolated from many aspects of society. Though he is enthusiastically greeted by the press, and the popular imagination equates him with "the Forerunner ... the one who comes before the millennium a stranger an outcast, an exile, bearing in empty hands the time to come," (TD 186), he feels walled in by the rigid class structure around him. At the same time, though, he is the only free person in a society "possessed" by the idea of possessing things. Paradoxically, it is in his exile on Urras that Shevek achieves the crucial breakthrough in his research, which in time will enable mankind to build the ansible, an instantaneous communication device. As readers of the other Hainish novels (which come later in the internal chronology of the series) know, the ansible will be the foundation and the symbol of that ultimate utopia of intercultural communication, the Ekumen of Known Worlds. When Shevek has found the decisive formula, he expresses the importance of the moment in a passage that simultaneously undermines the generic boundaries between utopia and dystopia:

> ... at this instant the difference between this planet and that one, between Urras and Anarres, was no more significant to him than the difference between two grains of sands on the shore of the sea. There were no more abysses, no more walls. There was no more exile. (TD 226)

The interrelation of exile and return is expressed in the very structure of this novel with its alternation of chapters set on Urras in the narrative present and Anarres set in the past. The first chapter depicts a departure, the last a return, but a return to a world that has changed during Shevek's exile on Urras. Like Shevek's research, which tries to reconcile simultaneity and sequence, the book attempts to portray both cyclical and sequential time. Odo's saying "true voyage is return" applies as well to this situation as her statement that home is a place where you have never been before. Exile, then, is not a temporary calamity, but becomes a metaphor for a world of eternal flux.

Exile in Le Guin's novels marks less an absence than the potential for utopian presence. Her characters exist in a world of the "not yet," to use a key term in the philosophy of Ernst Bloch. And indeed, Bloch's analysis of the utopian impulse (as being inherent in the principle of hope) is relevant to Le Guin's works. Bloch states that "reality is a process that consists in the complex mediation between the present, an unfinished past, and, particularly, the possible future" (I, 225, my translation). The decision to leave Omelas or Anarres subverts the idea of a stable utopia, or an end to history. The figure of the expatriate allows Le Guin to avoid the pitfalls of traditional utopias, while still preserving the image of a better society. Le Guin's work culminates in *The Dispossessed*, her utopia-in-exile, which, like Achilles in Zeno's paradox, must forever pursue a goal it can never reach.

Furthermore, Le Guin's novels of exile have to be considered within the context of the ideology expressed by many other American science fiction novels. The French critic Gerard Klein has pointed out in an article that Le Guin's work offers a sharp contrast to the empire-building so common within the pages of American science fiction (88). Le Guin's ethnological perspective and her cultural relativism offer an alternative to the fictional worlds which merely project nineteenth- and twentieth-century power politics onto a galactic scale. The figure of the exile is central to Le Guin's vision because he represents another utopia, not that of the technocratic empire, but a utopia of communication. By crossing literal and metaphorical boundaries, her exiles assert the necessity for cultural diversity. "*Utopia and SF*," as Gérard Klein writes, "*are literatures which consider the problem of cultural diversity, whether in order to exclude it, or to reduce it, or again to deny its benefits ... or finally to exalt it, as does Le Guin*" (96, italics in the original).

Le Guin's protagonists are worlds apart from the intergalactic Rambos that seem to dominate much of science fiction, yet their actions affirm the ability of individuals to influence their environment. While her later expatriates are no longer as obviously successful as Rocannon or Jakob, the deeds of Genly Ai and Shevek attain a more universal significance. Even though they return, their exile is a permanent one. Being in exile, as

Shevek recognizes, is a metaphor for living in an unfinished world, in which utopia will never be finally achieved: "There was process: process was all. You could go in a promising direction or you could go wrong, but you did not set out with the expectation of ever stopping anywhere" (TD 268).

Notes

1. The following abbreviations will be used in the text: *Rocannon's World* (RC), *Planet of Exile* (PE), *City of Illusions* (CI), *The Left Hand of Darkness* (LHD), *The Dispossessed* (TD), *The Language of the Night* (LN), and *The Wind's Twelve Quarters* (WTQ).

Works Cited

Bloch, Ernst. *Das Prinzip Hoffnung*. Vol. 1. 1959; Frankfurt: Suhrkamp, 1983.
Dietz, Frank. *Kritische Träume: Ambivalenz in der amerikanischen literarischen Utopie nach 1945*. Meitingen: Corian, 1987.
———. "Fantasy and the Poetics of Literary Utopia" Robert Graves' *Watch the North Wind Rise*." *Utopian Studies* 4. Ed. Lise Leibacher and Nicolas Smith. Lanham, MD: University Press of America, 1990.
Jameson, Fredric. "Progress Versus Utopia; or, Can We Imagine the Future?" *Art After Modernism: Rethinking Representation*. Ed. Brian Wallis. New York: The New Museum of Contemporary Art, 1984.
Klein, Gérard. "Le Guin's 'Aberrant' Opus: Escaping the Trap of Discontent." *Ursula K. Le Guin. Modern Critical Views*. Ed. Harold Bloom. New York: Chelsea House, 1986.
Le Guin, Ursula K. *The Dispossessed*. 1974. Reprint. New York: Avon, 1975.
———. *The Wind's Twelve Quarters*. New York: Harper & Row, 1975.
———. *The Language of the Night: Essays on Fantasy and Science Fiction*. New York: Putnam's, 1978.
———. *Five Complete Novels*. New York: Avenel Books, 1985.
———. "Up to Earth." *The Women's Review of Books* February 1989, 9.
Marin, Louis. *Utopics—Spatial Play*. Atlantic Highlands, New Jersey: Humanities Press, 1984.
Morson, Gary Saul. *The Boundaries of Genre: Dostoevsky's Diary of a Writer and the Traditions of Literary Utopia*. Austin: University of Texas, 1981.
Parrinder, Patrick. "Utopia and Meta-Utopia in H. G. Wells." *Science-Fiction Studies* 12:2 (1985): 115-128.
Ruppert, Peter. *Reader in a Strange Land. The Experience of Reading Literary Utopias*. Athens: University of Georgia Press, 1986.
Sinclair, Karen. "Solitary Being: The Hero as Anthropologist." *Le Guin: Voyager to Inner Lands and Outer Space*. Ed. Joe De Bold. Port Washington, NY: Kennikat Press, 1979.
Somay, Bulent. "Towards an Open-Ended Utopia." *Science-Fiction Studies* 11:1 (1984): 25–38.
Spencer, Kathleen. "Exiles and Envoys: the SF of Ursula K. Le Guin." *Foundation* 20 (1980): 32–43.
Suvin, Darko. *Metamorphoses of Science Fiction: On the Poetics and History of a Literary Genre*. New Haven: Yale University Press, 1979.
Wolfe, Gary K. *The Known and the Unknown: The Iconography of Science Fiction*. Kent: Kent State UP, 1979.

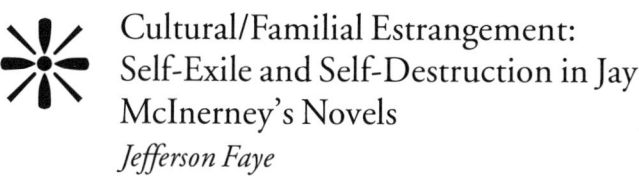 Cultural/Familial Estrangement: Self-Exile and Self-Destruction in Jay McInerney's Novels
Jefferson Faye

According to Malcolm Bradbury's *The Expatriate Tradition in American Literature*, fictional expatriation is a response to "a familiar American complaint about cultural barrenness, 'absence of forms,' the need for another culture . . . ." He describes expatriation not as the *act* of leaving but as "the desire to take the path of separatism, condemn the nation for culturelessness, materialism, or innocence, the gesture of protest" (6). In the 1980s we find this cultural disaffection is as strong as ever; in fact, it is the foundation of Jay McInerney's three novels: *Bright Lights, Big City; Ransom*; and *Story of My Life*, which use expatriation as an underlying metaphor for alienation. These novels contain the social awarenesses Terry Eagleton ascribes to upper-class and lower-middle class novels, both of which he said were "to some extent self-consciously hostile to what they see as the dominant cultural orthodoxy" (13). This cultural awareness is juxtaposed with what McInerney calls a heightened sense of the importance of familial influence on his protagonists' lives:

> I do think there's a kind of novel that starts with a character *without* a background—an existential novel, I suppose. My own feeling is that one's family history is hugely determinate, and I find that a very rich mine of character determination (Seidel 1986, 112).

Ransom literally treats an expatriate, largely American community in Japan. *Bright Lights, Big City* begins with an epigraph from that paradigmatic novel of expatriation, *The Sun Also Rises*, then McInerney introduces a protagonist whose cocaine-driven "brain at this moment is composed of brigades of tiny Bolivian soldiers" while his feet remain in

Manhattan. The character's mind is not merely in South America, but also in France with his expatriate wife. He even equates being fired from his job with receiving an "exit visa" (137) as if he were once again changing locales after the wanderings that brought him to New York. The protagonist of *Story of My Life* also exists in a state of spiritual exile, the result of identifying the link between family and culture, one which closely resembles Bradbury's and Eagleton's definitions. I will discuss this connection first in the context of Ransom's father-son conflict, which presents a clear representation of the running themes it shares with *Story of My Life* and *Bright Lights, Big City*. *Ransom*'s consideration of the outsider beset with family problems creates a perspective through which their cultural disaffiliations can be read; it has a more concrete sense of exile and clearly exemplifies characteristics of McInerney's work as a whole.

McInerney writes about dissatisfaction as it affects his characters, their families, and, in the process, their cultural perspective. Each novel may be considered a *bildungsroman* whose action revolves around a familial betrayal as it drives the main character to reject not only relatives, but self. What I intend to discuss is the means by which McInerney explains the rejection of family as a representation of culture: in alienating himself from his father, Christopher Ransom is reacting to the foundations upon which he was raised and questioning his own—as well as his father's and even society's—cultural priorities. He falls into self-destructive behavior because he has no beneficial support structure from which to operate; Ransom's inability to recover from his father's adverse influence and immediate social circumstances creates an atmosphere of self-alienation—his experiences make him attempt to escape everything, including himself, and he cannot.

Ransom is a death march in which McInerney connects family to culture straightforwardly. Christopher Ransom is an American living in Japan, a man whose name alone may be sufficient to explain his situation: Christ-for-ransom. The fact that he prefers to be called Ransom suggests the skewed reality in which he lives, a constant reminder not of the sanctity of his impending martyrdom, but of the price that is in the process of being paid. He is treading water, biding time before his death; more importantly, he is using his remaining time to criticize the priorities of predominant American popular culture on one hand and of his father on the other, two influences on his life that he finds difficult to separate and cannot change. He describes, ad infinitum, his father's "selling out," abandoning the honorable, or truer, art of playwrighting for the "diseased" world of television-screenplay writing. Ransom's rejection of American popular culture becomes hopelessly intertwined with his rejection of his father, as Chris cannot separate his father's abandonment of playwrighting from Chris's childhood, a time which he associates with neglect and his mother's death. Because of his father's attraction to the power games of Hollywood (and use of them elsewhere), Chris identifies Victor Ransom with its evils. Victor's name, too, is tell-tale: the victor is the ransom demand, economics wielding power over uncorrupted aesthetics.

There is more to Ransom's disaffection with power games and the influence of American culture, however. Through a series of flashbacks, the reader learns of Ransom's experiences during the earlier stages of his expatriation. Periodically, McInerney takes him back two years to the expatriate community in Pakistan, near the Khyber Pass: McInerney relates the disappearance of Ransom's friend Ian during a drug-purchasing trip into Afghanistan, and details Ransom's involvement in the accidental overdose of his lover, Annette. In Ransom's eyes Ian's absence was the result of power games: his desire to make a large amount of money very quickly led him to fall in with greedy drug smugglers, who in all likelihood killed him after his kidnapping. Annette died because she accepted her fate as being under the power of a stronger force. She saw heroin as an entity who had chosen her to be an addict; she had neither the strength nor resolve to try to elude its grasp. This sequence is important because it led Ransom to Japan in an attempt to salve his wounds and rediscover his soul. Unfortunately, in Kyoto's pre-rainy season humidity and distorted reality, his emotional injuries only reinforced the festering and spreading of his afflictions; the atmosphere is noxious, and hauntingly familiar.

The environment surrounding Christopher Ransom seems perverse from our perspective. As base as Ransom finds American television, he reacts more negatively to the complete lack of content standards in Japanese television; he also spends a substantial amount of time describing the Japanese emulation of American culture and its juxtaposition with the traditional, honor-framed Japanese language and customs: the picture he draws suggests that the Japanese have developed a polemical culture that is steeped in honor and tradition on one end of the spectrum and is countered by an entirely tasteless, borrowed and distorted popular culture. In fact, this dichotomy is common throughout McInerney's work; for example, it is similar to the perversion McInerney describes in the New York discotheque and party scenes of *Bright Lights, Big City* and *Story of My Life*, but in this situation McInerney emphasizes an ironic twist: the culture Ransom has rejected in the United States is actually the predominant influence upon which the more perverse Japanese television is based. The dark side of Japanese culture, then, manifests itself, in Jekyll-and-Hyde fashion, as abject commercialism—and it becomes apparent that for the same reasons Ransom does not like the United States he is not a perverse enough character to adapt to life in Japan. Not only is he unable to reconcile himself with his father's and his own failures, but in doing so he has lost the perspective necessary to survive—he cannot see that he hasn't the sense of humor to understand the dichotomy of popular culture: he cannot separate the self-serious from the satirical and merely entertaining.

Ransom's intolerance is obvious and very easy to understand, but equally clear is his inability to escape "trash" television's presence. It can be seen on the television sets of almost every bar he enters, apparently a necessary cog in the decadent American-influenced undercurrent of Japanese culture. And yet there appears to be a difference. American television has always had "tabloid" programs equivalent to those in the latest rage; "America's Most Wanted," "Cops," and even "A Current Affair" are recent examples, but in previous decades there was, among others, "You Asked for It." McInerney offers Japanese television's sardonic "equivalent" in tastelessness: "Sex Crimes."

> *What do we have tonight,* the host asked. He was wearing a pink tuxedo, a blue boutonnière and several pounds of hair spray.
> *One gang rape,* the woman responded brightly, *one double suicide, and a love-triangle murder. We'll be right back.*
> An ad for instant noodles came on, followed by back to back detergents. . . . The sensei . . . returned and asked what the lineup was (120).

This television show is a "dramatic re-enactment" of crimes taken directly from police files, and to Ransom it is little more than a blatant appeal to the same voyeuristic tendencies that make people stare at automobile accidents. With the possible exception of Ransom, it seems that no one is immune to its attraction and humor: even his karate sensei, the man with whom Ransom most closely connects the honor and tradition of Japanese culture, participates in this seduction through violence. This is the side of popular culture that Ransom cannot separate from his disappointment with Victor; while more flagrantly appalling than American versions of the same sort of programming, Japanese television's presentation of sex crimes is equal parts Monty Pythonian and cold-blooded appeal to base titillation as a means of selling laundry detergent and ramen noodles. But more than that, McInerney presents this brand of popular culture as both imitation of and influence on life—not only is it unclear which affects which, but which is more realistic.

To reinforce this point, motivated by concerns for his son's mental and physical condition, Victor has borrowed ideas from television and movies to coerce Ransom into returning to the United States. (He even subscribes to the great American myth that all problems are attributable to drug abuse.) Once Victor tried fooling him into flying to Los Angeles with a ridiculous story about a friend's "free companion ticket" received from her employers. When that didn't work, he sent an actress from Hollywood to pretend she was a Vietnamese refugee in trouble with the Yakuza (the Japanese Mafia). McInerney seems to be suggesting that it is dangerous for even a screenwriter to borrow ideas from old movies for use in the real world—it creates an artificiality which skews perceptions of reality. Sadly, for Ransom, when his father is the agent behind this mixing of unrealistic fantasy and reality, it creates more distance between them. His father's attempt to manipulate Ransom by appealing to his "sense of duty and honor" (243) only reinforces Ransom's perception of him, and makes Ransom realize that he has not been living so much as merely existing: he is in training for what he thinks is a battle of great importance between good and evil. Victor's ability to realize that purpose devalues, even cheapens it. Ransom is no longer living a quest, but instead his life has been reduced to a hackneyed good guys-bad guys movie plot; he now embodies this aspect of popular culture, and yet he cannot escape the fact that at one time he felt he had nothing in common with it.

For Ransom the world has become one of black and white, of hunger for power and humanity. There may have been degrees of grey, but they are still a part of the black; whether it is Victor, Japanese television and businessmen, or Ransom's enemy Frank DeVito, Ransom condemns them all in varying degrees for seeking power. Years before, Victor went to Hollywood for power, and he is unable to understand why his son thinks it tainted. Victor sees himself as strong because he is kinetic—his activity makes things happen—and he sees Chris as passively idealistic in a world Victor perceives as unresponsive to anything but power. Chris accuses Victor of being unresponsive to his needs, and of treating him as a vessel for Victor's own desires. He even calls Victor a lunatic, not realizing that he, too, is a lunatic for the opposite reason—they are equally distant from the "proper" cultural equilibrium. Each tilts at windmills, but neither understands what the other's windmills represent.

By reducing Ransom's life to preparation for a battle between good and evil, McInerney emphasizes the comparison between Ransom and DeVito, an ex-Marine with a colossal yearning for power. DeVito was drummed out of the Marines because he had neither a sense of duty nor honor (the qualities that drive Ransom's life), but instead an overdeveloped sense of self-importance and ruthlessness. DeVito is in Japan because he feels there are opportunities for him that exist nowhere else in the world. He sees Japan as a truly promising capitalistic domain: to DeVito money means power, because everything—with the possible exception of honor—can be obtained for a price. This is the lesson Victor learned, the lesson DeVito learns, and the lesson Ransom refuses to learn. DeVito hates Ransom because he believes Ransom represents everything holding him back: his rural Oklahoman roots, the morality that cost him his career in the Marine Corps, the social consciousness that reduces his influence and power. To DeVito, Ransom's honor represents his greatest shortcoming, so as Japanese tradition dictates, they must fight a duel for the purpose of saving face.

It is fitting, then, that DeVito kills Ransom. For just as Ransom represents DeVito's lackings, so DeVito represents everything Ransom has resisted (and run from) since before he left the United States. DeVito is the personification of the greed and desire for power that drove Victor to Hollywood, that brought about Ian's disappearance and Annette's death, that caused Victor to try to manipulate Ransom rather than reason with him. The final confrontation is fitting because Ransom has decided not to run any more, not to resist any more, and not to give in. He resigns in the face of incomprehensible odds; he knows that he cannot change the world, and he isn't about to continue "moping." It is fitting, too, that he dies as a result of DeVito's win-at-all-costs attitude. In effect he already has a moral victory when he undermines DeVito's assumed authority (he chooses the location of the duel against DeVito's wishes), then when he arrives at the duel's designated place without being observed, and finally when he draws first blood. In that world, however, moral victories are ephemeral; DeVito has the resolve to live and the savvy to fit perfectly in this world—Ransom does not. And Ransom dies unceremoniously, but with honor. That is all he has.

If Ransom is a misled or failed martyr as I have suggested, the protagonists in McInerney's other novels are survivors of their rites of passage, pilgrimage, failure, and self-sacrifice. In *Bright Lights, Big City*, the nameless protagonist begins the novel spiralling in a cocaine- and alcohol-driven whirlpool amid the Manhattan nightlife, but not just for the sake of "pure" hedonism. He is in exile from his "productive" cultural and familial ties: he is unable to cope with the emotional pain resulting from his mother's death after a battle with cancer; his job at an unnamed New York magazine promised a literary career in which "You wanted to be Dylan Thomas without the paunch, F. Scott Fitzgerald without the crack-up" (40), but delivered only dissatisfaction, drudgery, and failure; and his fairytale romance-turned-marriage with his fashion-model wife, Amanda, became a separation auspiciously categorized by her lawyer as "sexual abandonment" (77). These changes are manifested in his responses to popular culture, as he revolts against his instincts, rejecting the positive, and embraces the negative elements of his surroundings.

Bright Lights, Big City's narration reinforces the protagonist's self-division, exposing a process which Michael Ugarte considers an exile's characteristic self-discovery, a process which

> leads the writer, perhaps unwittingly, into a dialogue with him or herself on the very nature of writing and on the problems that arise from an attempt to record reality (19–20).

McInerney uses a second-person narrative in which the nameless protagonist refers conversationally to himself as "You," establishing a sense of an everyman—or perhaps an absence of being—through which the protagonist distances himself from his problems by talking to his reflection in the mirror, or to everyone else because he cannot face his own problems. The use of "You" creates an immediate discomfort for the reader. It shows a schism in which the protagonist is exiled from himself, an ethereal voyeur helplessly watching his own self-destruction from the outside. Unused to this language, the reader is seemingly incorporated in the text as still another powerless bystander, which further illustrates the divisive effects of the problem. McInerney literally draws a picture of this process in the description of the protagonist's

> dream about the Coma Baby.... The Coma Mom is stretched out on your desk in a white gown.... The gown is open around her midsection. You approach and discover that her belly is a transparent bubble. Inside you can see the Coma Baby. He opens his eyes and looks at you.
> "What do you want?" he says.
> "Are you going to come out," you ask.
> "No way, José. I like it in here. Everything I need is pumped in."
> "But Mom's on her way out."
> "If the old lady goes, I'm going with her.... They'll never take me alive," the Baby says (54–55).

As the Coma Baby incubates inside a near-dead mother, it awaits a court decision allowing it to be born by caesarian section at the cost of its mother's life. The protagonist faced a similar problem in attempting to fill his mother's expectations and desires before she died, rather than living his own life:

> marriage wasn't high on your list of priorities, although on Amanda's it was.... Then your mother was diagnosed and everything looked different. Your first love had given notice of departure and Amanda's application was on file.... And, in the end you may have confused what she wanted with what Amanda wanted (161).

The only way the Coma Baby or the protagonist can survive is if he accepts his mother's death and faces the conditions which have spawned his exile. Rather than allowing others to make his decisions, or set expectations for him, he must take his fate in his own hands. The protagonist does this by arriving at the realization that he must let his mother die. "'I tried to block her out of my mind. But I think I owe it to her to remember. . . . And I was just thinking that we have a responsibility to the dead'" (179), which is, for him, to go on living.

This is, of course, a decision which takes the protagonist the entire book to reach. Until then he is engaged in systematically dismantling his life. McInerney illuminates the protagonist's situation by explicating the formula for his self-destructive tendencies. In comparing the magazine and the Manhattan club scene, the yuppie equivalent to high culture, with the mass-cultural New York *Post*, McInerney focuses the narrative on the dichotomy of popular culture much the same way he did in *Ransom*, but more significantly. Aside from the actual *Post* headlines he reads, the protagonist periodically considers the embarrassing headlines that could result from his own bizarre experiences; although emotionally incapable of writing autobiographical fiction, he finds ironic comfort in considering the humorous possibilities his life presents as *Post* articles. In what has become a devastatingly pressure-filled existence, only the *Post* is a source of uncompromising pleasure.

> You get a seat and hoist a copy of the New York *Post*. The *Post* is the most shameful of your several addictions. You hate to support this kind of trash with your thirty cents, but you are a secret fan of Killer Bees, Hero Cops, Sex Fiends, Lottery Winners, Teenage Terrorists, Liz Taylor, Tough Tots, Sicko Creeps, Living Nightmares, Life on Other Planets, Spontaneous Human Combustion, Miracle Diets and Coma Babies (11).

McInerney's use of this tabloid as a means of providing and maintaining hope is much like Don DeLillo's in *White Noise*. The *Post* occupies a similar position to the protagonist's; its perspective is from the outside looking in, and relies upon a less self-indulgent, more facetious view of our culture and of life in general as its saving grace. It uses the conscientiously ridiculous to maintain a sense of perspective, extolling the idea that all is possible, but recognizes that most important is the style used to present its material: it is not obligated to limit itself to strictly documented events; the *Post* privileges truth over fact. These characteristics are spelled out in direct contrast with the obsessive directive of the protagonist's job at the Department of Factual Verification: the pursuit of correct accentuation, privileging fact over truth. It is depicted as absurdly anal-retentive and counter to his nature: in the protagonist's eyes, he "never stopped thinking of yourself as a writer biding his time in the Department of Factual Verification" (40), as opposed to some of the characters who actually *belonged* there. As a member of its staff, he is at best a misfit, more accurately an outsider, definitely an exiled prisoner.

The protagonist, like the *Post,* experiences a fundamental exile—just as the *Post* is not of the same ilk as the more mainstream newspapers or the magazine, he consistently finds himself on the perimeter of overzealous, tunnel-visioned groups, never quite meshing with their membership, yet unable to escape their influence. From the novel's first lines, McInerney is informing the reader that the protagonist does not fit in.

> You are not the kind of guy who would be at a place like this at this time of the morning. But here you are, and you cannot say that the terrain is entirely unfamiliar, although the details are fuzzy (1).

As the narrative continues, McInerney continually reiterates this idea; the protagonist feels incapable of escaping his failures, such as Amanda and the magazine. He is pressured by his inability to conform to the "normal" yearnings for a storybook existence; in essence, he fails to separate real life from idealized societal expectations, and the resulting sense of exile is consuming him. His perception of rejection, of unrealized dreams, as examples of our culture's (or life's) cruelty leads him into a world of decadence, but only as a fringe participant. His own idealism does not permit him to truly take part in the club scene: it is intellectually bereft and entirely unwholesome; he is looking for something more.

> The problem is, for some reason you think you are going to meet the kind of girl who is not the kind of girl who would be at a place like this at this time of the morning. When you meet her you are going to tell her that what you really want is a house in the country with a garden (3).

And yet he is unable to ignore the call of the hedonist Tad Allegash, who leads him to consume large quantities of cocaine and vodka—exiled drugs themselves—and spends each night tramping about Manhattan. He is a stranger, self-exiled from his rightful domain, thrust into the inescapable sub-culture that has enveloped his life, unable to wholeheartedly participate; he does not see a means of escape from what has become a failure-driven, self-destructive impulse. This is due to his only gradually developing awareness that he was used by Amanda.

Amanda, like the magazine, is a reminder of his failure to reach his surrogate dreams. The protagonist cannot help feeling humiliated; in Amanda he thought he was getting the perfect woman: eager to learn, beautiful, ingenuous, "she came right up and started talking to you. As you talked you thought: *She looks like a goddamned model and she doesn't even know it"* (69). He was mistaken. Early in their relationship she regarded modeling much the same way he thought of his job at the magazine: it was a means to an end, not a self-contained career. They shared the recognition that their jobs were ridiculous until modeling became Amanda's *career*, only a short time preceding his abandonment, and then he could not escape her/its presence. Walking along the street he saw mannequins molded after her, her face in advertisements, and people asked about her. He attempted to escape the images through his work at the magazine, but he was self-destructing there as well: "They want you to relax, go home. You don't want to go home. Your apartment is a chamber of horrors. There are instruments of torture" (80). For the protagonist it was not a home so much as a reminder of what was lost to him: he had no wife, no true friends, no mother. Even the dust in his apartment prevents his escape from Amanda's expatriation and his own exile.

Unlike the other novels, *Bright Lights, Big City* presents the only possible outcome for the protagonist if he continues on his present path. McInerney introduces Alex Hardy, who, as a dreamer shaped by society's mores, is a longtime editor at the magazine and a dark, alcoholic, exilic vision of the protagonist's future. Hardy is what the protagonist will become if he continues his self-destructive path; aside from some early success, and having shared an office with William Faulkner, Hardy's writing career has produced little despite initial promise—he spends his days stuporously reminiscing about the past rather than acting in the present, and "No one can say whether his drinking is a function of his decline or whether it is the other way around" (63). Hardy is unwilling to recognize the changing times and cannot extricate himself from his long-lost dreams of greatness, much like the protagonist; the difference is that the protagonist is unwilling to stand still. He, like the Coma Baby, is slowly coming to life, slowly rescinding his exile.

In what amounts to a rejection of his accustomed lifestyle's decadence, the protagonist eventually abandons everything that has been destroying him: he forces a release from his job, sees the end of his relationship with cocaine, recognizes Amanda's shallowness as she introduces a high-class male prostitute as her fiance. He recognizes Amanda and her kindred spirit, Allegash, as two who, knowingly or not, have been reinforcing his situation, blockading him from participation in the cultural mainstream, maintaining his exile. He has come to an important self-understanding about his goals and his past failures. He entered his present lifestyle by following the easy path, as Amanda approached him for her own gain, not his; the wrong job at the wrong kind of magazine was never a way to reach his literary goals; cocaine merely delayed and refocused the pain he was experiencing. He recognizes that "You will have to go slowly. You will have to learn everything all over again" (182), considering not what expectations are superimposed on him from without, but what comes from within.

Story of My Life is concerned with the more dangerous aspects of patriarchal American culture while maintaining much of *Bright Lights, Big City*'s flavor. It, too, describes a train of cocaine-fueled parties, this time colored with frequent, frank sexual interludes. Like *Bright Lights, Big City*, *Story of My Life* is a novel of self-abuse leading to an awakening, chronicling Alison Poole's struggle with the increasingly inescapable memories of being sexually abused by her father during her childhood; her constant effort to repress the pain he caused has driven her away from her family, the horse stables and suburban lifestyle that were her birthright, and into a numbing decadence. Alison is an emblematic representation of the position held by all women in a society run by men. This is not to say that all women are like Alison, but *Story of My Life* does present a lurid picture of the ease with which women can become disenfranchised—creating a class of exiles—in this society. Rather than chasing the concept of an ideal life (a la *Bright Lights, Big City*'s protagonist), or martyring herself for the salvation of integrity (as did the title character of *Ransom*), Alison's exile is a result of her attempts to avoid reminders of the past. Unlike McInerney's other protagonists, she has been physically exiled from what would normally be considered "home"—her father's psychological sickness has fostered her detachment from her accustomed family situation, leaving her adrift yet financially dependent on him. Alison is attempting to find a stolen innocence, (including reason, purpose and comfort); essentially, she is on a quest for a safe haven. The entire story creates an atmosphere in which Alison is so unable to separate her different self-abuses that she rambles through a stream-of-consciousness narration: she refers constantly to the men in her life who think of her as nothing more than a sexual playtoy (consequently contributing to her rootlessness), and she jumbles references to cocaine-filled parties with angry and disapproving allusions to her father. She can acknowledge vestiges of his pedophilia in his relationships with other women—"always gone for the young ones, haven't we, Dad?" (1)—but suppresses her memories of his sexually abusing her. She repeatedly hints that this molestation is the source of her self-destructiveness, but it is only at the end of the novel, when she is in treatment for cocaine addiction, that Alison's attitudes and behavior are directly explained.

Story of My Life, then, is a novel built around what Ugarte would call Alison's

> existential need to recover something lost (a land, an identity, a place of origin) results from the absence of an integral part of one's being—a fact that causes the exile to

perceive of him or herself as less than human.... In many ways exile also creates a new self; it creates the distance one needs to objectify the self, to look back at it from a different situation, a different land (20).

Alison's memories are the key to her behavior: periodically she hints at her father's sexual obsession with her during her time as an adolescent equestrian, and the combination of two passages, one at the beginning of the novel and the other at the end, creates a coherent narrative which explains her relationship with her father and her perceived need to escape him:

"When I was a kid I spent most of my time on horseback. I went around the country, showing my horses and jumping." (7)

"Back then my father bought anything for me. I was his sweet thing." (187)

Unfortunately for her father, the time spent on the road kept her away from him, and the majority of her time was spent on a particular horse:

"Dangerous Dan was the best.... I loved that horse. No one else could get near him, he'd try to kill them, but I used to sleep in his stall, spend hours with him every day." (187)

At this point the story could be the fantasy of any pre-teen or adolescent girl, taken directly from *National Velvet* or any other storybook.

"until Dangerous Dan dropped dead. I loved Dan more than just about any living thing since." (7)

"When he was poisoned I went into shock. They kept me on tranquilizers for a week." (187)

This teaches young Alison a lesson about how to escape pain, one which contributed to her future efforts to escape her memories.

I quit riding. A few months later, Dad came into my room one night. I was like, uh-oh, not this again. He buried his face in my shoulder. His cheek was wet and he smelled of booze. I'm sorry about Dangerous Dan, he said. Tell me you forgive me. He muttered something about the business and passed out on top of me and I had to go and get Mom." (187)

McInerney does not suggest that any action was taken against Alison's father, and does not say anything about what happened between Alison and her mother. Clearly the issue was not resolved, because it lingered on until Alison's drug treatment helped her to understand what had happened to her.

After a week in the hatch they let me use the phone.... So just for the hell of it I go, Dad, sometimes I wish you'd let me keep that horse.

He goes, I don't know what you're talking about.

I go, Dangerous Dan. You remember what you told me that night. After he died.

He goes, I didn't tell you anything.

> So, okay, maybe I dreamed it. I was in bed after all, and he woke me up. Not for the first time.... I'd love to think that ninety percent of it was just dreaming. (187–188)

Through the events surrounding Dangerous Dan's death, Alison learned that drugs and travelling were apparently efficient escapes from her feelings of betrayal, and subsequently she spent a significant amount of time doing both. Despite the fact that she feels economically bound to New York—"I owe everyone in the western hemisphere, I'm like a fucking Third World country" (177)—the novel is full of references to falsely foreign places she has been to escape her memories. She frequents clubs named Zulu (8), Indochine (9), and China Club (78), and travels by taxi cab on her nights out, so that from her

> apartment to Trader Vic's you get Cuban music, and then from Trader Vic's to Canal Bar you've got Zorba the Greek music and then Indian ragas from Canal Bar to Nell's, Scandinavian heavy metal on the way from Nell's up to Emile's apartment. After that you start singing the Colombian national anthem. (42)

Through the haze of her cocaine addiction Alison sees leaving as the most promising opportunity for the future. She has concerns for her younger sister, Carol, who may be jaded, but has not lost her innocence yet. In her fantasies, Alison would "have Carol kidnapped by Australian bushmen or something and raised by them before she turned out like the rest of us" (119). Mostly, however, she dreams of her own escape.

> I suddenly wonder how long it would take them to notice I was gone if I went out the fire escape or something. What if I just kept going, left New York entirely? I'm getting this really weird feeling like, I'm so involved in all this hysterical noise which is supposedly my life but it doesn't add up to anything, if you step back far enough it's just a dumb buzz like a swarm of mosquitoes.... From the planet Jupiter, none of it counts for shit. (147)

While Alison does not act on this impulse, this is a breakthrough for her, one in which she recognizes the pettiness that is surrounding her, and becomes the keystone upon which she builds up enough courage and desperation to actually seek help. She eventually escapes to a Minnesota hospital's detox program (186). As the above section indicates, until Alison reaches her breaking point, every event in the novel becomes interrelated in a network of nightmarish self-reflexivity, pushing her farther and farther—spiritually if not geographically—from an emotional reconciliation with herself; she has all the subconscious pieces to assemble a complete picture of her life, but lacks the fundamental self-awareness necessary to understand why she cannot function with any success in society, why she remains an exile. That is why her acting career is so important.

If her social life is an attempt to anesthetize herself, acting is a means of understanding and venting her pent-up emotions. She sees acting as a healing experience, rather than an exercise in denial:

> I just love it, getting up there and turning myself inside out.... It's like being a child again ... ever since I can remember people have been trying to get me to stifle my emotions but.... Acting is about being true to your feelings, which is great since real life seems to be about being a liar and a hypocrite. (7–8)

Alison has established a polemical approach to her past, and therefore her state of exile. She nearly admits by default that she is actively denying herself the benefits of being truthful with herself, and her acting is beginning to wear away the ropes which bind her reactions to her memories and feelings. The maintenance of this duality is contributing to Alison's stream-of-consciousness self-examination, a split which Ugarte says occurs naturally in exile:

> The gap between the reality and the description of what happened seems to grow wider as the exile writes.... Similarly, the rendition of the experience turns into the object of another description, as in the typically exilic apology for not recalling an event exactly as it took place. (20)

Her needs are being manifested in her acting lessons. She has already been separated from herself by her father's sexual abuse; it has forced her to subdivide her memories, repressing the times "he came into my room" (187), and effectively exile part of her being into a cerebral limbo. Drama school provides Alison with the opportunity to begin to heal; it is the means by which she can release the pent-up emotions and feelings of betrayal she experiences, and allow her to do so from an outside perspective. By learning about acting, she is enabling herself to create and escape the myths upon which our culture thrives: she is facilitating not only the expression of her own feelings, but those of anyone who observes her at work, conceiving of alternate realities in which they (and she) can find themselves. The acting allows her to vent her frustrations stemming from her treatment by her father and all the men with whom she associates, rather than lashing out at him/them. They are also a window into her pain:

> Anyway, I don't know—I'm just letting myself go limp in the head, then I'm laughing hysterically and next thing I'm bawling like a baby, really out of control, falling out of the chair and thrashing all over the floor ... a real basket case ... epileptic apocalypse, sobbing and flailing around, trying to take a bite out of the linoleum ... they're used to some pretty radical emoting in here, but this is way over the top, apparently. I kind of lose it, and the nurse says I'm overtired and tells me to go home and rest. (14)

Acting lessons represent Alison's positive interaction with the cultural mainstream; through it, she engages in a sort of self-analysis which allows her to continue living from day to day. Acting creates an alternative to, and provides an excuse for abstaining from, the destructive lifestyle in which she finds herself. Rather than taking in foreign substances and losing control over her mind, body and actions, acting makes her establish control over herself by channeling beneficial and detrimental emotions and memories into the creation of a physical state. This necessitates the exclusion of external stimuli and manifests a sense of self-reliance, even self-healing, which she must apply to her non-acting life if she is to survive.

Alison is in an awkward position. Her father's sexual abuse so entirely consumes her that she looks for a way to exorcise it by repeatedly associating with men and women like her father. Every one of her relationships is a power struggle in which she sees herself as the subject of aggressive behavior: she thinks her friend "Didi would make a really good Dictator of a Third World country" (41); her sister Rebecca is "the Tasmanian Devil, that character in Bugs Bunny cartoons that moves around in a tornado and demolishes everything in its path" (18); and her long-time friend Francesca as "like a force of nature, Niagara Falls or something" (50). Although each poses different threats, she feels that with each she must attempt to protect herself from conflict:

> "I could give a shit about the lifestyles of the rich and famous. I'm a lot more worried about survival of the fittest, and like whether I'm going to make the cut or join the club for dinosaurs and dodo birds." (164)

This hostile environment is the result of her attempts to live by a personal code which does not comply with the surrounding rules of order; but just as Ransom is a vessel for Victor's desires, Alison is an actual and metaphorical vessel for her father and those around her. Her resistance is an attempt to stifle the patriarchal tendencies of the culture in which she has inculcated herself. Because she is unable to succeed within the larger scope of her milieu, she is forced to seek outside help and is finally rescued.

McInerney's main characters' inability to respond positively or even in an openly constructive manner when faced with failure creates their need to abandon the mainstream/traditional family and cultural relationships. According to Michael Seidel, "An exile is someone who inhabits one place and remembers or projects the reality of another" (ix). In McInerney's novels, the protagonists share a (nearly) fatal mind set, rather than a spatial location, that makes them stumble and fall into an environment that will eventually destroy them if they cannot escape. Their flaw is a life-threatening inability to actualize their idealism. His protagonists are struggling against familial and societal pressures for an artistic freedom of sorts; decadence attacks them in the guise of abuses: cocaine, power, peer pressure. Alison Poole and the protagonist from

Bright Lights, Big City rectify their problems by changing environments, making the adjustments necessary for survival; the keystones in their survival are recognitions of the corrupting forces' limitations and the subsequent abandonment of the destructive situation created by an artificial world. Christopher Ransom, however, cannot change the way he is and has exhausted his possible safe havens; he is unable to reconcile the differences he has with the world around him (perhaps because he cannot partially attribute the problem to drugs), and therefore experiences a sort of spiritual resignation. In choosing his death at the hands of DeVito, he perversely satisfies all parties by either ensuring their safety from DeVito or making reality fit their expectations. Interestingly, McInerney spends very few lines describing Ransom's death; the important description has unfolded during the course of the novel, and the scraps are left to the tabloid television programs that represent the cultural affiliation of power, money, and tastelessness.

Works Cited

Bradbury, Malcolm. *The Expatriate Tradition in American Literature*. South Shields, England: British Association for American Studies, 1982.

Eagleton, Terry. *Exiles and Émigrés*. New York: Schocken, 1970.

McInerney, Jay. *Bright Lights, Big City*. New York: Vintage Books, 1984.

———. *Ransom*. New York: Vintage Books, 1985.

———. *Story of My Life*. New York: Atlantic Monthly Press, 1988.

Pinsker, Sanford. "Soft Lights, Academic Talk: A Conversation with Jay McInerney." *Literary Review* 30 (1986): 107–114.

Seidel, Michael. *Exile and the Narrative Imagination*. New Haven: Yale University Press, 1986.

Ugarte, Michael. *Shifting Ground*. Durham: Duke University Press, 1989.

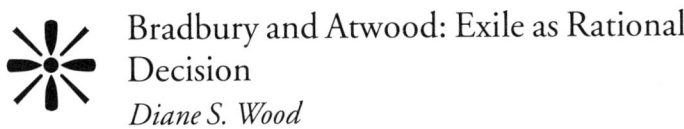 Bradbury and Atwood: Exile as Rational Decision
Diane S. Wood

Ray Bradbury's *Fahrenheit 451* and Margaret Atwood's *The Handmaid's Tale* depict the rational decision to go into exile, to leave one's native land, that is, the pre-exile condition. These novels present horrifying views of the near future where societal pressures enforce rigid limitations on individual freedom. Their alienated characters find their circumstances repugnant. Justice and freedom are denied them, along with the possibility for enriching their lives through intellectual pursuits. These speculative novels like Orwell's *1984* are dystopian in nature, showing how precarious are today's constitutional rights and how necessary it is to preserve these liberties for future generations. They depict ordinary people, caught in circumstances that they cannot control, people who resist oppression at the risk of their lives and who choose exile because it *has* to be better than their present, unbearable circumstances. Voluntary exile necessitates a journey into the unknown as an alternative to the certain repression of the present.

Both novels offer a bleak possible future for the United States. Bradbury, writing in the McCarthy era of the 1950s, envisions a time when people choose to sit by the hour watching television programs and where owning books is a crime. Atwood, in the 1980s, foresees a time when, in the wake of changes begun during the Reagan Administration, women are denied even the most basic rights of working and owning property.[1] Both novels thus present "political" stances in the widest sense of the word. In her address on Amnesty International, Atwood defines the word "politics" and how it comes to be incorporated into a writer's work:

By 'politics' I do not mean how you voted in the last election, although that is included. I mean who is entitled to do what to whom, with impunity; who profits by it; and who therefore eats what. Such material enters a writer's work not because the writer is or is not consciously political but because a writer is an observer, a witness, and such observations are the air he breathes. They are the air all of us breathe; the only difference is that the author looks, and then writes down what he sees. What he sees will depend on how closely he looks and at what, but look he must. (1982, 394)

To Atwood being "political" is part of the moral stance of the writer as truth teller. In his 1966 Introduction to *Fahrenheit 451*, Bradbury expresses moral outrage concerning bookburning: "when Hitler burned a book I felt it as keenly, please forgive me, as his killing a human, for in the long sum of history they are one and the same flesh. Mind or body, put to the oven, is a sinful practice...."[2] He sees the necessity to guard constantly against such practices:

For while Senator McCarthy has long been dead, the Red Guard in China comes alive and idols are smashed, and books, all over again, are thrown into the furnace. So it will go, one generation printing, another generation burning, yet another remembering what is good to remember so as to print again. (14)

Atwood stresses the qualities of authors which make them a danger to oppressive governments: "The writer, unless he is a mere word processor, retains three attributes that power-mad regimes cannot tolerate: a human imagination, in the many forms it may take; the power to communicate; and hope." (1982, 397)

The novels by Bradbury and Atwood examine the personal response of an individual who is in conflict with the majority in his society and whose occupation is abhorrent to him. *Fahrenheit 451* centers upon the personal crisis of Montag, a young fireman whose job consists of burning books. He finds his life increasingly meaningless and eventually comes to reject the too-simple, clichéd values of his milieu. He experiences loneliness in a society where people are constantly entertained without time given to reflexion and personal development, activities often associated with the reading process. The more complicated nuances of the world of books are available to him only when he leaves his reductionistic society. Atwood's novel recounts the story of a protagonist caught up in the rapid transition of her society. Dehumanized, stripped of her personal name and individual identity, and referred to only by the name of the man to whose household she is assigned, Offred (or Of-Fred), a handmaid, experiences firsthand an upheaval in the social order ending in limited personal freedom.[3] The new oligarchy uses Old Testament injunctions to justify extreme repression. Like the shock troops to which they are compared (144), handmaids are in the *avant garde* of the social reform and they undergo brutal re-education at the Rachel & Leah

Re-Education Centers, after which, like soldiers, they are "posted" to a commander's household. Even more than Montag, Offred's life is determined by her social role. As a fertile woman in a nearly sterile society, her function is to produce viable offspring and her entire life is regulated by her reproductive duties.[4] She describes herself and her fellow handmaids as "two-legged wombs, that's all: sacred vessels, ambulatory chalices" (1985, 176). There is nothing erotic about the handmaids, their mission is strictly biological: "We are for breeding purposes: we aren't concubines, geisha girls, courtesans" (176). Whereas Montag has to seek out an understanding of how his society developed, Offred lives through the transitional period and is thus acutely aware of the stages on the way to losing individual freedom. From the beginning of the narrative, she is literally a prisoner, watched at all times and even tattooed with a number: "Four digits and an eye, a passport in reverse. It's supposed to guarantee that I will never be able to fade, finally, into another landscape. I am too important, too scarce, for that. I am a national resource" (84–5).

In both novels the population is strictly regulated and the conduct of individuals is highly regimented. Indeed, in these repressive circumstances, it is not surprising that the protagonists would wish to flee, especially since, by the end of the novels, they have broken laws which would bring the death penalty if they were apprehended. "Mechanical Hounds" use scent to hunt down lawbreakers in Bradbury's fiction.[5] The hounds tear apart their prey. Montag narrowly escapes this fate but the police do not admit being outwitted. They stage his death for the benefit of the huge television audience which follows the developing story of his evasion.[6] The authorities murder an innocent derelict in Montag's place, so as not to disappoint the viewers and appear ineffectual. The authorities are motivated by the desire to maintain power at any cost and blatantly violate human rights.

Discipline is less mechanized in *The Handmaid's Tale* but no less ruthless. Cadres of brutal "Aunts," "Angels," "Guardians," and "Eyes" enforce order in Atwood's imaginary Gilead. Cattleprods punish uncooperative handmaids in the rehabilitation center. For particularly bad infractions, the handmaids' hands and feet are tortured: "They used steel cables, frayed at the ends. After that the hands. They didn't care what they did to your feet or your hands, even if it was permanent. Remember, said Aunt Lydia. For our purposes your feet and your hands are not essential" (118).[7] Other punishments are even more severe. A woman caught reading three times merits a hand cut off. Handmaids are executed for being unchaste, attempting to kill a commander, or trying to escape. Wives die for adultery or for attempting to kill a handmaid. As in the Middle Ages, cadavers of tortured prisoners are displayed on the town wall to encourage conformity to rules.[8] Offred describes her reaction to the cadavers hanging there:

> It's the bags over the heads that are the worst, worse than the faces themselves would be. It makes the men like dolls on which the faces have not yet been painted; like scarecrows, which in a way is what they are, since they are meant to scare. Or as if their heads are sacks, stuffed with some undifferentiated material, like flour or dough. It's the obvious heaviness of the heads, their vacancy, the way gravity pulls them down and there's no life anymore to hold them up. The heads are zeros. (43)

Execution is a public event, called a "Salvaging."[9] The local women are assembled to witness the execution by hanging of two handmaids and a wife. The authorities decide to depart from past procedure and not read the crimes of the condemned in order to prevent a rash of similar crimes. Offred comments on the unpopularity of this decision: "The crimes of others are a secret language among us. Through them we show ourselves what we might be capable of, after all" (354). The assembled women are required to assent to the punishment even though they do not know the nature of the crime. As part of the audience, Offred makes the ceremonial gesture of compliance with the execution: "I . . . then placed my hand on my heart to show my unity with the Salvagers and my consent, and my complicity in the death of this woman" (355).

An even more frightening public ceremony is that of "Particicution," where handmaids act as executioners of an accused rapist. Death is the punishment set in Deuteronomy 22:23–29. Offred paints the scene in terms of bloodlust: "The air is bright with adrenaline, we are permitted anything and this is freedom" (359). The women literally tear the accused apart with their bare hands. These brutal ceremonies serve to release violent emotion in a socially approved setting, since its normal expression is otherwise denied.

The major task of both Bradbury and Atwood is to portray convincingly in their futuristic novels how the abridgement of freedom evolved in the United States. As such, the novels are strong political statements warning of the consequences of what seem dangerous trends to the authors. One has only to look at the statistics for television watching, witness the decline of interest in reading among our students, and read current reports about ecological damage to verify the gravity of the dangers this country faces at the present time. In the world of *Fahrenheit 451* people have given up thinking for mindless pursuits. No revolution or *coup d'etat* brings about the loss of freedom. Rather, individual laziness precipitates a gradual erosion. This evolution takes place long before the birth of Montag, who grows up in a society where books are proscribed. His superior, a fireman, explains the trend of increasing simplification as the result of the influence of the mass media: "Things began to have *mass*.... And because they had mass, they became simpler.... Once, books appealed to a few people, here, there, everywhere. They could afford to be different. The world was roomy. But then the world got full of eyes and elbows and mouths (61). In a vast generalization which is itself a simplification, he tells how the modern era brought a movement to speed up and condense everything:

> Then, in the twentieth century, speed up your camera. Books cut shorter. Condensations. Digests. Tabloids. Everything boils down to the gag, the snap ending. ... Classics cut to fit fifteen-minute radio shows, then cut again to fill a two-minute book column, winding up at last as a ten- or twelve-line dictionary resume.... Do you see? Out of the nursery into the college and back to the nursery; there's your intellectual pattern for the past five centuries or more (61)

The rich value of books is thus denied when they are reduced to brief summaries. Happiness to this fireman comes from eliminating all dissension, especially that caused by books: "'Colored people don't like Little Black Sambo. Burn it. White people don't feel good about Uncle Tom's Cabin. Burn it. Someone's written a book on tobacco and cancer of the lungs? The cigarette people are weeping? Burn the book. Serenity, Montag. Peace, Montag. Take your fight outside. Better yet, into the incinerator'" (65–6). Yet this society does not produce happiness. Montag is perpetually lonely and his wife attempts suicide.

Whereas Atwood's society ceremonializes violence, in Bradbury's book the society eliminates all cause for unhappiness and sweeps unpleasantness away, including those which are an integral part of the human condition: "'Funerals are unhappy and pagan? Eliminate them, too. Five minutes after a person is dead he's on his way to the Big Flue, the Incinerators serviced by helicopters all over the country. Ten minutes after death a man's a speck of black dust. Let's not quibble over individuals with memoriams. Forget them. Burn all, burn everything. Fire is bright and fire is clean'" (66). Television concerns itself with the ephemeral present and thus follows the trend toward forgetting the past.[10] Books by their very essence preserve and memorialize those who have lived before. Bradbury would probably agree with Atwood's comments that all repressive governments eliminate authors because they are so dangerous.[11] The fireman views fire as a means of purging and cleansing emotions in his society. Political dissension is eliminated by giving only one side of the argument (66). War is not even talked about (66). People are reduced to thinking about simple facts, meaningless data: "Cram them full of noncombustible data, chock them so full of 'facts' they feel stuffed, but absolutely 'brilliant' with information. Then they'll feel they're thinking, they'll get a *sense* of motion without moving. And they'll be happy, because facts of that sort don't change. Don't give them any slippery stuff like philosophy or sociology to tie things up with. That way lies melancholy" (56). Through simplifying and reducing ideas, he feels that the firemen produce happiness for the society: "we're the Happiness Boys, the Dixie Duo, you and I and the others. We stand against the small tide of those who want to make everyone unhappy with conflicting theory and thought. We have our fingers in the dike. Hold steady. Don't let the torrent of melancholy and drear philosophy drown our world'" (67).

Balancing this reductionist apology are the views of another character in the novel, a retired English professor who "had been thrown out upon the world forty years ago when the last liberal arts college shut for lack of students and patronage" (76). He traces the lack of reading to apathy: "Remember, the firemen are rarely necessary. The public itself stopped reading of its own accord. Your firemen provide a circus now and then at which buildings are set off and crowds gather for the pretty blaze, but it's a small sideshow indeed, and hardly necessary to keep things in line. So few want to be rebels anymore. And out of those few, most, like myself, scare easily" (87). The professor's personal experience bears witness to the gradual nature of the transition from a reading to a non-reading culture. One day, there are simply no more students:

> That was a year I came to class at the start of the new semester and found only one student to sign up for Drama from Aeschylus to O'Neill. You see? How like a beautiful statue of ice it was, melting in the sun. I remember the newspapers dying like huge moths. No one *wanted* them back. No one missed them. And then the Government, seeing how advantageous it was to have people reading only about passionate lips and the fist in the stomach, circled the situation with your fire-eaters. (88)[12]

Whereas in *Fahrenheit 451* the government acted opportunistically, taking advantage of the lack of passionate readers to outlaw books, the government in *The Handmaid's Tale* actively shapes lifestyles through public policy. Atwood's protagonist recalls the governmental action that declares women may no longer own property and hold jobs (227–31). Offred is fired, along with every other woman in the country. Her money can be transferred to her husband, but she no longer may control the funds accessed by her plastic card. The government deprives women of the right to work and to own property simultaneously, to prevent a mass exodus (231). These freedoms were not the first to be lost, however. Offred explains the progressive loss of the women's constitutional rights, perpetrated by an ominous invisible group she identifies as "they":

> It was after the catastrophe, when *they* shot the president and machine-gunned the Congress and the army declared a state of emergency. *They* blamed it on the Islamic fanatics, at the time. . . . That was when *they* suspended the Constitution. *They* said it would be temporary. There wasn't even any rioting in the streets. People stayed home

at night, watching television, looking for some direction. There wasn't even an enemy you could put your finger on. (225, emphasis mine)

Still the transition is gradual and required the complicity of the populace: "We lived, as usual, by ignoring. Ignoring isn't the same as ignorance, you have to work at it. Nothing changes instantaneously: in a gradually heating bathtub you'd be boiled to death before you knew it" (74).[13] The protagonist finally decides that the conditions of the military state are untenable and unsuccessfully tries to escape to freedom with her husband and child, only to find that it is too late. When captured, she is separated from her family whom she never sees again, and is forced to take her place as a handmaid.

In both novels books represent important artifacts of the past and the act of reading becomes a heroic gesture. This is not surprising since both authors are avid readers and have described the importance of books in their lives. In fact, *Fahrenheit 451* was written in the UCLA library (15).[14] One of the most crucial passages in the novel shows a woman willing to die for her books. Montag is stunned when she sets fire to her library and immolates herself along with her precious volumes.[15] This experience causes Montag to question what there is in books that is worth dying for and ultimately leads to his becoming a preserver of books instead of a destroyer.[16] Allusions to being denied the right to read occur throughout *The Handmaid's Tale*. As a handmaid, Offred is forbidden to read, a hardship for a person whose former job was in a library. The only words she sees are "faith" on the petit point cushion in her room and "*Nolite te bastardes carborundorum*" (Don't let the bastards get you down) which is scratched in tiny letters near the floor of her cupboard. During the course of the novel Offred recalls reading and having access to books and regrets her former blasé attitude toward them. Because they are now denied to her, they become very precious whereas once books were commonplace and taken for granted. In the middle of the novel her Commander (the Fred of Offred) invites her to forbidden soirées in his private study. He permits her to read old women's magazines. Offred philosophically reflects on the promise that the old magazines once held:

> What was in them was promise. They dealt in transformations; they suggested an endless series of possibilities, extending like the reflections in two mirrors set facing one another, stretching on, replica after replica, to the vanishing point. They suggested one adventure after another, one wardrobe after another, one improvement after another, one man after another. They suggested rejuvenation, pain overcome and transcended, endless love. The real promise in them was immortality. (201)

The Commander not only lets Offred read magazines but plays scrabble with her. This is the ultimate in forbidden games in a society where women are not allowed to read: "Now it's dangerous. Now it's indecent. Now it's something he can't do with his Wife. Now it's desirable. Now he's compromised himself. It's as if he's offered me drugs" (179).

When the Commander allows Offred to read magazines, the experience is equated to the orgiastic pleasures of eating or of sex: "On these occasions I read quickly, voraciously, almost skimming, trying to get as much into my head as possible before the next long starvation. If it were eating it would be the gluttony of the famished; if it were sex it would be a swift furtive stand-up in an alley somewhere" (239, and see 1988, 110). The Commander, who watches the illicit reading, is described as a sort of pervert: "While I read, the Commander sits and watches me doing it, without speaking but also without taking his eyes off me. This watching is a curiously sexual act, and I feel undressed while he does it. I wish he would turn his back, stroll around the room, read something himself. Then perhaps I could relax more, take my time. As it is, this illicit reading of mine seems a kind of performance" (239).

These magazines somehow escaped the government's attention, although house-to-house searches and bonfires were conducted on the orders of the oligarchy in order to remove all reading material from women (202). The government of Gilead denied women access to the printed word as a means of controlling them.[17] Only the vicious Aunts are allowed to read and write as a part of their role in re-educating the handmaids (166). The effect of this is to silence the women, or as Atwood has said elsewhere: "The aim of all suppression is to silence *the voice*, abolish the word, so that the only voices and words left are those of the ones in power." (See 1982, 350)

In her essays Atwood speaks out against suppression of reading and writing, abhoring fascism on anyone's part.[18] This view is paralleled in the novel where Offred remembers as a young girl attending a magazine burning with her mother, who is recalled as a quintessential feminist demonstrator of the 1970s. As the pornographic material burns the image evoked is particularly poetic: "I threw the magazine into the flames. It rifled open in the wind of its burning; big flakes of paper came loose, sailed into the air, still on fire, parts of women's bodies, turning to black ash, in the air, before my eyes" (51). Offred's views toward women's rights are much less activist in nature than her mother's. The mother/daughter relationship is fraught with tension and their opposing viewpoints brings into question some of the tactics of the women's movement including the bookburning. After attending a "Birthing," a particularly grotesque woman's ritual in Gilead, Offred ironically comments: "Mother, I think. Wherever you may be. Can you hear me? You wanted a women's culture. Well now there is one. It isn't what you meant, but it exists. Be thankful for small mercies" (164) Her feminist mother probably dies a victim of the new regime, but when Gilead comes into being, there is no triumph on the part of the rightwing opponents to the woman's movement like the Commander's Wife Serena Joy. These women also find no happiness in the new society.

Despite the fact that the social order is founded on biblical references, women are not allowed to read the Bible: "The Bible is kept locked up, the way people once kept tea locked up, so the servants wouldn't steal it. It is an incendiary device: who knows what we'd make of it, if we ever got our hands on it? We can be read to from it, by him [the commander], but we cannot read" (112). Even the familiar reading passages read by the commander hold their attraction for those hungering for the written word: "He's like a man toying with a steak, behind a restaurant window, pretending not to see the eyes watching him from hungry darkness not three feet from his elbow. We lean towards him a little, iron filings to his magnet. He has something we don't have, he has the word. How we squandered it, once" (114). Tapes of biblical readings are an integral part of the re-education in the Rachel and Leah Centers. The quotations, however, have been changed to further the goals of the oligarchy. Offred notices transformations in the Beatitudes: "*Blessed be the poor in spirit, for theirs is the kingdom of heaven. Blessed are the merciful. Blessed be the meek. Blessed are the silent.* I knew they made that up, I knew it was wrong, and they left things out, too, but there was no way of checking. *Blessed be those that mourn, for they shall be comforted.* Nobody said when" (115). Her ironic comments underscore her frustration with the prohibition against reading and her resistance to indoctrination.

Just as the Beatitudes are rewritten, Marx's comments about the distribution of property are attributed to the Bible in order to justify the distribution of the precious and scarce handmaids in Gilead: "Not every Commander has a Handmaid: some of their Wives have children. *From each*, says the slogan, *according to her ability; to each according to his needs.* We recited that, three times, after dessert. It was from the Bible, or so they said. St. Paul again, in Acts" (151).

The author's ironic use of religious terms becomes comic when she creates the franchise "Soul Scrolls" where prayers are continually spewed out on printout machines called "Holy Rollers" and paid for by pious citizens. Like the flavors in an ice cream store, there are five different prayers: "for health, wealth, a death, a birth, a sin" (216). The state religion distortedly caricatures fundamentalist beliefs, including having a former television gospel singer as the Commander's Wife.

Each novel ends with the protagonist's escape and the beginning of his exile from repression. There is some ambiguity, however, since the alternative order is not elaborated on. Montag watches his city being destroyed by a nuclear explosion. He joins a group of vagabonds who memorize the books with which they have escaped. No attempt is made to follow his further development in these difficult circumstances or to predict the course the future holds for society or the survivors.[19] The implication is clear, however, that intellectual freedom is worth the inconvenience of life outside the modern city. Because he left, Montag survives the death of the mindless masses who stayed behind. Offred's fate is even more ambiguous. In the last lines of her tale she describes her feelings as she steps into the Black Maria which has come for her: "Whether this is my end or a new beginning I have no way of knowing: I have given myself over into the hands of strangers, because it can't be helped. And so I step up, into the darkness within; or else the light" (378). The postscript "Historical Notes on *The Handmaid's Tale*" provides information that the heroine survives to record her story on cassette tapes.[20] She is rescued by the Mayday organization of the Underground Femaleroad (381–2). Her ultimate fate is unknown to the scholars of 2195 who, in an academic conference, comment on the handmaid's story as a historical document from the past.[21]

The appeal of these two highly acclaimed novels stems from the main characters' difficult situation in a repressive future United States. The plausible explanations given by both Bradbury and Atwood for the ghastly turn taken by American society in the futures they portray serves as a vivid reminder that freedom must be vigilantly guarded in order to be maintained. Apathy and fear create unlivable societies from which only a few courageous souls dare escape. "Ordinary" says one of the cruel Aunts of *The Handmaid's Tale* "is what you are used to" (45). The main characters never are able to accept the "ordinariness" of the repression which surrounds them. They are among the few who are willing to risk the difficult path of exile.

Notes

1. Arthur A. Davidson in "Future Tense: Making History" (in 1988, 113) points out how "the appalling future [is] already implicit in the contemporary world." It is the very plausibility of these futures that make them so terrifying.

2. Not all critics see the political nature of this novel. For Wayne L. Johnson, "The book is about as far as Bradbury has come in the direction of using science fiction for social criticism" (See 1980, 85). He considers "Montag's spiritual development" to be the main focus of the novel (87).

3. Roberta Rubenstein points out that Offred's name always is akin to "offered" and views the name as encoding "her indentured sexuality." See her "Nature and Nurture in Dystopia" in 1988, 103.

4. Rubenstein relates the female anxieties in the novel to "female ambivalence about childbearing in patriarchy" (102).

5. Donald Watt comments on the symbolic nature of the hounds who lurk in the dark and then relentlessly pursue and execute "those who seek to shed some light on their age" in his "Burning Bright: *Fahrenheit 451* as Symbolic Dystopia," (1980, 201).

6. Watt considers the audience to be more menacing than the Mechanical Hound (212). Peter Sisario terms the television entertainment "tapioca-bland" (in 1970, 201).

7. Rubenstein discusses how bodies are objectified and reduced to their parts, a critique begun in Atwood's *Bodily Harm* (1982, 103–5). She also draws an interesting parallel with the binding of female feet among the Chinese.

8. The novel thereby suggests that such tactics are a part of the modern world, a notion Atwood has underscored in her essays "Witches" (332–3) and "Amnesty International" (396) in *Second Words*.

9. Rubenstein demonstrates the ironic resonances of "salvaging" with "*salvage, salvation*, and *savaging*" (104).

10. See Marvin D. Mengeling's "The Machineries of Joy and Despair" (in 1980, 95). David Mogen sees this "reductionist, materialist image of human nature and human culture reinforced through mass entertainment media" as a peculiarity of American culture (in 1986, 107).

11. Because of her view of the role of the author, Atwood has strong words to say about torture:

> One of the few remedies for it is free human speech, which is why writers are always among the first to be lined up against the wall by any totalitarian regime, left or right. How many poets are there in El Salvador? The answer is none. They have all been shot or exiled. The true distinction in the world today is not between the so-called left and the so-called right. It's between the governments that do such things as a matter of policy, or that wink at them when they are done, and those that do not. ("Witches" in 1982, 332).

12. Atwood addresses the problem of apathetic readership in her essay "An End to Audience?" (in 1982). She posits the concept "free reading" as a corollary to free speech (354).

13. Davidson sees the protagonist as an essentially passive character who goes along with the changes until the situation becomes untenable (116). She complies rather than instigates action.

14. Willis C. McNelly speaks of Bradbury's "lifelong love affair with books," equating Montag with the author in "I. Ray Bradbury—Past, Present, and Future" (in 1980, 19).

15. Watt sees this woman demonstrating for Montag "the possibility of defiance and the power of books" (198). See also 201–2.

16. Watt sees the group outside the city as the preserver of human culture (210). Mengling terms Montag's metamorphosis as a change "from book-burner to living-book" (86).

17. Atwood's praise of Tillie Olsen's *Silences* in *Second Words* bears witness to her concern about silencing women (313–5). Barbara Hill Rigney finds that the principal subject of this novel is "the suppression of language, especially language used by women" (in 1987, 131).

18. Helen N. Buss speaks to the question of the bookburning: "The caution here is that if feminists seek fascist solutions they are ultimately condoning fascism" in her forthcoming article "Maternity and Narrative Strategies in the Novels of Margaret Atwood." Rigney concurs with Buss's assessment of Atwood's criticism of the tactics of certain feminists: "In *The Handmaid's Tale*, as in the actual and current situation, some feminist groups exercise the same faulty judgment, thereby forfeiting their own freedom along with that of both the writers and the reading audience" (134).

19. Johnson points out the uncertainty of the novel's ending both for Montag and for the future of the society (88).

20. Rubenstein makes the pertinent comment that Offred's story is an act of self-generation which opposes the procreation duties required of a handmaid (105).

21. Davidson's article offers insight into Atwood's presentation of the academic community in the epilogue. He notes the pessimism implicit in this ending (120). Rubenstein, on the other hand, sees its comic aspects (111–2).

Works Cited

Atwood, Margaret. *Bodily Harm.* Toronto: McClelland and Stewart, 1977.
———. *The Handmaid's Tale.* New York: Fawcett Crest, 1985.
———. *Second Words, Selected Critical Prose.* Toronto: Anansi, 1982.
Bradbury, Ray. *Fahrenheit 451.* New York: Simon and Schuster, 1967.
Buss, Helen N. "Maternity and Narrative Strategies in the Novels of Margaret Atwood," *Atlantis* 15 (1): [forthcoming].
Greenberg, Martin Harry and Joseph D. Olander. *Ray Bradbury.* New York: Taplinger, 1980.
Johnson, Wayne L. *Ray Bradbury.* New York: Frederick Ungar, 1980.
Margaret Atwood, *The Handmaid's Tale.* New York: Fawcett Crest, 1985.
Mogen, David. *Ray Bradbury.* Boston, Twayne, 1986.
Olsen, Tillie. *Silences.* New York: Laurif Seymour Lawrence, 1983.
Peter Sisario. "A Study of Allusions in Bradbury's *Fahrenheit 451,*" *English Journal* 59 (1970): 201.
Rigney, Barbara Hill. *Margaret Atwood.* Totowa, NJ: Barnes & Nobel, 1987.
VanSpanckeren, Kathryn and Jan Garden Castro. Eds. *Margaret Atwood, Vision and Forms.* Carbondale and Edwardsville: S. Illinois University Press, 1988.

Daniel Moyano's *Libro De Navíos Y Borrascas:* The Expression of Territorial Exile
Linda L. Hollabaugh

Literature by writers exiled from their native countries has enjoyed a recent surge of critical attention. It offers a particularly rich field for hispanists—for the varieties of exile experience, even among compatriots, have been vast. The writings by Spanish American exiles of the seventies are especially interesting and not yet fully explored. Argentine Daniel Moyano is one of the most talented of these exiles. The present article will apply the criteria established by John Spalek in his study, "The Varieties of Exile Experience: German, Polish, and Spanish Writers" to Moyano's most recently published novel, *Libro de navíos y borrascas* [*Book of Ships and Storms*].[1]

Although Spalek treats European refugee writers living in South America, his comparative analysis notes several features common to much literature of exile: preoccupations with autobiography, time, and the motif of return. "Exile" in Spalek's essay refers to writers forced to leave their native country because a political system, either of the extreme Right or Left, denies them freedom of expression. Daniel Moyano clearly falls within this category. Forced to leave his native Argentina in 1976 because his ideology was considered subversive by the military regime, he has lived in exile in Spain since that time. Moyano's *Libro de navíos y borrascas*, his first novel entirely produced since his emigration, thus belongs fully to the traditional realm of literature of exile.

According to Spalek, such literature often takes the form of diary, autobiography, or autobiographical fiction. Neither diary nor autobiography, however, suits Moyano's purpose; for he avoids explicit chronicling of reality, like his narrator, Rolando in *Libro de navíos y borrascas*.

Rolando tries unsuccessfully to write a *diario de a bordo* and is disgusted by a puppet show about Lavalle and Dorrego: "La verdad, me parece de mal gusto ventilar estas cosas tan íntimas en alta mar. Me da vergüenza. [The truth is, I think it's in bad taste to air such intimate things openly (literally, on the high seas). It embarrasses me]" (124). Autobiographical fiction, however, affords the author a means of expression about the reality that surrounds him while removing him somewhat from the agony caused by his exile. Moyano's fifth novel, therefore, is both testimonial and imaginative fiction.

By stating that *Libro de navíos y borrascas* is not autobiographical, perhaps Moyano wishes only to insist on the fictional nature of his novel; for the parallels between the author and his narrator are so close that comparison is unavoidable.[2] Both are violinists forced to leave La Rioja, for reasons they do not understand, on a ship full of undesirables bound for Europe. Mention in the novel of other persecuted writers, such as Rodolfo Walsh and Haroldo Conti, compatriots with whom Moyano had close contact, further connects the novel to the author's own exile.

Moyano expresses a need to relate his experiences, in hopes that the horrors he has endured will not be repeated in the future. He repudiates Argentina's *Ley de Olvido* [Amnesty Law] and asserts: "No se puede, no se debe olvidar [One cannot, one should not forget]."[3] However, he chooses to reflect, rather than project, reality and stresses the imaginative properties of his writings. Therefore, in an effort to assuage the pain of exile, the pseudofictitious Rolando tells his readers to imagine sitting in an old fishing shack on a stormy European winter night: "Y tomando prestado el clima de los viejos relatos sobre fantasmas mi burda historia real puede ganar en fantasía y entrar decentemente en el mundo de la comprensión, contándola como al descuido y un poco para olvidarme de ella. [And taking on the atmosphere of old ghost stories, my true, ordinary account, is able to gain in fantasy and decently enter the world of comprehension, telling about it offhandedly so I can forget it a bit]" (10). The thoughts and feelings Rolando expresses, as he relates the story of his voyage to Spain, undoubtedly reveal Moyano's own *Weltanschauung*;[4] but because of the fictional makeup of the novel, references concerning the treatment of exile are, of course, to Rolando.

The title and format of *Libro de navíos y borrascas* imply a heterogeneous structure. The subject matter suggested by the title is reminiscent of the diaries and exaggerated autobiographical accounts from the Spanish American colonial period. The epithet, *libro de* [book of], brings to mind both the learned form of Spanish Medieval narrative lyric poetry and the Golden Age *libros de caballería* [books of knight errantry]. The narrator's name, Rolando, perhaps alludes to the French epic, *Chanson de Roland*; and the suggestion of a *chanson de geste* brings to mind the Spanish *Cantar de mío Cid*, one of the first works of Spanish literature to treat the theme of exile. With the symbolism of the sea and ship and storms, the voyage motif also recalls numerous literary masterpieces. The narrative, itself, combines the spontaneous, popular flavor of the early epics with subjectivity and lyricism. The novel, however, does not treat amorous, chivalric, or heroic adventures. Moreover, Rolando is not an epic hero, but an aspiring troubadour of his own experiences; and, of course, the novel is not written in verse, nor intended to be sung or recited. Rolando narrates the story of his exile with a dual purpose. He aspires to leave a legacy for future generations and, in so doing, to achieve metaphysical transcendence of his human condition.

Because Rolando avoids explicit descriptions of reality, he has great difficulty expressing certain aspects of his voyage. For example, he changes from first-person to third-person narration, naming his companion Bidoglio as narrator, in order to reveal his sexual fantasies without facing them as directly as first-person narration would require. The graphic chapter concerning the torture of the Uruguayan, Sandra, is prefaced in the following way: "Bueno, este capítulo puede resultar un tanto fuerte. [All right, this chapter may turn out to be a little bit rough]" (191). He prefers to eschew ostentation and soften reality. For this reason, he suggests that those who want more details consult Amnesty International.

In his alienation from the concrete details of his world, music serves Rolando better than words as a means of expression: "Lo mío es la música, antes que las palabras [I am more in my element with music than with words]" (11). His narrative even resembles a musical score in some ways. There are several movements, such as a puppet show (written as a script within the text), and a lyrical, balletlike episode between the ship and the way, symbolic of lost innocence.[5] The exiles also compose a story based on a popular song of the forties in order to help ease the pain of one of their comrades preoccupied with the disappearance of his son. Likewise, there are a number of recurring motifs, such as discussions about the possibility of return, the exiles' origins, the *desaparecidos* (those out of favor with the regime who have mysteriously disappeared), and Rolando's memories of schooldays and his grandfather's voyage from Europe to the New World. Rolando has difficulty concluding his story; therefore, he resorts to Beethoven-like modulations in order to avoid an abrupt ending. Here, the episodes related out of sequence have the effect of digression in the narrative. After the series of modulations, Rolando ends the novel in a diminuendo with the exiles' diaspora (1984, 153).

Some of Rolando's text, in fact, is written in musical notation to elucidate the verbal expression of his feelings. To illustrate, for example, the affinity of his voyage and his grandfather's, he employs the musical staff with an E sharp and an F natural as tied notes. They represent the same sound with a different annotation. Also, Rolando prefers an ineffable name for his imagined son to prevent his being called by name and taken from home. Therefore, he proposes a minor triad as a name because it is impossible for a single human voice to execute its sound. He then decides on certain sounds that most musical instruments are incapable of producing and a few can achieve only with great difficulty, such as a tetrachord composed of large intervals. In this way, music facilitates Rolando's expression of his account.

Rolando creates a polyphony of memories and current existence, as is characteristic of autobiographical accounts in literature of exile which "often dwell on the past, on childhood, on the origins of the writer" (Spalek 1983, 77). Rolando's feeling of severance is so strong that he compensates subconsciously by linking past events with the present: "Esos malditos recuerdos que uno tiene y que a veces lo estropean todo. Y la manía de vincularlos con sucesos actuales [Those damned memories that one has and that sometimes upset everything. And the crazy need to tie them to current events]" (242). Thus, Rolando repeatedly employs memories from his childhood or past to overcome the feeling of interruption produced by his exile. The topic of origin and identity is also frequently treated. Rolando's method of recalling the past to explain the present, his criticism of *porteños* [inhabitants of Buenos Aires] and of military figures, and his inclusion in the narrative of grievances expressed by other exiles aboard, all illustrate Spalek's assertion that the autobiographical accounts of exiles "represent a reassessment, justification, and often a confrontation with the culture and the period in which their authors originated" (Spalek 1983, 77).

One aspect of Rolando's exile which he continually evaluates is the feeling of severance. By comparing rupture from his homeland to an infant's weaning, he is able to understand better the essence of exile. Rolando knows that he is on his own and must find a way of coping with his exile. He later describes himself as: "argentino destetado que decide romper formalmente con la madre [a weaned Argentine who decides to formally break away from his mother]" (201).

Infancy and childhood, however, are not merely metaphors for Rolando but are accompanied by specific memories. His departure from Argentina brings to mind childhood lessons in geography and map coloring. He uses this motif numerous times to describe the vastness of the sea, the changing colors of the continent as his ship draws away from the mainland, and his fear of the unknown, which is compared to a return to childhood:

> El marrón para los bordes del continente, el celeste para la bandera idolatrada, y el azul oscuro para el mar. Entonces debemos estar muy cerca del borde marrón, donde no era necesario apretar tanto el lapíz. Y mucho cuidado con las entradas de las bahías sin olvidar puntas y cabos, tiene un cero Rodríguez, se ha tragado usted nada menos que la bahía de Samborombón. Atravesando, valijita en mano la línea marrón, o sea a un paso del azul intenso. Es que salir del país en estas condiciones, con dudoso volver, tan dudoso como fue el salir, es volver a la infancia.

> [Brown for the borders of the continent, sky-blue for the idolatrized flag, and dark blue for the sea. Now we must be very near the brown border, where it was no longer necessary to hold the pencil so tightly. And be very careful with the entrances to the bays, but don't forget the points and capes, Rodríguez has a zero, you have swallowed up the whole bay of Samborombon. Crossing, with the little suitcase in hand, the brown line, or rather one step away from the deep blue. It's just that leaving the country under these circumstances, uncertain about returning, as uncertain as leaving was, is a return to infancy] (22).

The exile is childlike in his vulnerability and innocence of the (new) world in which he is to live. The map-coloring motif serves Rolando to explain the permanent condition of his exile and to mock the notion that armies preserve freedom. Leaving Argentina is likened to having spilled ink on the map. Further recollection of his childhood education results in a minor de-mythification of Argentine culture:

> tan linda la imagen de Colón en primer plano y al fondo el convento de La Rábida cuando el almirante lo único que buscaba era salvar almas indias, tan bueno como todas las cosas buenas que nos enseñaba la maestra con patriótico entusiasmo a pesar de los seis meses de sueldo que le debían.

> [so pretty the image of Columbus in the foreground and in the background the convent of La Rabida when the only thing the admiral wanted was to save the souls of the Indians, so good like all the good things the teacher would teach us with patriotic enthusiasm despite the six months worth of salary they owed her.] (151)

Similarly Rolando's fear of the soldiers escorting him to the ship is linked to his childhood: "Largo el corredor no entre paredes, formado por soldados que parecían de plomo cada cual con su fusil, muy bien parados, no como los que teníamos en la caja de zapatos, a casi todos les faltaba una pata [A long corridor without walls, formed by soldiers that seemed to be made of lead, each with his rifle, not like the ones we used to keep in the shoebox, almost all of them lacked a foot] (19).

The history of Rolando's violin likewise provides him with a means of linking the past with his present condition as an exile. His Gryga once belonged to a Hungarian violinist exiled to South America. The memory that rats ate the strings of the Hungarian's violin reinforces Rolando's feeling of permanent severance. He compares the feeling he has when he boards the ship, accidentally dropping his suitcase in the water, with the reaction of the Hungarian's woman after the Hungarian departs early one morning, leaving her and his violin behind. All that is connected with the past is lost: "Hungría, dice la tonta, y no puede representarse nada, no hay significado, es una palabra que no le entra en la cabeza, es nada más que un sonido ronroneante que revolotea alechuzándose como el vuelo de las nuncas. [Hungary, says the silly woman, and it can't mean anything, it has no meaning, it's a word that won't enter her mind, it's nothing more than a purring sound that flutters like an owl's flight into nothing]" (39).

Rolando recalls having mailed letters for his grandfather that were addressed to relatives in Villanueva de la Serena and tries to find a link with the present by comparing the ship he is on with the vessel that carried his grandfather's letters to Spain. Similarly, he seeks a connection between past and present by imagining the ship that brought his grandfather to South America: "Un barquito que se pareciese más al de mi abuelo para poder vincularme a un tiempo verdadero [A little ship that might seem more like my grandfather's so that I could connect myself to a true time period]" (61).

Rolando often reassesses the unreality of his situation. He remembers waiting to see if his name appeared in the *Libro Negro* [Black Book] or on one of the *listas negras* [black lists] and criticizes the unjust methods government officials use in interrogations. He states that the interrogators often cause one wrongly to confess guilt. In this way the innocent enter a "fictitious reality." Rolando now is able to see that the only method of combatting this type of situation is to beat the interrogator at his own game:

> Uno se agarra la cabeza, acepta lo que todavía no sabe y cae en la realidad ficticia. Una regla práctica: antes de que el interrogador acabe de dar forma a su primera frase hay que sorprenderlo con las palabras nuestras, acoplándolas a las suyas y en su mismo tono, o sea en su misma irrealidad, como si fueran nuestras las palabras que él estaba por decir: *precisamente quería hablar con usted de eso*. Es un poco como estar ocupando su lugar, de igual a igual. Nos metemos de entrada en su irrealidad y las cosas así pueden salir un poco más equilibradas.
>
> [One grabs his head, accepts what he doesn't know yet, and fades into a fictitious reality. A practical rule: before the interrogator has a chance to finish his first sentence we have to surprise him with our words, connecting our words to his and in his same tone, or rather in his same unreality, as if the words he was about to say were ours: I was *wanting to talk to you about that very thing*. It's a little like occupying his place, as an equal. We enter his unreality first thing, and in this way things can turn out a little more balanced.] (47)

Other figures in Rolando's narrative harbor similar grievances (to which Rolando is sympathetic) and reveal reassessment of their exile and confrontation with their cultures as well. The cook on board the ship, who had been exiled from Spain during the Civil War forty years previously, expresses ill feelings toward a powerful and unjust government and condemns the state's deceitful measures for carrying out its plans. The cook resents the suffering he has endured because he dared to disagree with those in power; and, although he feels that the oppressed are the only ones who can ameliorate their situation, their liberty to do so has been taken from them. Comments about torture are also made by those on board and illustrate the exiles' reevaluation of their governments' dehumanizing treatment of those considered subversive. Bidolgio remarks, for example, that torture violates a person's innermost being. Sandra, an Uruguayan exile, compares the moral illness of her torturers to the god they worship: "un dios podrido y enfermo como ellos [a rotten, sick god like them]" (195). While Sandra wants to forget the repulsive events from her past by not discussing them, the exiled Jewish psychologists and psychiatrists on board refuse to suppress their feelings. Rolando agrees that the atrocities committed should not simply be forgotten. He is so repulsed when Sandra tells him about her torture that he wants to throw not only the mute for his violin overboard, but the instrument as well, and shout or cry instead of softening reality. He is ashamed of having evaded reality in order to alleviate his pain. Rolando also regrets not having taken action against the oppressors of his people: "Que hacía yo rascando el violincito en mi provincia pobre? Andar por la vida con sordina refugiados en la inocencia por no querer reconocernos idiotas. [What was I doing fiddling around in my poor province? Going through life with a mute, we found refuge in innocence by not recognizing that we were fools]" (193).

The *provincianos'* [inhabitants of the provinces] feelings of having endured unjust treatment by the *porteños* are vented in the puppet show the exiles perform. The play treats the events leading to the hanging of the Argentine campesino, Dorrego, at the hands of the corrupt official of the capital, Lavalle. The reenacted dispute between city and province questions which side constitutes civilization and which one barbarism. Although Rolando is uncomfortable watching the play because of the feelings it exposes, it is evident that he sympathizes with the *provincianos.* Again employing the past to explain the present, he affirms that the provincials' sufferings began because Dorrego was unable to combat the unrealistic world created by those of the capital.

One of the most frequently discussed topics among the exiles is that of *los desaparecidos.* Rolando likens the term to a shipwreck without survivors and later recalls the affinities between George Orwell's novel *1984* and the political situation in his country. Paredes, another of the exiles aboard, proposes a definition for *desaparecidos:* "Estrictamente, no están ni muertos ni vivos. Pero esto no significa que no tengan realidad. Están en otro plano. [Strictly speaking, they are neither dead nor alive. But this doesn't mean that they aren't real. They are on another plane]" (86). For Bidoglio, however, the term cannot be defined; therefore, it is not possible to help Contardi overcome his feelings about his lost son, Haroldo (Haroldo Conti?). Contardi's explanation for *los desaparecidos* is that they are dead; but because their death was unnatural, their souls cannot rest until the bodies are found. Therefore, he likens the situation to a vigil. El Gordito concludes that those who have disappeared are dead and infers that Contardi has lost his mind.

Rolando's narrative not only treats the subject of the physically displaced, but deals with psychological displacement as well. His already cited compulsion to find symmetry between the past and the present is symptomatic of his own lost sense of identity. Further, as Rolando is leaving Buenos Aires and has difficulty making out the facial features of those on shore, he realizes that those staying behind are also having difficulty distinguishing the exiles one from another: "Todos éramos óvalos borrosos. [We were all fuzzy ovals]" (32). They figuratively and literally lose their identities.

The insane young exile, el Masoca, expresses his loss of identity by pleading for a compass so that he will know where he is. Sandra states that she has no identity: "No sé, no soy nada, no soy una persona . . . [I don't know, I'm nothing, I'm not a person]" (286). Rolando relates a feeling of self-negation when he looks at the sea. In order to preserve some sense of identity, he is compelled to look at himself in the mirror: "Verme en un espejo para saber como era yo para ellos, y a la vez para reencontrarme, físicamente me estaba olvidando de mí mismo [To see myself in a mirror in order to find out what I looked like to them, and at the same time to rediscover myself, I was forgetting what I looked like]" (96–97). That Rolando does not recognize himself when he looks in the mirror confirms to him his severance from the person he once was. Feelings of *ninguneo* [nothingness] are also evident in Rolando's reference to those on board as unimportant trifles and "inocentes inútiles que nadie necesita ni en el Cono Sur ni en cualquier parte, porque el mundo se juega con una baraja diferente. [useless, innocent ones that no one needs, not in Argentina or anywhere else, because the world plays with a different deck of cards]" (182).

This sense of lost identity leads to the exiles' discussion about their origins. They deliberate on different theories on the origin of man which brings about further discussion on their origins as South Americans. Their drowned roots and lost past are underscored in the helmsman's postulate that their ancestors were from Atlantis: "Ustedes no tienen ni cara, ni habla, ni costumbres europeas. Tampoco son indios. Qué problemas tienen entonces para considerarse atlantes? Tienen la cara justa para eso, lo pensé en cuanto los vi subir al barco. [You don't have European faces, speech, or customs. You aren't Indians either. What problems do you have then considering yourselves Atlanteans? Your faces are just right for that, I thought that as soon as I saw you board the ship]" (144).

Like most exiles, Rolando seeks justification for his plight; but he finds an answer only in terms of fate. He mentions the ship's portholes (*ojos de buey*—literally, ox eyes), which links the ship to the symbol of the ox, signifying cosmic forces (Cirlot 1981, 247). The exiles' notion of being manipulated by forces beyond their control is evident as they approach the equator and note that the stars are changing. Bidoglio and el Gordito, for example, hope the change in their zodiacal sign will alter their fate. Rolando's attitude is not fatalistic, however, for he affirms that one must know how to play the hand one has been dealt: "Hay que saber darles su valor a las cartas. Dos de oros, de ojos de buey. [You have to know how to read the cards. Two of diamonds, two of ox eyes]" (28).

The ox, often connected in literature with the moon and darkness, may also be symbolic of sacrifice (Cirlot 1981, 248). The notion of the exiles as innocent, sacrificial victims is apparent throughout Rolando's narrative, and he speculates about the possibility of their sacrificed bodies being returned home in the future. He describes the Jewish exiles aboard as goats, and the helmsman of the ship seems to Rolando like a shepherd. El Enfermo is, likewise, described as a sacrificial victim: "Barbita crecida, ojos de animal entrando en el degolladero, no tendría ni veinticinco años. En esa actitud, la peor que hubiera podido elegir, gritó que era inocente. [His little beard grown out, eyes like an animal entering the slaughterhouse, he probably wasn't even twenty-five years old. In that attitude, the worst that he could have chosen, he cried out that he was innocent]" (45). In Rolando's exposition on the impossibility of declaring one's innocence, he makes an analogy between the exiles' innocence and sacrifice: "ya que la desesperación suele ligarse a la culpabilidad, como biblicamente se relaciona la inocencia con la degollación. [since desperation is usually linked to guilt, just as, biblically, innocence is related to beheading]" (46). The exiles' sacrifice does not signify a spiritual cleansing, however, for Rolando ironically remarks to himself: "y el destino final es el sacrificio, de aquí salimos limpitos y bien pelados como un pollo. En el inmenso gallinero o matadero, este tipo de fantasías te ayuda a sorportar mientras te llega el turno.[and the final destiny is sacrifice, from here we come out squeaky clean and well plucked like a chicken. In the great big chicken coop or slaughterhouse, this kind of fantasy helps you hold up while you wait your turn]" (198-99).

This sentiment of a forced rebirth is also evident in Rolando's portrayal of the ship as a second mother: "este barco que por ahora es nuestra segunda madre .... [This ship which for now is our second mother ...]" (152). The stairs of the ship are described as an umbilical cord: "escalera umbilical [umbilical stairs]" (41); and Rolando perceives the ship as giving birth when he and the other exiles arrive at the shores of Europe. Their rebirth, however, does not signify a desired change. Their exile is by no means voluntary. The Jewish exiles, referred to as Jewish gauchos, dispute Borges' statement that Jews have an innate will for exile: "los sacaron de sus casas y consultorios a punta de fusil. Se equivocaba Borges, se equivocaba. [They took them out of their homes and doctors' offices at gunpoint. Borges was wrong, he was wrong]" (176). Furthermore, Rolando fears unknown territory and is comfortable in the womb of the ship: "Y yo en mi nubarrón, tibio y protector como líquido fetal, con miedo de salir de allí [And I in my big black cloud, lukewarm and protective like amniotic fluid, afraid of going out of there]" (69). His delivery to Europe, therefore, is likened to a birth with forceps: "y aquí se trata de un nacimiento, una salida, con forceps pero salida al fin, parto inminente [and here we have a birth, an exit, with forceps but, nonetheless, an exit, an imminent delivery]" (153-54).

The question of return, which Spalek cites as a theme common especially among Spanish exiled writers, appears several times throughout Rolando's narrative. Like Moyano who states: "no hay regreso en los exilios [There are no returns with exile],"[6] Rolando senses a permanent severance from his homeland. His narrative includes various opinions about the possibility of return. For example, el Gordito explains the permanent condition of exile to him in terms of death, "se muere y se acabó [you die and that's that]" (36). Sandra, on the other hand, does not give up hoping that the sociopolitical situation will change and she can resume her life in Uruguay. For Contardi, the hope of return is a form of torture: "Es la tortura por la esperanza.... [It's torture by means of hope ...]" 57). Rolando also ruminates on the concept of returning:

> No volver más. Ademas de la tía Adelina está también Cleto, mi compadre, a él jamás le entraría en la cabeza lo de no volver. Al decirme que podaría mi viñita daba por sentado que la mantendría en buen estado hasta mi regreso, un par de años o algo así, a lo sumo cuatro o seis para ponerle un plazo largo. Absurdo pensar que un ofrecimiento así se hace para toda la vida. Se ofreció porque sabía que había un término, estaba claro que se refería a que la cuidaría hasta mi regreso. Y mi compadre es de esos hombres que raramente se equivocan. Pero suponiendo que fuera cierto lo de no volver, unos traerán de vuelta cuando haya pasado mucho tiempo? ... Y para que querrán, digo yo,

un montón de huesos blancos, por más necrofílicos que seamos? No vamos a volver ni de una forma ni de otra.

[To never go back. Besides Aunt Adelina there's Cleto, too, my buddy, it probably never entered his mind, the idea of my not coming back. When he told me that he would prune my little vineyard, he meant that he would maintain it in good condition until I got back, a couple of years or so, at most four or six if we stretch it. It's absurd to think that someone would make an offer like that for a lifetime. He offered because he knew there was a set time period, it was clear he meant he would take care of it until my return. And my buddy is one of those men who is rarely wrong. But supposing this business of not returning were true, will they bring us back after a long period of time has passed? And for what purpose, I say, could they possibly want a heap of white bones, regardless of how necrophilic we might be? We are never going to go back, not in this form or any other.] (40)

Rolando's mania for linking past and present causes him to inversely perceive his exile to Europe as a kind of return to his grandfather's European heritage. He laments that people forget the past and that history absurdly repeats itself: "aquí damos vueltas todos una y otra vez y siempre, nos contamos las mismas cosas al revés, borramos el crucigrama hecho para volver a hacerlo dentro de unos meses, cuando hayamos olvidado un poco las palabras [here we're all going around in circles over and over again, we tell the same things backwards, we erase the crossword puzzle we've done just to do it over again in a few months, when we've forgotten the words a little]" (179). The exiles' "return" to Europe is in fact senseless repetition.

This concept of repetition is further exemplified in Paredes' observation that the Spanish ship bound for South America, which they passed midway through their voyage, arrives at its destination at precisely the time they arrive in Europe. Also, el Gordito dryly compares their arrival to the arrival of Spanish Civil War exiles in South America: "Como en el 36 cuando llegaban allá los exiliados españoles y se juntaban veinte mil gallegos en el puerto para esperarlos y había amistad y laburo para todos. Igualito [As in '36 when the Spanish exiles arrived there and 20,000 Galicians gathered at the port to wait for them and there was friendship and work for all. Exactly the same]" (308). Rolando perceives exiles as flotsam being swept back and forth from one continent to another. For this reason, he feels that time is at a standstill.

This sense of a continuous present is another common feature of literature of exile. Spalek cites Alberti's poetry, for example, as expressing time "as an endlessly stagnating, hypertrophic present, as a life in parentheses, between the memories of the past and an uncertain future" (83). The result is a feeling of circular rather than forward motion. Rolando, in fact, describes his situation as one of oscillation: "ahí debí quedar oscilando, al fin y al cabo ésa es la verdadera situación. [There I had to keep oscillating, after all that's the true situation]" (71). He describes elapsed time as being in parentheses: "Entrar en el camarote, por fin, como volver a casa, a una casa, y ver que lo sucedido entre el dejar el violin bajo la parra y entrar en el camarote quedaba entre parentésis [Entering the berth, finally, like going back home, to a house, and seeing that what had happened between leaving the violin under the grapevine and entering the berth was in parentheses]" (103).

Rolando's narration of his exile affords him a means of transcendence. The plunge into the unconscious, symbolized by navigation on the sea, and severance from the mother, represented by his exile from Argentina, bring him to a negative kind of self-discovery. His odyssey affirms that he has no identity. The voyage of the exile goes nowhere—it is circular. There is, consequently, a common need among the exiles for metaphysical release from their misfortune. After the helmsman of the ship explains his belief in *maravillas* (wonders), Rolando understands Sandra's hope in a demigod as a kind of *maravilla*. Rolando, however, provides his own salvation through narration. Therefore, he has difficulty ending his tale:

> Desde que empecé a contar esta historia del barquito me he ido yendo de mi con las palabras. No soy el mismo que la empezó, las palabras me han ido transformando. De alla salió un Rolando contando Buenos Aires y es otro el que llega contando Barcelona. He venido en una deriva de palabras. Y no por duplicar las cosas o explicarme nada; mas bien para ser o seguir siendo navegándome, saltando de Rolando en Rolando. Y como navegué hacia el este, a lo mejor gane un Rolando no previsto que me servirá para ir tirando en el exilio. Aquí mas que la historia importan las palabras, esas olas que nos transportaron. Vamos a sobrevivir según tengamos esas olas.
>
> [Ever since I began telling this story about the little ship, I have been overflowing with words. I am not the same person that began it, the words have been changing me. From there, one Rolando left, telling about Buenos Aires, the one arriving in Barcelona is another. I have gone adrift with words. And not by duplicating things or for the sake of explaining anything to myself, but rather in order to be or to continue being by steering my course, jumping from Rolando to Rolando. And since I sailed toward the east, probably an unforseen Rolando will win out that will help me keep on pulling through in exile. Here, more important than the story are the words, those waves that transported us. We are going to survive in the measure with which we have those waves.] (294)

He will continue his story and, thereby, transcend his miserable condition. In fact, Rolando alludes to a second part of his story.[7] "Y entonces de ningún modo puedo poner la palabra *Fin* cuando en realidad las cosas empiezan a suceder en ese momento de la llegada a Madrid. [So there is no way I can write "The End" when in reality things begin to happen at that moment of arrival at Madrid]" (279).

Although he had at first felt that only music could provide his release from an unreal world, Rolando has discovered a similar outlet in narration.

Separated from his violin, which he was forced to leave behind in La Rioja, words are now his instrument which he leaves as a legacy. Rolando, thus, combats the unreality of exile with fiction: "Ficción contra ficción, algo parecido a acoplar palabras propias a las del interrogador, para descolocarlo y hablar de igual a igual. [Fiction against fiction, something like joining your own words to those of the interrogator, in order to displace him a little and speak as equals]" (61).

Notes

1. All translations from this text are my own.
2. In the interview, "Un caballo blanco anda por las escaleras," with Delgado Aparaín, Daniel Moyano states that a documentary on exiles, aired on the Spanish program "Vivir cada día," took *Libro de navíos y borrascas* as its source on his exile. He remarks: "Se trató de la peripecia del exilio, entroncada con Navíos y borrascas, ya que en el libro, por mas que no es autobiográfico, trato del exilio y sus motivos."
3. Personal communication from Daniel Moyano, January 20, 1988.
4. Moyano stated in personal communication, January 20, 1988: "No tengo ideología. Invento historias." While Moyano certainly does not entertain a given school of thought, his perspective of the world with respect to his situation in it is evident.
5. In his article, "Libro de navíos y borrascas," Eduardo Romano calls the episode between the bay and the ship an "especie de ballet."
6. Personal communication from Daniel Moyano, January 20, 1988.
7. In the previously cited interview with Delgado Aparain, Moyano states that there is a second part to *Libro de navíos y borrascas* entitled *Libro de caminos y de reinos:* "En el fondo, escribí Navíos y borrascas por error. Yo quería escribir otra cosa y me salió eso. Lo que deseaba en realidad, era escribir la segunda parte, la historia de un grupo de exiliados que se pasean por una calle de Madrid en una 'bañadera.'"

Works Cited

Cirlot, J. E. *A Dictionary of Symbols.* New York: Philosophical Library. 1981.
Delgado Aparaín, Mario. "Un caballo blanco anda por las escaleras." *Clarín* 29 (August 1985): 4–5.
Moyano, Daniel. *Libro de navíos y borrascas.* Buenos Aires: EditorialLegasa. 1983.
Romano, Eduardo. "Libro de navíos y borrascas." *Cuadernos hispanoamericanos* 406 (1984): 4–5.
Spalek, John M. "The Varieties of Exile Experience: German, Polish, and Spanish Writers." *Latin America and the Literature of Exile: A Comparative View of the 20th-Century European Refugee Writers in the New World,* ed. Hans-Bernhard Moeller, Reihe Siegen 47. Heidelberg: Carl Winter Universitätsverlag, 1983: 71–90.

 When the Gods Abandon Us: Dissolution in *The Hill of Devi, Pharos and Pharillon,* and *Alexandria*
Kathleen Collins Beyer

On January 1, 1912, E. M. Forster turned thirty-three. He was in a slump, writing little, sexually confused, tied to his home and widowed mother. When the opportunity arose to see India with his former Cambridge tutor, Goldsworthy Lowes Dickinson, Forster, hoping to unsnarl himself, decided to go. He sailed from Naples in October 1912 and began a trip that lasted until April 1913. The trip was full of rich experiences; among the most memorable was the warm welcome at the court of Tukoji Rao, the young Rajah of Dewas, a small princely state in central India near Ujjain. In 1921, Forster had once again come to an impasse with his writing and he was casting for a career. In February he received a wire from Dewas asking him to assume temporarily the position of Private Secretary to Tukoji Rao. Forster went and stayed from March to November of 1921.

Forster's published record of these two trips is contained primarily in *The Hill of Devi* (1953), a book with many threads. Indeed, because it contains writings from three periods of Forster's life—the letters of 1912–13 and of 1921 from India as well as the additional sections from the early 1950's when Forster was composing the book—the volume is an important key to persistent themes in Forster's canon. Strong affinities, for example, mark the central section of *The Hill of Devi* and Forster's Egyptian books, *Pharos and Pharillon* (1923) and *Alexandria* (1922), especially as these texts present one of Forster's overarching themes, the fragility of earthly kingdoms.

Assuming his post in Dewas in 1921, Forster found that things had changed "for good and for evil" (1953, 79). Tukoji Rao had been raised to the rank of Maharajah after eagerly assisting the Allies during World War I. What touched the ruler more profoundly was the failure of his marriage. In 1908 he had married a fourteen-year-old princess from Kolhapur and thus forged an important political link with a large and prestigious Marathan state. The young prince was elated. Forster records that letters from the new husband to Malcolm Darling, the Maharajah's former tutor, "breathe unqualified rapture: he has been never so happy: may he succeed in making his wife happy!" (1953, 72). He didn't. Troubles brewed in the zenana when one spiteful maid insisted to her mistress that the Maharajah had slept with a second maid. The Rani, who had hardly known Tukoji Rao when she married him, was not convinced by his arguments of innocence. The confused wife was inconsolable and from then on the marriage was precarious. The final crash came in 1916 when the Maharajah "sent his wife back to Kolhapur" (1953, 79).[1]

The Maharajah had always suffered from loneliness, and his tendency to gloom was exacerbated by his marital problems and compounded by the fact that he now found himself the enemy of Kolhapur, the powerful state he had earlier wooed. The Maharajah "needed some friend who stood outside the court and its intrigues" (1953, 80), and so he asked Malcolm Darling to return to Dewas as his Private Secretary. Darling declined but recommended Colonel Wilson, an administrator well-versed in Indian languages. Wilson took the post, but in 1921 had to return to England on sick leave (1953, 80–81).

Thus, India again opened a door for Forster. In 1916 the Maharajah had asked Forster if he would consider being his Private Secretary, but Forster refused because he was working for the Red Cross in Egypt (1978, 2:27). By 1921, Forster was home, but he was working without success or direction. He had gone as far in 1920 as writing the Maharajah to inquire into the possibility of a court appointment. In February 1921 he was holidaying with Lowes Dickinson when Dewas wired asking him temporarily to assume Wilson's job. Forster cabled his acceptance the same day (1978, 2:64–67). He packed, among other things, two pillows, four pillow cases, two pairs of sheets, two blankets, and four towels, and on March 4 sailed aboard the *S. S. Morea*.[2]

Once he settled down in Dewas, the schedule was easy-going, the pace leisurely. His work hours were 8 to 10 or 11 a.m.[3] Nonetheless, Forster was a working member of a Native State, and he was getting a rare, intimate glimpse into a bizarre political set-up. In the central section of *The Hill of Devi*—"The State and Its Ruler" and "Letters of 1921"—

Forster lays heavy stress on the fantastical qualities of his new home. There were, for example, actually two states of Dewas, the Junior Branch and the Senior Branch. Each ruler had "his own palace and court and army and national anthem" (1953, 56). Until the 1940s when their territories were reshuffled (1963, 289), the area they controlled was divided "not by towns or sections, but by fields and streets: In Dewas City, S.B. would own one side of a street and J.B. the other." Forster was amused by the oddity: "The arrangement must have been unique, and an authoritative English lady, who knew India inside out, once told me that it did not and could not exist, and left me with the feeling that I had never been there" (1953, 55–56).

When Forster wrote home in 1921 that he would "never be at an end of the queernesses" (1953, 163), this political hodgepodge was just one of the peculiarities which he had in mind. Another which boggled Forster was the comparative extravagance of courtly life. In 1907 Malcolm Darling had been shown the Crown Jewels, an event Forster recreates in *The Hill of Devi:*

> Watched by a committee of six nobles, he inspected trays of necklets, bracelets, nose rings, anklets, all of gold, also rubies and uncut diamonds, and there were ropes and ropes of pearls: for instance ten ropes each four feet long, knotted at the ends with gold: there was a string of watery emeralds as large as marbles: there was a sword studded with diamonds, and a dagger set with rubies: there were the silver trappings for the elephants—three men were needed to lift one: there were gold caparisons for the horses, and trenchers and flagons of gold. Total estimated value: £60,000. (1953, 214)

Darling's own account in his memoirs, *Apprentice to Power*, adds that at Lord Curzon's Delhi Durbar, one long strand of pearls "got caught in the Rajah's diamond-studded sword and broke. After the Durbar, pearls were shaken out of his dress, but a number were lost, for the Durbar was hardly the moment to hunt them" (143). Noblesse oblige.

When Forster assumed his post as interim Private Secretary, "scarcely any" (1953, 214) of these state jewels remained. The aura of wealth lingered, but the finances of Dewas were seriously strained because of poor management and expensive living, and the ambiance was one of decline and disintegration.

Forster, in his official role, was responsible for monitoring many of Dewas's finances, and he was repeatedly irked by what he considered exorbitant waste. Approximately one thousand pounds were spent to celebrate the birth of a daughter to Bai Saheba, the Maharajah's "Diamond Concubine." If the baby had been a son, Forster ruefully complained, the cost could have risen to two thousand pounds (1953, 118). The expense involved in Gokul Ashtami, a religious festival, also alarmed him. Roughly thirty pounds were spent on new clothes, a bed, and mosquito curtains for a six-inch statue of Krishna. Over one hundred pounds were spent on installing electric lights. To pay for all of this, there was talk of closing the one state high school.[4] When the Maharajah of Gwalior paid a visit, Forster worried about the "expenditure both of money and exertion. All real work gets postponed to these regal tomfooleries—red carpets, special dining rooms, dancing girls from Bombay."[5] There was "so much muddling and such genuine emptiness of the State Coffers" that it was even difficult to scrape together Forster's own salary:

> I have just had my salary for April—that too not through the Finance, but from the Superintendent of Police who playfully poured it (300 silver rupees) into my topi. I am to pay it back to him if or when the Finance pays it to me.[6]

Descriptions of what Forster considered financial recklessness thread their way through the 1921 section of *The Hill of Devi* and are reinforced there and elsewhere by descriptions of physical ruin: "The New Palace . . . is still building, and the parts of it that were built ten years ago are already falling down. You would weep at the destruction, expense, and hideousness, and I do almost" (1953, 86). Darling once claimed that the peculiarities of Dewas rivaled those of Wonderland (1953, 56), and certainly Forster paints the inside of the Palace as a set for the Mad Hatter's tea party. Forster describes

> two pianos (one a grand), a harmonium, and a dulciphone, all new and all unplayable, their notes sticking and their frames cracked by the dryness. I look into a room—dozens of warped towel-horses are stabled there, or a new suite of drawing-room chairs with their insides gushing out. I open a cupboard near the bath and find it full of teapots . . . . (1953, 87)

Forster wrote to Lowes Dickinson and complained, " . . . I swim in the Ocean of Milk itself, where every one becomes anything or nothing. It is impossible to get one thing done, and I feel in despair." Continuing this letter, Forster brooded: "Tea looms. The palace has been empty of attendants for hours—can't even get a commode emptied . . . and a large rodent, thought to be a civet-cat, gnaws the canvas ceiling in my verandah."[7]

From Forster's perspective, life in Dewas in 1921 was "queer beyond description" (1953, 86). Examples of confusion and chaos abound in the central section of *The Hill of Devi,* and they are tinged sometimes with black humor: Forster helped decorate for a religious festival and later fretfully recalled the glass battery cases which he had

> filled with water and live fish and into which some humanitarian idiot dropped handfuls of flour so that the fish should not starve. You couldn't have seen a whale. Oh, such an emptying and slopping to get it right, and two of the fish died through

overeating, and had to be buried in a flowerpot in case H.H. [His Highness] should see them. (1953, 165–66)

Wails of frustration punctuate this section of *The Hill of Devi*: "Little is clear-cut in India" (1953, 58); " . . . I live in a haze" (1953, 93); "To check the idleness, incompetence and extravagance is quite beyond me" (1953, 99); "I could never describe the muddle in this place. It is wheel within wheel" (1953, 115).

When we first read the outlandish accounts of his 1921 stay, we may feel that Forster was using comedy to convey his deeper sense that the Westerner cannot fully fathom the East. The spirit of India seemed, indeed, so elusory, that even in India Forster was stymied when he tried to add to his early chapters of *A Passage to India:* "they seemed to wilt and go dead and I could do nothing with them" (1953, 238). But more than comedy or confusion haunts the central section of *The Hill of Devi*. There is also Forster's sense of disintegration and collapse. In 1913 Forster had come away from his first Indian trip convinced that muddledom ruled. During his 1921 stay that feeling was accentuated by his first-hand involvement with the day-to-day workings of Dewas. In particular, it seemed clear that the state was careening towards disaster because of the dangerously haphazard approach to money. Dewas was still a rare and "wonderful" place to be, but part of its allure was that it was "the fag end" of an era (1953, 106). In 1953, when he wrote the Preface to *The Hill of Devi*, Forster made that point in the thumbnail sketch of his book: it was to be a "record of a vanished civilisation. Some," he admitted, "will rejoice that it has vanished." His own sentiments are barely veiled: "Others will feel that something precious has been thrown away amongst the rubbish—something which might have been saved" (1953, 8). The central section of the book is underscored by a sad note of transience. Things did not connect in Dewas. In November 1921, Forster left, convinced that "H.H. will certainly reign for the rest of his life in a ruin . . ." (1953, 209).

The disarray in Dewas was a reality that cannot be questioned. But one cannot help wondering whether Forster's emphasis on this disorder would have been so emphatic if it did not mirror, if only in microcosm, his interest in the breakdown of civilizations which had been so much a part of his life in Egypt. As John Colmer has said, Forster found in Dewas "an objective correlative to his own consciousness of belonging to the end of another great civilization, 'to the fag-end of Victorian liberalism'" (152). Forster, it would seem, had his theme even before he arrived in Dewas. His work as a Red Cross volunteer in Alexandria involved listening to and recording wartime experiences of wounded soldiers. Professionally, Forster was spending his time documenting what he felt was the unravelling of his own civilization. Privately, his own writings turned to the same theme—things fall apart. While in Egypt, he became intrigued with the history of Alexandria itself, and he dealt with it in two books, *Pharos and Pharillon* (1923) and *Alexandria* (1922). In the latter, subtitled *A History and a Guide*, Forster inevitably found himself charting the decline of an impressive city and culture, and when he left for India in 1921 he carried with him the weight of his war experiences and his long thoughts about the passing of whole worlds.[8]

It is clear that while in Egypt Forster felt himself to be under the mantle of the East and that the temptation to draw comparisons with India was irresistible. Most often, Egypt paled: "To one who has been in India, it is almost irritating—the 'real East' seems always vanishing round the corner, fluttering the hem of a garment or the phantom of a smell."[9] To his mother he conceded that "the wonderful sunsets" in Egypt surpassed any he had seen in India, but his brief sketch of Alexandria was hardly inviting.

> One can't dislike Alex (to give it its slang abbreviation) because it is impossible to dislike either the sea or stone. But it consists of nothing else, as far as I can gather: just a clean cosmopolitan town by some blue water—no coast line, not even sand. The whole has an artificial and uninspiring effect.—And Egypt (as seen from hours of train)—a feebler India, as flat but without the sense of immensity.[10]

In 1919, after he was home in England, Forster sorted out his comparison of Egypt and India in an article for *The Athenaeum*. The piece is curious, for while the details are Egyptian, the essence is lyric praise of India.

> There are a hundred Indias, but only two or three Egypts. Now and then one has the illusion that Egypt also is multiform and infinite, and that the Nile, like the Ganges, flows from the hair of God through men into Hell. At evening perhaps; in the Delta: when the animals, suddenly sacred, walk in short processions through the purple air—a donkey, two sheep, a buffalo; a goat, a buffalo, three sheep; the owner following. Or perhaps at mid-day, in the desert; when the little flat stones jump and quiver, and pieces of sky slop into the sand. Or under the arcades of some huge mosque at Cairo or Rosetta; worshippers are kneeling on pale yellow rushes in a pale grey light. Then the imagination and the theories that attend upon it awake, and one says: "This is the East," or "This is Romance," or "Here, too, is an entrance into life and all that lives." The illusion soon passes. The valley of the Nile may be long, but it is narrow, very narrow. Day after day one meets in it the same faces and fields and thought, and the towns that are strung about it are of the Nile's substance, not jewels out of unattainable treasuries. ("Two Egypts" 393)

Whenever Forster was in India, its reality evaded him. This passage is a striking summary of what India remembered meant to Forster—the "multiform and infinite," "Romance," "an entrance into life and all that lives."

In general, Egypt was an impoverished East to Forster. But if Egypt in the present failed to impress, there was the Egypt of the past alluringly at hand. Forster, who claimed Gibbon as a favorite author, had long been interested in history. In 1900 he had passed the Classics Tripos, Part I, at Cambridge, and in 1901 the Historical Tripos, Part II. In 1906 he wrote the Introduction and Notes to E. Fairfax Taylor's translation of *The Aeneid*, and he was a fan of guide books, "particularly the earlier Baedeckers and Murrays" (1922, xv). Antiquities roused him. Indeed, in Dewas one of his few hushed moments came when he looked at the old royal tombs. In the Old Palace in the heart of the city

> was the dynastic shrine, and above it lay the Durbar Hall with the sacred bed by which a lamp always burned. Here too was the ancient armoury. The place had the quality known as "numinous": it carried one away from the bleak light into another of the Indias.... (1953, 75)

When Forster was in Alexandria, the past tugged at him, too: "visions kept coming as" he "went about in trams or on foot or bathed in the delicious sea" (1922, xvi). Assuredly, one could not turn with much joy to present history in Alexandria. It is true that in his personal life Forster found unique fulfillment and pleasure there. He socialized; became friendly with the poet C. P. Cavafy (1975, 143); and had his first intimate sexual relationship. But over it all hung the gloom of war, and that meant for Forster consistent despair.

From the beginning, World War I had depressed him. It was not only the war itself which alarmed him, but the herd-instinct it fostered (1978, 2:1). He despised the thought of "young men killing one another while old men praised them" (1978, 2:18). Yet, while at home in England, his conscience smarted for contributing so little to the war effort, and he felt he should give up his job as part-time cataloguer at the National Gallery and help directly. He considered joining an ambulance unit in Italy but then decided to sign up with the Red Cross in Egypt where supplies for the Dardanelles campaign were based and where a quarter million troops were stationed to protect the Suez Canal. Thus it was that Forster arrived in Alexandria late in 1915, ready to begin work as a "hospital searcher" who would interview wounded soldiers in hopes of gleaning information about those reported missing (1978, 2:19–21).

Forster eventually stayed until January 1919 and was deeply troubled by the war. On December 5, 1915, after just two weeks of working in the hospital, he jotted down for himself "Incidents of War" which the wounded had confided to him.

> Scraps. The earth is full of dead—their arms and legs sticking out. When a mine is exploded they are so mixed that when the digging recommences one has often to cut through corpses. They lie between the trenches after a charge and the smell of them is

awful when there's a hot sun and a bit of wind. Sometimes a shot hits them, increasing the stench—they get blown all over the place. Two men, while sheltering from Turkish shells, came across a packet of them in a gully, and preferred the shells. Another man, suffering from jaundice, had helped to bury many and cannot get the smell out of his nose.[11]

Writing to those at home, he spoke with thoughtful conviction. He told Dickinson that war "entails an inward death. It has taken the place of all the old healthy growths—love, joy, thought, despair—deluding men by its semblance of vitality . . . and tempting them not to mind . . . what ought to be minded down to such depths as one has of soul."[12] Premonitions of other wars dogged him. In 1916 he wrote Dickinson, "'We must fight again as soon as we are strong enough' is all I expect the war to teach Europe."[13] In November 1918, after the fighting stopped, Forster voiced to his mother his fear "that no one has learnt anything and that any moment another war might start."[14] His own philosophy was bleak; what hopes he had reflected his Bloomsbury years:

> Nothing that any of us wants and strives for will have the least effect on the course of events. I have read History too carefully to believe it. It's like ants tugging and pushing at a piece of food: the piece moves, but not in the direction than any ant wished. All I can do now is to learn, and to help the individual.[15]

Alexandria offered some escape from this mushrooming horror. Forster began to feel "the magic and the antiquity and the complexity of the city, and determined to write about her" (1922, xv). He did this in two ways. He frequently submitted essays to *The Egyptian Mail*, which mainly catered to English-speaking foreigners. He collected six of these essays along with eight others dealing with Alexandria into a small volume, *Pharos and Pharillon*, and explained his title: "Pharos, the vast and heroic lighthouse that dominated the first city—under Pharos I have grouped a few antique events; to modern events and to personal impressions I have given the name of Pharillon, the obscure successor of Pharos . . ." (1923, 12). He also began writing *Alexandria, A History and a Guide*, which was, as Rose Macauley claimed, "full of scholarship, spirit, poetry, humour, and prejudices" (137). That text surveyed Alexandria from the Graeco-Egyptian period to the modern and provided a guide to specific points of interest in the city and nearby.

In reading *Pharos and Pharillon* and *Alexandria*, we are struck by Forster's historical expertise, but what we finally remember are not facts and figures. Forster aims primarily to convince us that ancient Alexandria was "a city of the soul," and he relies as much on rhetoric as on research. Throughout both books it is clear that he is keen to make "vanished glory" reappear (1923, 89), and striking descriptions are myriad. But one description, found in both books and written with marked enthusiasm, is the description of the lighthouse on Pharos Island. In *Alexandria*, the details are presented more matter-of-factly, but even there Forster reminds us that in its time the lighthouse was "the wonder of the world" (1922, 145) and boldly claims "that the antique world never surpassed it . . . " (1922, 146). Centuries later, its powers were still felt: "It beaconed to the imagination, not only to ships at sea, and long after its light was extinguished memories of it glowed in the minds of men" (1922, 145).

Clearly, the lighthouse fired Forster's imagination. He not only gave its name to the historical section of *Pharos and Pharillon*, in that book he also used the full weight of his prose to capture its impressive grandeur. Designed by Sostratus and dedicated circa 279 B.C. during the reign of Ptolemy Philadelphus, it was a massive, four-story building topped at the height of 400–500 feet by a statue of Poseidon. Later Arab stories (1922, 147) told of even more fantastic statues, one "whose finger followed the diurnal course of the sun," and one "who gave out with varying and melodious voices the hours of the day . . . " (1923, 21).

These artistic toys, however, were not the real marvel. What so excites curiosity is the

> mysterious "mirror" . . . even more wonderful than the building itself. Why didn't this mirror crack, and what was it? A polished steel reflector for the fire at night or for heliography by day? Some writers describe it as made of finely wrought glass or transparent stone, and declare that when they sat under it they could see ships at sea that were invisible to the naked eye. A telescope? (1923, 20)

Forster prefers to leave history a haze on this last point. It is the visionary mystique of the building which he stresses:

> it is not clear whether a divine madness also seized the builders, whether they deliberately winged engineering with poetry, and tried to add a wonder to the world. At all events they succeeded, and the arts combined with science to praise their triumph. Just as the Parthenon had been identified with Athens, and St. Peter's was to be identified with Rome, so, to the imaginations of contemporaries, "The Pharos" became Alexandria and Alexandria the Pharos. Never, in the history of architecture, has a secular building been thus worshipped and taken on a spiritual life of its own. (1923, 18–19)

Over the centuries, the mirror fell and broke, and earthquakes toppled the lower stories. Forster mourns the passing: "its stones have vanished and its spirit also" (1923, 24).

Vanished glory. This elegiac motif keynotes Forster's Egyptian books because in writing about Alexandria's past and present, he inevitably charted declining grandeur. Concluding *Pharos and Pharillon*, he anticipated the tone of *Alexandria*:

> A serious history of Alexandria has yet to be written, and perhaps the foregoing sketches may have indicated how varied, how impressive, such a history might be. After the fashion of a pageant it might marshall the activities of two thousand two hundred and fifty years. But unlike a pageant it would have to conclude dully. Alas! The modern city calls for no enthusiastic comment. (1923, "Conclusion")

He picked up his threads and tied his knot in *Alexandria*:

> Her future like that of other great commercial cities is dubious. . . . The Library is starved for want of funds, the Art Gallery cannot be alluded to . . . . [N]either the Pharos of Sostratus nor the Idylls of Theocritus nor the Enneads of Plotinus are likely to be rivalled in the future. (1922, 103)

The lighthouse at Pharos represented for Forster the essence of antique Alexandria—its intellectual, scientific, and architectural self-confidence. Its collapse is clearly a reminder to him of how much a plaything of history man's world could be: like ants, we do little more than push and pull. World War I taught that lesson every day, Alexandria's past confirmed it, and the unsettled state of affairs that Forster found in Dewas only made him wary again. Forster never talked about the three—the war, the history of Alexandria, or the disarray in Dewas—in the same breath, but it is certain that dissolution was the theme at the nexus of his writings about them and that his view of history was well set by the time he sailed for India in 1921. Two words near the end of *Pharos and Pharillon* told his story: "Everything passes . . ." (1923, "Conclusion"). If *The Hill of Devi* had to be summarized, that too would be its theme. Indeed, Forster's realization that he was witnessing "the fag end of a vanished civilisation" (1953, 106) in Dewas would not have been so marked if he had not already felt the same sadness as he gazed at the ruins of Alexandria and if he had not already felt the fragility of earthly kingdoms. In both the Egyptian and Indian writings from this period, 1915–1921, Forster's message is clear. Time is relentless; just as it overwhelmed the Pharos, so too it will overwhelm the Maharajah.

Over the years, the confusions in Dewas spiralled out of control. An uneasy relationship between the Maharajah and his son, the Yuvraj, had caused scandalous notoriety. Even worse, financial carelessness, four years of agricultural decline, and an international depression left Dewas bankrupt (1953, 255; 1963, 277). In 1933, the Government of India ordered a commission of inquiry. The Maharajah, as Forster takes great pains to point out, was brutally humiliated by the turn of events but was too noble to concede to the British; using illness as an opportunity, he went into self-imposed exile in Pondicherry, French territory. Forster plays the account of the monarch's desperate and determined stand for all its dramatic worth in "Catastrophe," the climactic, closing section of *The Hill of Devi*. However foolish the Maharajah seems for his refusal to return to Dewas and sort out the state's crisis under the stern gaze of the British, he is finally a figure of heroic spirit. His self-definition leaves him adamant: "I am a Rajput and I should be false to all my traditions if I compromised my honour" (1953, 261).

Tukoji Rao's role in his own fate recalls a poem by C. P. Cavafy which Forster greatly admired, "The God Abandons Antony." Forster had included it in both *Pharos and Pharillon* and *Alexandria*, never guessing, of course, that it might someday be applicable to that young Rajah he had first met in Dewas in 1912. The poem is set at midnight when Hercules, signaling his desertion of Antony, departs Alexandria in the midst of the music and voices of an unseen choir (1922, 29). Antony, now about to lose the city, is admonished in the poem to assume his destiny with calm dignity. He is told not to pretend that his life's dreams have not been wrecked, not to cower, not even to lament. Twice he is exhorted to behave "like a brave man," and, finally, he is urged to walk decisively to the window. There he is to listen to the choir and, confronting both his deep emotions and his fate, he is to "bid farewell" (1923, 55).

Cavafy's poem, with its stately cadences, is shot-through with the doctrine of tragic acceptance. Its tone offers an adumbration of Forster's assessment and depiction of Tukoji Rao's last days and suggests again the haunting thematic links between Forster's Egyptian and Indian writings. When history threatens and the gods abandon us, we can only look to ourselves.

Notes

1. Accounts of the failure of the marriage vary. See 1963, 272.
2. E. M. Forster, Letter to J. R. Ackerly, October 24, 1923, E. M. Forster Collection, Harry Ransom Humanities Research Center, The University of Texas at Austin.
3. E. M. Forster, Letter to J. R. Ackerly, March 12, 1924, E. M. Forster Collection, Harry Ransom Humanities Research Center, The University of Texas at Austin.
4. E. M. Forster, Letter to Goldsworthy Lowes Dickinson, August 6, 1921, E. M. Forster Collection, King's College Library, King's College, Cambridge, England. Also see Lago 2:10.
5. E. M. Forster, Letter to Florence Barger, May 20, 1921, E. M. Forster Collection, King's College Library, King's College, Cambridge, England. Also see Lago 2:9.
6. E. M. Forster, Letter to Alice Clara Forster, May 17, 1921, E. M. Forster Collection, King's College Library, King's College, Cambridge, England.
7. E. M. Forster, Letter to Goldsworthy Lowes Dickinson, April 14, 1921, E. M. Forster Collection, King's College Library, King's College, Cambridge, England. Also see *Lago* 2:3–5.
8. Since even the writing of Forster's Egyptian and Indian materials overlapped to some extent, it is not surprising that they often seem all of a piece. Forster was correcting proofs of Alexandria while in Dewas (1978, 74), and he only completed the book while on a stopover in Egypt on his return to England from India (Pinchin 1977, 107).
9. E. M. Forster, Letter to Florence Barger, April 28, 1916, E. M. Forster Collection, King's College Library, King's College, Cambridge, England.

10. E. M. Forster, Letter to Alice Clara Forster, November 21, 1915, E. M. Forster Collection, King's College Library, King's College, Cambridge, England.

11. E. M. Forster, "Incidents of War," from an untitled manuscript which includes accounts of the war by soldiers Forster visited in hospitals in Egypt, November 1915 to July 1917, E. M. Forster Collection, King's College Library, King's College, Cambridge, England.

12. E. M. Forster, Letter to Goldsworthy Lowes Dickinson, October 9, 1916, E. M. Forster Collection, King's College Library, King's College, Cambridge, England.

13. E. M. Forster, Letter to Goldsworthy Lowes Dickinson, April 5, 1916, E. M. Forster Collection, King's College Library, King's College, Cambridge, England.

14. E. M. Forster, Letter to Alice Clara Forster, November 14, 1918, E. M. Forster Collection, King's College Library, King's College, Cambridge, England.

15. E. M. Forster, Letter to Alice Clara Forster, February 2, 1918, E. M. Forster Collection, King's College Library, King's College, Cambridge, England.

Works Cited

Thanks to The Provost and Scholars of King's College, Cambridge, England, for permission to include the E. M. Forster materials, for which they hold the copyright. Thanks also to Doubleday for specific permission to quote from *Alexandria* and to the Harry Ransom Humanities Research Center, The University of Texas at Austin, for the use of Forster letters in their collection.

E. M. Forster Collection. King's College Library, King's College, Cambridge, England. Copyright © The Provost and Scholars of King's College, Cambridge.

E. M. Forster Collection. Harry Ransom Humanities Research Center, The University of Texas at Austin. Copyright © The Provost and Scholars of King's College, Cambridge.

Colmer, John. *E. M. Forster: The Personal Voice*. London and Boston: Routledge and Kegan Paul, 1975.

Darling, Malcolm. *Apprentice to Power: India, 1904–1908*. London: Hogarth Press, 1966.

Forster, E. M. *Alexandria: A History and a Guide*. [1922.] Gloucester, Mass.: Peter Smith, 1968.

———. *The Hill of Devi*. New York: Harcourt, 1953.

———. *Pharos and Pharillon*. [1923.] London: Hogarth, 1972.

———. "Two Egypts." Review of *Recollections and Reflections* by Coles Pasha, and *Through Egypt in War-Time* by Martin S. Briggs. *The Athenaeum*, 30 May 1919, 393–4. Signed E. M. F.

Furbank, P. N. *E. M. Forster, A life: Volume One, The Growth of the Novelist (1879–1914)*. London: Secker and Warburg, 1977; *Volume Two, Polycrates' Ring (1914–1970)*. London: Secker and Warburg, 1978.

Lago, Mary and P. N. Furbank. *Selected Letters of E. M. Forster, Volume One, 1879–1920*. Cambridge: Belknap Press of Harvard, 1983. *Volume Two, 1921–1970*. Cambridge: Belknap Press of Harvard, 1985.

Macauley, Rose. *The Writings of E. M. Forster*. [1938.] London: Hogarth, 1972.

Malgonkar, Manohar. *The Puars of Dewas Senior*. Bombay: Orient Longmans, 1963.

Pinchin, Jane Lagoudis. *Alexandria Still: Forster, Durrell, and Cavafy*. Princeton: Princeton University Press, 1977.

# Parricide and Exile: Tracing Derrida in Augusto Roa Bastos' *Yo el Supremo*
John Incledon

> *Written discourse [is] born out of a primary gap and a primary expatriation, condemning it to wandering and blindness, to mourning.*
>
> Derrida, *Of Grammatology*

I

The theme of exile is as old as Western literature and Western mythology itself. The story of Oedipus, besides treating the topics of parricide and incest, is framed by the question of exile: Oedipus is banished by his family at birth because of the warning by the oracle; and, upon learning of his unintentional crimes, he goes into a self-imposed exile from Thebes. In the following discussion, I shall attempt to show, first, how the linguistic theory of Jacques Derrida is related to this thematics of exile and, second, how the Paraguayan writer, Augusto Roa Bastos, appropriates this theme, as filtered through the work of Derrida, in his discussion of power and politics in Latin America in *Yo el Supremo* [*I the Supreme*].

The topics of exile and the Jewish diaspora are treated directly by Derrida in his essay, "Edmond Jabès and the Question of the Book." The theme also appears indirectly in his discussion of marginality and marginalization in "Living On Border Lines," an essay which contains a marginalized or exiled text in the form of a footnote running the entire length of the essay. However, the question of exile is central to Derrida's critique of the sign, the starting point of his philosophical project.

Western thought according to Jacques Derrida has always manifested itself in the form of binary oppositions: good *versus* evil, mind *versus* matter, nature *versus* culture, and so on. The relationship between the two terms in these philosophical oppositions, he says, is never neutral; one term always dominates the other. Moreover, by putting these oppositions side by side, a pattern can be found. Barbara Johnson, in the Introduction to her translation of *Dissemination*, describes it as follows:

> In general, what these hierarchical oppositions do is to privilege . . . *presentness* over distance. . . . In its search for the answer to the question of Being, Western philosophy has indeed always determined Being as *presence*. (*Dissemination*, 1981 viii)

If *presence* is valorized over *absence*, the reason is that *presence* is immediately at hand, is manageable and controllable. In short, the hierarchical categorization of Western thought into these philosophical oppositions is first and foremost an exercise of power, a political act—the valorization of one term and the banishment or exiling of the other.

Derrida's critique of Western thought focuses on language and on one philosophical opposition in particular: the privileging of the spoken word over the written word. In modern linguistics as described by Ferdinand de Saussure speech is valorized because of its proximity to meaning, its *presence*. "From this point of view," says Derrida, "the voice is consciousness itself. When I speak, . . . I am conscious . . . of keeping as close as possible to my thought. . . . The exteriority of the signifier seems reduced" (*Positions* 1981, 22). Speech, the ever-faithful son, stays close to its source, the thought which fathered it. Writing, on the other hand, being the representation of speech, is at two removes from meaning. It is the signifier of a signifier, and as such must be orphaned, banished, exiled. "Written discourse," says Derrida, "[is] born out of a primary gap and a primary *expatriation*, condemning it to wandering and blindness, to mourning" (1976, 39). Writing does not know its source, its father, and harbors an underlying animosity toward him. Derrida himself compares writing to the figure of Oedipus (*Dissemination* 1981, 131). "From the position of the holder of the scepter," he says, "the desire of writing is . . . denounced as a desire for orphanhood and patricidal subversion. . . . The father is always suspicious and watchful toward writing. . . . Writing is parricidal" (*Dissemination* 1981, 77, 76, 164).

Derrida "deconstructs" the concept of the sign in the linguistic system of Saussure, showing that the phonic signifier (speech) suffers the very same distance and exteriority from meaning (the signified) as the graphic signifier (writing). By pointing out the contradictions in Saussure's system, he destabilizes its very foundation. Exile—distance from meaning, from the center—is a condition of *all* signifiers, he argues. It is a profoundly unsettling and subversive notion. Augusto Roa

Bastos, himself living in exile since 1947, draws on the problematics of the exiled signifier as described by Derrida and uses it in his masterful discussion of power and politics in *Yo el Supremo*.

II

Notwithstanding the large amount of criticism that has been written on *Yo el Supremo* since its appearance in 1974,[1] Augusto Roa Bastos is arguably his own best critic. In an important essay, "Algunos núcleos generadores de un texto narrativo" ["Some Nuclei Which Have Generated a Narrative Text"] Roa Bastos provides a critical orientation for the reading of the novel:

> La lectura de un texto es ya una tarea difícil y compleja. . . . Todo texto nos reenvía al origen arcaico de la escritura, a esa *huella* o *trazo* que se reabsorbió y esfumó sin desaparecer en la transcripción e inscripción fonética y alfabética. Y nos reenvía al mismo tiempo a uno de los tres grandes debates que dominan nuestra modernidad: . . . el de Saussure y Derrida; es decir . . . oralidad/gramatología. (167)
>
> [Reading a text is at once a difficult and complex task. . . . Every text sends us back to the archaic origin of writing, of that *imprint* or *trace* which was reabsorbed and faded without disappearing in the alphabetic and phonetic transcription. At the same time it sends us back to one of the three great debates which dominate our modernity: . . . the one between Saussure and Derrida; that is to say . . . between orality and grammatology.]

After ten years of exile and creative silence, Roa Bastos' contact with the explosion on the French critical scene in the mid- and late-60s, especially with the work of Jacques Derrida, provided a key impetus for the resumption of his literary work. Derrida's critique of the sign and his examination of the opposition of speech and writing in Western discourse, gave Roa Bastos the starting point from which he could mold and remold material which had lain idle within his psyche for many years.

In "Algunos núcleos generadores de un texto narrativo," Roa Bastos states unequivocally: "No se debe olvidar que *Yo el Supremo* es un texto bifronte o bivalente que se pretende surgido al mismo tiempo de la oposición cultura/naturaleza, tradición escrita/tradición oral" (179) ["It should not be forgotten that *I the Supreme* is a bifrontal or bivalent text which develops out of the nature/culture opposition as well as from the opposition between oral tradition and written tradition"]. From the opening words of the novel, from the very title itself, the problematics of speech versus writing and their relationship to meaning are set into motion: "Yo el Supremo Dictador de la Repub[ca] ordeno que al acaecer mi muerte mi cadaver sea decapitado; la cabeza puesta en una pica por tres días en la Plaza de la Rebública . . . Al termino del dicho plazo, mando que mis restos sean quemados y las cenizas arrojadas al río . . ." (1974, 7) ["I, the Supreme Dictator of the Republic, order that on the occasion of my death my corpse be decapitated; my head placed on a pike for three days in the Plaza de la República. . . . At the end of the aforementioned period, I order that my remains be burned and my ashes thrown into the river . . ."] (1986, 3). These are the words found on a sign nailed to the door of the cathedral. Who has written them? Who is responsible for this treason? The problem is that the words are written, distanced from their source. Unlike the spoken word, that faithful son which stays close to its father, the meaning it dutifully represents, writing, on the other hand, is subversive and parricidal. The pasquinade orders the defilement of the remains of a dictator in the final days of his reign. Its author, that disloyal citizen/son, must be sought out and punished. "Empéñate . . . en cazar al pérfido escriba" ["Start looking for the perfidious scribbler"], El Supremo orders his personal secretary, Patino. "Darle su ración de carucho" (20–21) ["Give him his full ration of bullets"] (15–16). Just as the novel opens with this problem, so too does it end with it. "¿Qué pasa con la investigación del pasquín catedralicio?" (425) ["How is the investigation of the cathedral pasquinade going?"] (396), asks El Supremo in the final pages. The problem is one of writing. "Si alguien debe quejarse de las letras," says El Supremo, "ése soy yo, puesto que en todo tiempo y en todo lugar sirvieron para perseguirme" (445) ["If anyone has a grievance against the written word, I am that person, since everywhere and always it has served to persecute me"] (414). Writing, the unfaithful, illegitimate, parricidal son must be sought out and destroyed, for government, says El Supremo, "no devora a sus verdaderos hijos. Destruye a sus bastardos" (340) ["does not devour its true children. It destroys its bastards"] (340).

El Supremo relies on speech, his voice as the seat of his power: "El Supremo Dictador habla siempre a los demas. Dirige su voz delante demás sí para ser oído, escuchado, obedecido" (24) ["The Supreme Dictator continually talks to others. He projects his voice before himself so as to be heard, listened to, obeyed"] (18). He is a dictator/dictater. "Escribir," on the other hand, "es depegar la palabra de uno mismo" (67) ["To write is to disconnect the power of words from oneself"] (59). Nonetheless, El Supremo finds it necessary to preserve a written record of everything he says, even to take up writing himself in his personal notebook. "Al principio," he says, "no escribía; únicamente dictaba. Después olvidaba lo que había dictado. Ahora debo dictar/escribir; anotarlo en alguna parte" (53) ["In the beginning, I did not write; I only dictated. Then I forgot what I had dictated. Now I must dictate/write; note it down somewhere"] (45). El Supremo, in Nixon-like fashion, has every utterance he makes recorded by his "fide-indigno" ["trust-unworthy"] scribe, Patiño. Needless to say, trouble follows.

"¡No, que no y no!" screams El Supremo. "No es eso de ninguna manera lo que dije. Has trabucado como siempre lo que dicto" (41) ["No, no, no! That isn't what I said at all. As usual, you've mixed up what I dictated" (35)]; and "¡Ah imbécil y malvado Patiño! Todo lo trabucas y confundes.... Lo de la querida fue agregado por ti, mulato irreverente, vocinglero canalla" (359) ["Patiño, you confounded imbecile! You muddle and mix up everything.... That part about the turtledove was added by you, you irreverent mulatto, you vulgar prattler"] (332). The real problem is one of meaning, the distance of the signifier from the signified. "Cuando te dicto," El Supremo says to Patiño, "las palabras tienen un sentido; otro, cuando las escribes" (65) ["When I dictate to you the words have (one) meaning; when you write, another"] (57). To which Patiño replies, by way of excuse: "Mientras escribo lo que me dicta no puedo agarrar el sentido de las palabras. Ocupado en formar con cuidado las letras de la manera más uniforme y clara posible, se me escapa lo que dicen. En cuanto quiero entender lo que escucho me sale torcido el renglón. Se me traspapelan las palabras, las frases. Escribo a reculones" (41) ["As I write what you dictate to me I don't grasp the meaning of the words. Occupied as I am in carefully forming the letters in the clearest and most uniform manner possible, what they say escapes me. Whenever I try to understand what I'm listening to, the lines come out all crooked. I misplace the words, the sentences. I write backwards"] (35). Again, writing, the graphic signifier, is at two removes from the signified, having lost its relationship to meaning, as Patiño admits. "Ya es bien triste," says El Supremo, "que nos veamos reducidos a envasar en palabras, notas, documentos, contra-documentos, nuestros acuerdos-desacuerdos. Encerrar hechos de naturaleza en signos de contranatura. Los papeles pueden ser rotos. Leídos con segundas, hasta con terceras y cuartas intenciones. Millones de sentidos" (227–28) ["It is quite sad enough to see ourselves reduced to bottling up our accords in words, notes, documents, counterdocuments.... Papers can be torn up. Can be read between the lines, and even between the lines between the lines. Millions of meanings"] (210). Rather than being under control, the meaning of writing is slippery; it disappears in a garden of forking paths. This is precisely the danger of the written word—its treachery, its subversive quality, its distance from definitive meaning, from the "transcendental signified."

El Supremo tries to remedy the problem by giving Patiño a writing lesson. (Roa Bastos, by the way, refers to this section of the novel as "the writing lesson,"[2] alluding to the opening of Part II of Derrida's *Of Grammatology*, which is an extended commentary on "The Writing Lesson," a chapter in Claude Lévi-Strauss' *Tristes Tropiques*.) "Escucha. Atiende," says El Supremo, "Te enseñaré el difícil arte de la ciencia escriptural" (66) ["Listen. Pay attention. I am going to teach you the difficult art of scriptuary science"] (58). The Dictator tries his best to get Patiño back on track: "Lo que te pido, mi estimado Panzancho, es que cuando te dicto no trates de artificializar la naturaleza de los asuntos. . . . Escribes lo que te dicto como si tu mismo hablaras por mi en secreto al papel. Quiero que en las palabras que escribes haya algo que me pertenezca. . . . No emplees palabras impropias que no se mezclan con mi humor, que no se impreganan de mi pensamiento" (65, 64) ["What I beg of you, my dear Sancho Pauncho, is that you not try, when I dictate to you, to artificialize the nature of the matter being dealt with but [that] . . . You write what I dictate to you as though you yourself were speaking in secret on the paper. I want there to be something of myself in the words you write. . . . Don't use improper words that are not in my style, that are not steeped in my thought"] (57,56). But all this is to no avail. At the end of the lesson, El Supremo catches Patiño doodling: "acabas de escribir soñoliento YO EL SUPREMO" (67) ["You have just drowsily written: I THE SUPREME"] (59). His own closest servant is now unconsciously mimicking the treacherous pasquinade. Or is he, perhaps, its author?

The lack of control implicit in writing is threatening. El Supremo has created a system of order and government. "Si se ha de formar un centro de unidad," he says, "ese centro no puede ser otro que el Paraguay" (235) ["If a center of unity is to be formed, that center can be none other than Paraguay"] (208); and "El Paraguay será invencible mientras se mantenga cerrado compactamente" (397) ["Paraguay will be invincible as long as it remains hermetically sealed"] (368). Like the Chinese emperor described by Borges in "La muralla y los libros," ["The Wall and the Books"], El Supremo creates a wall around Paraguay, referred to in the novel as "La muralla china" ["The Great Wall"]. He is the only one allowed access to books and to writing paper within the Republic. When the pasquinade appears on the cathedral, El Supremo casts a suspicious glance towards Patiño, wondering how it is that paper from his own royal treasury has been obtained on which to write the heretical message. In his obsession for absolute power, he will tolerate no deviance from the system. "Yo disculpo ciertos errores," he says, but "No tolero a aquellos que atentan contra el intocable, el inatacable sistema en que están asentados el orden de la sociedad, la tranquilidad pública, la seguridad del Gobierno" (180–81) ["I pardon error, but I do not tolerate those who seek to undermine . . . the inviolable system on which the order of society, public peace, the security of the Government are firmly founded"] (166–67). In every way possible, he seeks to shore up and maintain his absolute power, going even so far as to invent the "pluma recuerdo" ["memory-pen"].

Something like the light pens used to read computerized bar codes, the memory-pen optically "reads" and records the objects over which it passes, the objects it "writes." Like the aleph in the story of the same name by Borges, like Morel's holographic camera in Bioy-Casares' *La invención de Morel* [*The Invention of Morel*], or like José Arcadio Buendía's spinning dictionary in *Cien años de soledad* [*One Hundred Years of Solitude*], the memory-pen is an attempt to capture, control and dominate reality. "El Supremo," Roa Bastos tells us in "Algunos núcleos generadores...," "busca empecinadamente un lenguaje fónico, visual: un lenguaje cuyos signos son los objetos mismos que designa, y no solamente su representación gráfica.... De estos delirios surgieron sin duda los objetos miticos como la 'pluma recuerdo'" (183) ["El Supremo stubbornly searches for a visual, phonic language, a language whose signs are the designated objects themselves and not just their graphic representation.... Surely mythic objects like the 'memory pen' were the result of this delirium"]. The memory-pen is a failed dream, a symbol of the failure of El Supremo's totalizing vision. The memory-pen, as it is described in the passage, is now broken and does not function—if, indeed, it ever did. Its nub is scratched and blurred. Light no longer passes evenly through it, and it is unable to read/write reality as originally intended.

An equally striking symbol of El Supremo's desire for total control is the meteor he has chained to his desk. "Cuando al comienzo de la Dictadura Perpetua vi caer el aerolito a cien leguas de Asunción, lo mandé cautivar. Nadie comprendió entonces, nadie comprenderá jamás el sentido de esta captura del bolido migrante.... La fuerza del poder consiste entonces, pensé, en cazar el azar.... Está ahí. Meteoro-azar engrillado, amarrado a mi silla.... Sólo que después de este meteoro no pude cazar ningun otro" (109, 107, 111, 113) ["When at the beginning of the Perpetual Dictatorship I saw the aerolite fall a hundred leagues from Asunción, I ordered that it be taken captive. Nobody understood then, nobody will ever understand the meaning of this capture of the migrant meteor.... The force of power lies then, I thought, in chasing down chance.... It is here. Chance-meteor in chains, bound to my chair.... The only hitch is that after this meteor I was never able to hunt down another one"] (98, 96, 99, 101). Francia's obsessive desire to realize his vision of Paraguay forces him to go to greater and greater lengths to consolidate and centralize his power. Says Roa Bastos, "Me interesó el mito del Poder Absoluto que el Doctor Francia encarnó paradigmáticamente. Me impulso a excavar en su envoltura metafísica" ("Algunos núcleos...", 192) ["I was interested in the myth of Absolute Power, and Dr. Francia was its paradigm. It forced me to dig deeper into his metaphysical casing"].

Total control is indeed the mark of his government. The relationship between El Supremo and his subjects, like that between the signified (meaning) and the phonic signifier (speech), is that of a father and his sons. "Como Gobernante Supremo también soy vuestro padre natural" (38) ["As Supreme Governor I am also your natural father"] (32), he declares. Roa Bastos speaks at some length on the relationship between Francia and the populace in "Algunos núcleos generadores...": "La figura histórica del doctor José Gaspar Rodríguez de Francia... era... y lo sigue siendo, una presencia importante, la más importante y capital—debería agregar, puesto que encarna la figura del padre en el seno de la sociedad paraguaya.... Gaspar de Francia es el Padre-Ultimo-Primero" (170) ["The historical figure of Dr. Jose Gaspar Rodriguez de Francia... was... and continues to be an important presence—one of capital importance, I should add, given the fact that he embodies the figure of the father in the soul of Paraguayan society.... Gaspar de Francia is the First-and-Last Father"]. The problem is that all of his sons are not loyal. "En treinta años," El Supremo says in the novel, "mis venales Sanchos Panzas me han dado más guerra que todos los enemigos juntos de adentro y de afuera.... A racha de hacha voy a talar este bosque de plantas parásitas.... Voy a empezar por el falsario que tengo más a mano; mi amanuense y fiel de fechos que anda tejiendo sus maquinaciones e intrigas para alzarse en cuanto pueda con el gobierno provisorio de fatuos" (367–68) ["In thirty years my venal Sancho Panzas have caused me more trouble than all my enemies within and without put together.... I shall hack with my ax and cut down this jungle of parasitic plants.... I'm going to begin with the double-dealer closest at hand: my amanuensis and confidential clerk, who's been weaving his plots and intrigues so as to throw his lot in with the provisory fatuous government and stage a rebellion as soon as he can"] (340–41). Patiño's swollen feet (1974, 436–37; 1986, 407), as Roberto González Echevarría has pointed out, mark him as an Oedipal figure (*The Voice of the Masters,* 78). (Oedipus, in Greek, means "swollen foot.") El Supremo dictates Patiño's own death sentence to him, though he (Patiño) manages to survive Francia's reign, only to hang himself in a jail cell some years later.

Thus, the relationship between El Supremo and his subjects—especially with his closest subject, his personal secretary, his scribe, Patiño—plays out in very real human as well as socio-political terms the same problem which is played out in Western metaphysics from Plato to the present: the problem of maintaining at all cost the close tie, the intimate relationship between the signifer and the signified, the problem of distinguishing those signifiers which are indeed faithful to meaning (the vocal signifiers) from those treacherous signifiers which are not (the written). "No es necesario notar," Roa Bastos says in "Algunos núcleos generadores...," "que toda la novela... es un libelo implacable contra la escritura como grafía de la 'palabra cadavérica'" (183) ["It's hardly necessary to point out that the entire novel... is an implacable libel against writing as the graphic representation of 'the dead letter'"]. As in the case of Derrida, it is not a question of restoring writing to its rightful position, but of subverting the system which would denigrate it to a lesser position because of its lack of presence. Roa Bastos shows how the whole problematics of the denigration of writing is not just a linguistic problem, but is pertinent to deeply-rooted socio-political problems endemic to Latin American culture and politics.

III

Patiño is not the only "son" who is trying to overthrow El Supremo in the novel. In a manner reminiscent of Cervantes' explanation of how he came into possession of the manuscript of the *Quijote*, the segment on the memory-pen relates how it passed into the hands of Patiño, then to Patiño's great-great-great grandson, Raimundo "Loco-Solo" (an obvious reference to Raymond Roussel, author of *Locus Solus* and other works which presage much in the modern novel, including *Yo el Supremo*) and finally to the "compiler" of the novel, that is, its author, Augusto Roa Bastos. The notion of the author as "compiler" highlights the intertextual nature of the novel and calls into question the idea of an author as source or origin. But unlike Cervantes, who used this narrative strategy to decenter and throw into question the idea of authorship in a very different way (that is, by positing a "lying Moorish historian," Cide Hamete Benengeli, as author, and himself as "second author" or editor of the novel), it is important for Roa Bastos' purposes that he clearly establish himself as author/compiler of the text, for his relationship to Francia is deeply personal and dates back to childhood:

> Mi vida de niño, como la de la mayoría de los niños del Paraguay, sufrió en carne viva esta influencia en un hogar donde la memoria de José Gaspar de Francia, el maldito e infernal *Karai-Guasú* (gran-jefe-o-señor, en guaraní) había sustituido con ventaja al cuco.... A la menor falta... el índice severo de mi padre me fulminaba implacable: '¡Ahí lo tienen al futuro tirano! ¡Cachorro del Karai Guasú!'.... acabé identificando en mi miedo al superyoico padre carnal con el supremo padre de la colectividad sin pasado y sin futuro. De este modo, Gaspar de Francia pasó de los albores de mi vida a los primero esbozos de mi literatura. El antecedente más antiguo que puedo recordar es un cuento... escrito a los trece años, que inaugura precisamente mi narrativa y que permanece inédito hasta hoy. (171)

[My life as a child, like that of most children in Paraguay, suffered this influence in the flesh in a home where the memory of José Gaspar de Francia, that damned and infernal Karai-Guasú (great-chief-or-lord, in Guaraní) had in fact taken the place of . . . the bogeyman. At the slightest misdeed . . . my father would shake his index finger at me wrathfully: 'Look at him, the future tyrant! Offspring of the Karai Guasú!' . . . . in the midst of my fear I wound up identifying my own flesh and blood father with that collective father without a past and without a future. It was in this way that Gaspar de Francia passed from the dawn of my own life to the initial pages of my literary work. The first piece I can remember is a story . . . written at the age of thirteen, which in fact inaugurates my narrative and which remains unpublished even today.]

Roa Bastos published the story, entitled "Lucha hasta el alba," ["Fight until Dawn"], in 1977. In yet another Cervantine gesture, he explains in a note preceding the story that he rediscovered it as he was beginning to "compile" *Yo el Supremo*. He found it, he says, between the pages of a copy of Leonardo's *Treatise on Painting*, a book "que me enseñó a ver el sentido del mundo como un vasto jeroglífico en movimiento pero cuyos signos son tal vez indescifrables" (1979, 3) ["which taught me to see the meaning of the world as a vast set of hieroglyphics in motion, whose signs are perhaps indecipherable"]. Speaking about the relationship of the story and the novel, Roa Bastos explains, "El cuento primerizo, inédito y olvidado durante más de cuarenta años . . . podría ser considerado tal vez como el más lejano antecedente generador o suscitador de la novel *Yo el Supremo*" (1977, 173) ["This first attempt at a story, unpublished and forgotten for more than forty years . . . might be considered the most distant source of the novel, *I the Supreme*"]. The story deals with a child's dream and the theme of parricide. Like the biblical Jacob, the boy dreams of a struggle from dusk until dawn with a monster whose face first resembles that of Francia and then his father's: "Ha 'visto' al dios oscuro," says Roa, "ha contemplado como en una pesadilla al dioscuro, al demiurgo de los paraguayos. Ha dado muerte al Padre Ultimo-Primero, al Primer Padre" (1977, 171) ["He has 'seen' the dark god. As if in a nightmare, he has contemplated the demiurge of the Paraguayan people. He has killed the First-Last Father, the First Father"]. The boy awakens at dawn knowing he has killed the paternal monster. Roa Bastos says that on the back of one of the manuscript pages of the story he found the following sentences: "El Supremo es el Hombre-Dueño-del-susto. Papá dice que es un hombre que nunca duerme. Escribe día y noche y nos quiere al revés. Dice también que es una Gran Pared alrededor del mundo que nadie puede atravesar. Mamá dice que es una araña peluda siempre tejiendo su tela en la Casa del Gobierno. Nadie escapa de ella" (1977, 173) ["El Supremo is the Man-Who-Owns-Fear. Father says he is a man who never sleeps. He writes day and night, and his feelings for us are the opposite of love. He also says that he is a Great Wall around the world from which no one can escape. Mother says he is a hairy spider who spends his time weaving a web in the House of Government. No one can escape from it"]. The exact same words, purportedly confiscated from a schoolchild during Francia's reign, appear in *Yo el Supremo*. The author/compiler of the novel thus establishes a clear connection between "Lucha hasta el alba" and *Yo el Supremo*. Says Roa Bastos, "Cuarenta años después, estos pensamientos pasaron después, casi intactos a la novela. Pero en aquel entonces sentí de igual manera que jamás podrá escribir la historia del Dictador Perpetuo del Paraguay, salvo que volviera a cometer un parricidio mítico" (1977, 173) ["Forty years later, these thoughts passed nearly intact into the novel. But at that time I also felt that I could never write the history of the Perpetual Dictator of Paraguay except by committing a kind of mythical parricide]." *Yo el Supremo* is indeed Roa Bastos' attempt to "finish off," to kill once and for all that mythic father who had been haunting him for a lifetime and his countrymen for generations, to exorcise the ghost of El Supremo: "Para usurpar al Supremo el narrador-compilador ha debido suprimirlo, dandole muerte novelesca" (191) ["In order to usurp the position of El Supremo, the narrator-compiler has had to suppress him, give him a novelistic death"]. Roa Bastos describes the process by which he "kills" the dictator, usurping his power:

> Es necesario que El Supremo esté muerto para que el narrador-compilador pueda hablar de sí mismo como si hablara de El Supremo, invirtiendo los papeles y los signos. . . . Imagino que el proceso de sustitución y usurpación de los roles o funciones centrales debío de producirse de la siguiente manera. . . . [El] compilador-narrador se convierte en El Supremo novelesco y convierte en el amanuense Patiño a su doble exterior. Desde adentro, El Supremo Usurpador le dicta lo que debe escribir, lo que debe hacer, lo que debe compilar, lo que debe callar, lo que debe mentir. El único desquite que le queda al compilador exterior es delizar de tanto en tanto su mano intrusa entre los papeles del Compilador-Supremo para enrostrarle su traición, sus mentiras, su negatividad. (191)

> [It is necessary that El Supremo die in order for the narrator-compiler to talk about himself as if he were El Supremo, inverting the roles and the signs. . . . I imagine the process of substituting and usurping the central roles or functions must have taken place in the following manner. . . . (The) compiler-narrator is transformed into the novelistic El Supremo and makes the amanuensis Patiño into his external double. From inside, the Usurper El Supremo dictates to him what is to be written, what is to be done, what is to be compiled, what is to be hushed up, what is to be lied about. The only compensation which remains for the external compiler is to here and there insert his intrusive hand into the papers of the Supreme Compiler in order to confront him with his treason, his lies, his negativity.]

The takeover occurs slowly at first: the pasquinade on the cathedral door, little messages written in the margins of El Supremo's personal notebook. But gradually Roa Bastos paints a portrait of the private man that is far different than the persona he displays in public. We learn that writing is a constant occupation for him, not just a memory-aid to preserve his pronouncements. Rather than a man who wants to wipe out chance, we find him avidly playing dice and cards. In his quiet moments, safe behind closed doors and in complete privacy, El Supremo shows us that he is well aware of "the supplement at the source," as Derrida calls it. He knows full well that there is no endpoint, no definitive meaning (signified) to which the signifier leads. Instead, he finds one more signifier in a long chain. Says Roa Bastos, "Convertir al Supremo Dictador, en la novela, en sujeto y objeto al mismo tiempo del discurso narrativo. Esta propuesta me atrajo . . . por las posibilidades . . . de paleografiar la escritura henchida de signos" (1977, 192–93)["Converting the Supreme Dictator in the novel at once into the subject and the object of narrative discourse. That was the proposition that attracted me . . . because of the possibilities . . . for 'paleographing' a writing filled with signs"]. As "compiler" of the novel, Roa Bastos attempts to put to rest the myth of Absolute Power created by Dr. Francia, a myth which he says is still alive today in the collective unconscious of the Paraguayan people. He tries to "kill" El Supremo by deconstructing the philosophical opposition on which his system and source of power is based, the same philosophical opposition that can be found running through Western thought since Plato: the logocentrism implicit in the opposition of speech *versus* writing.

IV

Though I have focussed my discussion on this one question, central though it is in Derrida's philosophy, there are other important allusions to Derrida in *Yo el Supremo*, most notably to the discussion of the pharmakon and memory in the essay, "Plato's Pharmacy," in *Dissemination*. Roa Bastos draws heavily on the philosophy of Derrida. This can be seen explicitly in "Algunos núcleos generadores sobre un texto narrativo," in which he clearly points the way to a Derridean reading of *Yo el Supremo*; and it can be seen implicitly in the novel itself.

In his portrait of the final days of Dr. Francia, Roa Bastos has brought to life some of the most pressing philosophical issues of our time by showing their relevance to cultural, historical and political issues which are pertinent to Paraguay and Latin America in general. The problem of absolute power, of authoritarianism in government, is one which has plagued Latin America since colonial days. Claudio Véliz calls it "the centralist tradition," Richard Morse "the neo-Thomist patrimonial state." Sociologists and political scientists have been studying the phenomenon for decades, and longer.[3] Today, as in the past, Latin America is struggling to find a way out of its tradition of authoritarianism in government. Unlike other "dictator novels" or works of political literature, which simply decry existing conditions, *Yo el Supremo* is a more subtle and powerful attempt to undo the source of that absolute power.

Notes

1. See, for example, the following collections of articles: Margarita Balansa de Ocampos (ed.), *Comentario sobre* Yo el Supremo (Asunción: Ediciones Club del Libro núm. 1, 1975); S*eminario sobre* Yo el Supremo *de Augusto Roa Bastos* (Poitiers: Publications du Centre de Recherches Latino-Americaines de l'Université de Poitiers, 1976); *Textos sobre el texto (2⁰ seminario sobre* Yo el Supremo *de Augusto Roa Bastos)* (Poitiers: Publications de Centre de Recherches Latino-Americaines de Universita de Poitiers, 1980); various articles in Jacques Leenhardt (ed.), *Litterature latino-americaine d'aujourd'hui: Colloque de Cerisy* (Paris: Union Generale d'Eds., 1980); and Saúl Sosnowski (Compilador), *Augusto Roa Bastos y la producción cultural americana* (Buenos Aires: Ediciones de la Flor, 1986). Fine individual studies on the novel are available by Jean Andreu, Rubén Bareiro Saguier, Gerald Martin, Jacques Leenhardt, Alain Sicard and Sharon Ugalde, among others. Also important is Francisco Tovar, *Las historias del dictador:* Yo el Supremo, *de Augusto Roa Bastos* (Barcelona: Edicions del Mall, 1987).

2. See (1977, 177), translations of which are mine. This passage from *Yo el Supremo* is anthologized in Augusto Roa Bastos, *Antología personal* (Mexico, D.F.: Editorial Nueva Imagen, 1980) under the title, "Lección de escritura."

3. See Claudio Véliz, T*he Centralist Tradition of Latin America* (Princeton: Princeton University Press, 1980) and Richard Morse, "The Heritage of Latin America," in Louis Hartz (ed.), *The Founding of New Societies* (New York: Harcourt, Brace & World, 1964).

Works Cited

Derrida, Jacques. *Dissemination.* Chicago: University of Chicago Press, 1981.
———. "Edmond Jabès and the Question of the Book." In *Writing and Difference.* Chicago: University of Chicago Press, 1978.
———. "Living On Border Lines." *Deconstruction and Criticism.* New York: Seabury Press, 1979.
———. *Of Grammatology.* Baltimore: Johns Hopkins University Press, 1976.
———. *Positions.* Chicago: University of Chicago Press, 1981.
González Echevarría, Roberto. *The Voice of the Masters.* Austin: The University of Texas Press, 1985.
Roa Bastos, Augusto. "Algunos núcleos generadores sobre un texto narrativo." *Escritura* 4 (1977): 167–93.
———. *Antología Personal.* Mexico, D.F.: Editorial Nueva Imagen, 1980.
———. *I the Supreme.* Tr. by Helen R. Lane. New York: Alfred Knopf, 1986.
———. "Lucha hasta el alba." *Texto Crítico* 12 (1979): 3–9.
———. "Writing: A Metaphor of Exile." *On Modern Latin American Fiction.* Edited by John King. New York: Farrar, Straus and Giroux, 1987.
———. *Yo el Supremo.* Mexico, D.F.: Siglo XXI, 1974.

Notes on the Authors

HELEN M. BUSS, a native of Canada, earned the Ph.D. at the University of Manitoba where her dissertation topic was "Canadian Women's Autobiography." She has published on Canadian Literature and on women's autobiography in the United States and Canada, including "Canadian Women's Autobiography: Some Critical Directions," in *A Mazing Space*, "Frameworks for the Literary Study of Women's Personal Narratives in Archival Collections," in *English Studies in Canada*, and "Canadian Feminist Autobiographers," forthcoming in *Biography*. She is the author of *Mother and Daughter Relationships in the Manawaka Works of Margaret Laurence*. At present she is a Canada Research Fellow at the University of Calgary, doing research on women's autobiographical documents in archival collections.

FRANK DIETZ received his Ph.D. in American Literature from the University of Wurzburg/Germany. He was co-editor of the German Science-Fiction magazine *Cosmonaut* and has also co-edited a science-fiction anthology, *Die Kinder Utopias* (Munich). He published *Kritische Traume: Ambivalenz in der Amerikanischen Literarishen Utopie nach 1945* (Meitingen), a study of contemporary American utopian fiction. He has published articles on Robert Silverberg, Robert Graves, utopian science fiction, allohistorical fiction, and the image of medicine in utopian literature in various journals. He is currently teaching at Austin Community College in Austin, Texas.

SHOSHANAH DIETZ received her B.A. in Russian and M.A in German at the University of Texas at Austin and is now a doctoral student in Comparative Literature. Her specialities include early twentieth-century German and Russian literature, literature and ideology, modernism, and Jewish Studies. She has published reviews and articles in *Jewish Folklore* and *Ethnology Review, TTR,* and is working on a translation of Max Brod's literary memoirs *Der Prager Kreis*. She was assistant editor of *Slavic Review* in 1987–88, and studied at Leningrad State University in the summer of 1989. She is currently an instructor in the Department of Germanic Languages at the University of Texas as Austin.

JEFFERSON FAYE is a native of Michigan who earned the M.A. at Northwestern University. Currently he is a Ph.D. candidate at the University of Cincinnati, where he specializes in Postmodern American literature. He has read his fiction at the Ann Arbor Chapter of The Baker Street Irregulars and at the Grier School in Tyrone, Pennsylvania. He has read papers at Ohio Wesleyan University, Miami University, Iowa University, and Youngstown State University.

LINDA HOLLABAUGH is Assistant Professor of Spanish at Midwestern State University and has taught Spanish and French at the high school, junior college, and university levels. She earned the Ph.D. in Spanish from Texas Tech University. Her current research involves Argentine writers who were exiled as a result of the military repression of the 1970s.

JOHN INCLEDON is Associate Professor of Spanish at Albright College in Reading, Pennsylvania. He earned the B.A. at Colgate University and the Ph.D. at State University of New York at Binghamton. He has published articles on such writers as Gabriel Garcia Marquez, Julio Cortazar, Alejo Carpentier and Salvador Elizondo in journals such as *Revista Iberoamericana* and collections such as *Critical Perspectives on Gabriel Garciá Marquez* (Nebraska). He has also published a number of translations and done subtitling of foreign films. He has been awarded four NEH grants and a Fulbright.

ROBERT S. NEWMAN earned the Ph.D. in English literature at UCLA. He has taught at San Fernando Valley State College and is currently Associate Professor of English at the State University of New York at Buffalo. He has published on irony in seventeenth-century English drama, Ursula Le Guin's anarchist utopia and contemporary Central European writers. At present he is working on a study of recent ideological criticism.

JANET PÉREZ holds the M.A. and Ph.D. in Romance Languages from Duke University. She taught at Duke, Trinity College (of Catholic University), Queens College (City University of New York), and the University of North Carolina at Chapel Hill before coming to Texas Tech, where she is Paul Whitfield Horn Professor of Spanish and Associate Dean of the Graduate School. Her books include volumes on Ortega y Gasset, Ana María Matute, Miguel Delibes, and Gonzalo Torrente Ballester. A past or present member of some thirty editorial boards, she has edited or co-edited nearly 100 volumes in the Spanish section of the Twayne World Authors Series. Her articles have appeared in *Hispania, Romance Notes, Hispanofila, Kentucky Romance Quarterly, Revista de Estudios Hispánicos, Journal of Spanish Studies: Twentieth Century, The American Hispanist, Cuadernos hispanoamericanos*, etc. She is current Vice President of the Twentieth Century Spanish Society of America and consultant to the Council for International Exchange of Scholars. She has recently published *Contemporary Women Writers of Spain* and is now working on a companion volume concerning the women poets of Spain.

SHU-MEI SHIH was born of Chinese descent in South Korea and educated in Korea, Taiwan and the United States. She taught American literature at Tunghia University in Taiwan, Chinese language at UCLA extension, Korean language and European literature at UCLA as a teaching assistant. At present, she is a graduate student in the Ph.D. Program in Comparative Literature at UCLA. She has published articles on Lu Xun and Zheng Zhenduo in the Journal of Asian Culture. Her review of four volumes of contemporary Chinese women's writing will soon appear in *International Examiner*, and her translation of Wang Zengqi's story "Revenge" is to be published in *Renditions*. Chinese Literary Modernism is the subject of her dissertation.

MARY VÁSQUEZ earned the M.A. and Ph.D. at the University of Washington. She has taught at Kendall College (Chicago), Florida State University, and Arizona State University. She has published a number of articles on the Spanish writer Ramón Sender and edited a collection *Homenaje a Ramón J. Sender, 1901–1982*. Vásquez is founding editor of the journal *Letras Peninsulares* and on the editorial board of *Letras Femeninas*. She is currently preparing a book on the work of U.S. Cuban writer Roberto G. Fernández.

WARREN STANLEY WALKER received his Ph.D. in English from Cornell University. He has been Chairman of Humanities and English at Blackburn College, and then Chairman of Humanities and Dean of Arts and Sciences at Parsons College. He has written, translated, or edited books on Nigerian folktales, James Fenimore Cooper, twentieth-century short-story explication, the Erie Canal, *The Book of Dede Korkut*, prose lyrics, and Turkish folklore. He is currently Director of the Archive of Turkish Oral Narrative, cofounded by him with Barbara Walker and Ahmet E. Uysal at Texas Tech University, where he is also Horn Professor of English, Emeritus.

DOLORA WOJCIEHOWSKI is an Assistant Professor of English at the University of Texas at Austin. She received her Ph.D. in Renaissance Studies from Yale University, where she concentrated her study upon Comparative Literature, intellectual history, and literary theory. Wojciehowski's dissertation, which has been revised for publication, is entitled "Old Masters, New Subjects: Early Modern and Post-Structuralist Theories of Will." Her other publications include articles on early modern theology and sixteenth-century science. She is currently studying ideologies of censorship and feminist axiology.

DIANE WOOD, Associate Professor of French at Texas Tech University, earned the Ph.D. from the University of Wisconsin-Madison. She has published studies of Helisenne de Crenne (1538-1560), and contemporary writers Marion Zimmer Bradley, Vonda N. McIntyre, and Jean Auel, in journals such as *Journal of Medieval and Renaissance Literature, Explorations in Renaissance Culture, World Literature Today, Rocky Mountain Review,* and *Extrapolations.* Currently she is preparing studies on De Crenne and the Parisian printer Denys Janot.